Ee. 199

Fe 199

Knowledge, Mind, and Nature

An Introduction to
Theory of Knowledge
and the Philosophy of Mind

F.e.199

CONSULTING EDITOR

V. C. Chappell

THE UNIVERSITY OF CHICAGO

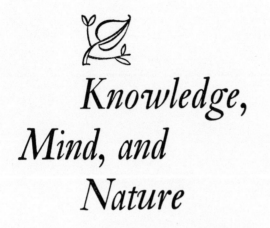

Knowledge, Mind, and Nature

An Introduction to Theory of Knowledge and the Philosophy of Mind

Bruce Aune

UNIVERSITY OF MASSACHUSETTS

Random House NEW YORK

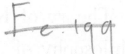
FIRST PRINTING

© *Copyright, 1967, by Random House, Inc.*
All rights reserved under International and Pan-American Copyright Conventions. Published in New York by Random House, Inc. and simultaneously
in Toronto, Canada, by Random House of Canada Limited
Library of Congress Catalog Card Number: 67-10906
Manufactured in the United States of America
by The Book Press Incorporated, Brattleboro, Vermont

DESIGN BY LEON BOLOGNESE

TO *Wilfrid Sellars*

preface

*M*y original purpose in writing this book was to develop and clarify my views on the subjects indicated in the title. As my ideas took shape on the typewriter, it became clear to me, however, that my discussion would be of use to the student and of interest to the educated layman. To maximize this appeal to the nonprofessional, I therefore introduced orienting sketches of the historical situation in which the problems I discuss originally arose, and I also described the general strategy of recent attempts to solve them. In addition to this, I took special pains to relate my particular philosophical conclusions to familiar issues in neighboring subjects such as theoretical psychology, cybernetics, and even physics. Although the argument of certain chapters, especially VIII and IX, inevitably became somewhat technical at times, I was nevertheless able to simplify matters by introducing numerous analogies from common life and by relegating everything involving special symbolism to footnotes. Having presented the material of these more difficult chapters to undergraduate as well as graduate students at three universities—Pittsburgh, Michigan, and Minnesota—I am confident that they can be understood by the nonprofessional reader.

Although every honest author must acknowledge that the book

he sends out into the world is not quite the one he hoped to write, I have done my best to organize the following pages into a unitary whole. The reader should therefore read this book in the order in which it is presented. If he jumps in somewhere in the middle to see what I have to say about the topic that interests him most, he will not appreciate the grounds on which the words he reads are ultimately based. The whole book constitutes a long, complex argument, and it is in the earlier chapters that my basic premises are worked out. Without some understanding of what I say in these chapters, the often controversial claims I make later on are bound to be unconvincing.

As it stands, this book is a pared-down version of a much longer manuscript, which has occupied a good share of my attention for the past four years. In writing it I have been deeply indebted to my teachers, friends, and students, as well as to various institutions and foundations that have provided financial assistance. My greatest intellectual debt is to Wilfrid Sellars. It is largely from him that I have inherited my conception of what philosophy is all about, and I can only hope that this book does justice to his teaching and example. Aside from my students, whose sharp eyes have forced me to rework countless passages, I am also greatly indebted to Herbert Feigl, another of my teachers, for the generous help and kind encouragement he has given me ever since I first conceived the task of writing this book. Finally, I owe a special debt to my friend Jeffrey Sicha, who engaged in a virtual day-by-day discussion with me while I was working out the argument of the last five chapters.

The preparation of the first half of this book and of another long chapter on concepts and propositions, which I decided not to include, was greatly facilitated by two Charles E. Merrill Summer Fellowships awarded by the University of Pittsburgh. For these I must thank the Charles E. Merrill Foundation and also Dr. Charles H. Peake, Vice-Chancellor of Academic Disciplines at the University. Professor Kurt Baier, Chairman of the Philosophy Department at the University of Pittsburgh, and Dr. Frank Wadsworth, Dean of the Humanities, also provided valuable aid and encouragement, and for this I am grateful. The second half of the book was written in Oxford, while I was a John Simon Guggenheim Fellow. I wish to express my gratitude to the Guggenheim Foundation for its generous support. While at Oxford I enjoyed many talks with

Professors William Kneale and Gilbert Ryle, and I want to thank both men for reading and commenting on certain chapters, as well as for their many personal kindnesses. I must also express my gratitude to the President and Fellows of Corpus Christi College for their generous hospitality during the year I visited them. Professor V. C. Chappell, Consulting Editor in Philosophy for Random House and Alfred A. Knopf, has also earned my gratitude for his extremely helpful comments on the manuscript. The patience and understanding of my wife, Ilene, requires an acknowledgment that I lack words to express.

Thanks are also due to Professor Roderick Chisholm, who kindly allowed me to include his latest criterion of intentionality, and to Professor Norman Malcolm, who clarified certain matters in private correspondence and permitted me to quote at length from his important review of Wittgenstein's *Philosophical Investigations*. Permission to quote from his review was also granted by the editors of *The Philosophical Review*, in which it was first published, and by Prentice-Hall, Inc., Englewood Cliffs, N.J., publishers of Malcolm's *Knowledge and Certainty: Essays and Lectures*, in which the review is reprinted, with additions. I must also thank George Allen & Unwin, Ltd. for permission to reprint in Chapter IV much of the material from my essay, "On the Complexity of Avowals," which was published in *Philosophy in America*, edited by Max Black.

BRUCE AUNE

Amherst, Massachusetts
March, 1967

contents

Knowledge, Mind, and Nature

An Introduction to
Theory of Knowledge
and the Philosophy of Mind

I

Introduction

The purpose of this introductory chapter is to pose a basic problem concerning our knowledge of ourselves and the world around us. Like most philosophical problems, this one is extremely difficult to state in a clear, straightforward way. Formulated vaguely, many contemporary philosophers would regard it as senseless, gratuitous, or completely ruled out by the latest methods of critical analysis. My main task will be to show that it can be stated in such a fashion that it is not only legitimate but actually as alive today as it ever was. To do this in a reasonably convincing manner, I shall begin with some orienting comments on the history of modern empiricism, then describe the general grounds on which recent philosophers have attacked a root assumption of this tradition, and finally argue that their attack has not clearly succeeded. Having demonstrated this lack of definite success, I shall then pose my basic problem. This done, I shall sketch out a natural solution based on traditional empiricist principles. This sketch will serve as the first step of a thorough reappraisal of traditional empiricism, which will be continued in a more critical vein in Chapters II and III. My criticism of traditional empiricism will apply to some of the chief assumptions of contemporary philosophy, and it will provide the essential groundwork on which my positive views regarding knowledge, mind, and nature will subsequently be built.

I. SENSE DATA AND RECENT PHILOSOPHY

One of the oldest contentions of critical philosophy is that our knowledge of the world around us is based on the data of sensory experience. Although this contention seems to be entirely obvious and unproblematic, it has actually been a notorious source of philosophical puzzlement. This puzzlement grows naturally from the observation that the data of sense are not always entirely reliable. We sometimes seem to see, smell, or hear things that are simply not there. Historically, the favored explanation of this phenomenon is that what we immediately perceive, in sensation, is not the outer world itself but rather certain effects that the world produces in our consciousness. A red object normally produces a distinctive sensation in a standard observer, but sometimes this sort of sensation may be produced when no red object is present. This may happen either because of something unusual in the perceiver, such as too many martinis, or because of something unusual about the conditions under which the perception occurs, such as the presence of a peculiar reddish light.

Once it is granted that the immediate objects of perception are sensations, or sense data, rather than the public objects that are said to produce them, the question naturally arises as to how we can be sure that these public objects have the qualities we take them to have. If we do not immediately perceive them, how indeed can we be sure that they exist at all? Attempts to answer these questions have led to the remarkable variety of philosophical positions distinctive of the period since the Renaissance. Some philosophers, such as Descartes, have argued that the goodness of God assures us that, under certain conditions at least, our claims about the world must be true. Others, like Berkeley, have argued that it is an illusion to suppose that there even is a public world of the sort described by Descartes. The world that actually exists must rather be understood as some kind of construct out of sensory experiences. As this idea was later expressed, to speak of public objects is to speak of systems of actual and possible sense data. Other philosophers have frankly embraced a form of skepticism, arguing that if there is an outer public world, we really cannot know anything about it. We may assume, as a matter of custom, that such a world exists, but there is no rational way of proving that it does.

Any idea leading to such peculiar claims about the world is bound to come under sharp attack sooner or later, and this has happened in recent years. In opposition to the idea that the immediate data of sense are essentially subjective, the trend has been to defend a view that might be called "direct realism." As its name implies, those accepting this view are inclined to argue that public reality is actually open to direct inspection. We know that a common world exists, and we know what it is like, because we directly perceive it. The old idea that we really perceive only our own sensory experiences is simply false, springing from a hasty and seriously confused analysis of the concepts involved in assessing perceptual claims.

This recent revolt against the traditional assumptions concerning perception, though very rapid once under way, was not just a blind stampede. It was actually forced by a barrage of novel arguments, which reflect a radical reappraisal of what the philosophical problems of perception really are. A close scrutiny of these arguments will be given in later chapters, but their general thrust and flavor can be indicated by locating the source from which they spring: namely, a profound conviction that philosophers have unwittingly trapped themselves in useless, even hopeless difficulties by the contrived and unnatural terminology in which they pose their basic problems. In the early years of this century the problems of perception were posed in the terminology of "sense data," and the chief question debated was whether anything other than sense data could possibly be perceived or known. Anyone with a deep distrust of technical terminology would naturally regard this so-called sense datum language with extreme suspicion, and this is exactly the way recent philosophers have come to regard it. For most of them it has in fact become somewhat of a dogma that one may legitimately employ the sense datum terminology, if at all, only when one is actively prepared to explain every aspect of its meaning in the ordinary, nontechnical idiom of everyday speech —the latter being, in effect, a programmatic touchstone of good philosophical sense.

It is not difficult to see in a general way how this hard-hearted attitude toward traditional terminology could have led to the actual repudiation of subjective data as objects of immediate perception. Once it is decided that talk of such things as sense data is strictly meaningful only to the extent that it can be satisfactorily translated into the language of everyday life, it becomes necessary to lay down conditions of adequacy for these translations. Since a commitment to subjective sensory objects has lain at the root of so many discouraging traditional problems, it was natural that these conditions of adequacy should be made very stringent. For many spokesmen of the new movement, only one form of translation for the distasteful idiom of sense data was grudgingly admitted as legitimate. This may be called "the appearance analysis." According to it, locutions such as "The object X presented Jones with a red sense datum" were reluctantly allowed in philosophical discussions of perception only if they meant something like "The object X looked or appeared red to Jones." Contrived statements purporting to concern the so-called unattached sense data of hallucinatory experience, such as "I am now apprehending a solitary red datum," were similarly regarded as permissible (though not, of course, happy) only if they were clearly understood as signifying nothing more mysterious than the claim, "It is *as if* I were actually seeing something red."[1]

Anyone admitting only an appearance analysis of sense datum language is plainly not committed to regard sense data, or indeed any sort of sensory experience, as objects of immediate perception. Neither of the favored forms of speech, "X looks red to Jones" and "It is *as if* I or he were seeing something red," mentions any such objects at all. It may be granted, of course, that there are sensory *experiences*—experiences of seeing, or seeming to see, something red—but these experiences are not a kind of object standing between us and the world. If I am experiencing, or seeing, something red, the thing that is red is not my experience, it is *what* I experience—and this may be a fire-engine. Similarly, when I seem to see something red, my experience of seeming-to-see is not red; in fact, in this case no red thing may be present at all. On this view there is thus no commitment to any object of perception other than the objects that constitute our common world. For this reason, philosophers holding the appearance analysis view could emphatically insist that our knowledge of the existence and nature of a public world may be firmly grounded in direct perception.

This often militant insistence that sensory experiences are not themselves objects of perception led, however, to a certain paradox when coupled with the traditional assumption that our basic means of gaining knowledge is by perception. This paradox concerns the possibility of knowing anything at all about sensory experiences. If we cannot directly perceive them, why should we think that they actually exist? In the past twenty years it has become fashionable in certain quarters to answer this question by interpreting sensory experiences, and indeed mental states generally, as constructs out of behavior. This approach gains plausibility from the common assumption that the language of everyday life, the accepted touchstone of good philosophical sense, is essentially a public one, whose intersubjective character can be preserved only by the requirement that the claims formulated in its terms be intersubjectively confirmable. Since the activities of human beings open to public scrutiny are in principle limited mainly to overt behavior—the faces they make, the sounds they utter—it becomes natural to argue that talk about sensory and mental phenomena must be construed as highly abbreviated talk about complicated patterns of behavior or about "polymorphous" dispositions to behave in various ways.[2] As G. A. Paul concluded in an extremely influential article, "What we call someone else's seeing a sense datum is his behaving in certain ways in certain situations, his reacting in certain ways to certain stimuli."[3]

This kind of behaviorism may seem to be about as bizarre a position as any defended by traditional philosophers. Yet it cannot be denied that it carries with it certain theoretical rewards that might, for certain thinkers, prove almost irresistible. If, as Paul said, talk about private experiences merely introduces "pointless imagery," we are obviously no longer threatened by solipsism or by a form of skepticism regarding the external world, and we are immediately able to provide quick and easy solutions to such age-old problems as Other Minds and the Relation between Body and Mind. This being so, it is entirely understandable that philosophers concerned mainly with abstract, theoretical problems might actually become convinced that behaviorism is a highly liberating position to defend.

2. AN ALTERNATIVE BASIS FOR SENSE DATA

Although a good share of the detailed analysis supporting the recent revolt against sense data is extremely subtle and persuasive, its general strategy is unlikely to be convincing to a hard-headed defender of traditional empiricism. Not only does the emphasis on how *we* speak and on the logic of *our* language have an unmistakable air of circularity when brought to bear against a philosopher for whom solipsism is a living issue, but the behavioristic tendency of the approach does patent injustice to the myriad phenomena of subjective experience, the enormous variety of which is catalogued in the endless annals of phenomenology and introspective psychology. Moreover, the new approach to sense data fails to appreciate some of the major considerations that have led empiricists to insist upon such entities. These considerations have little to do with the analysis of language, and they do not concern (at least directly) the problem of explaining perceptual error. Their source is rather a speculative, scientific one, and they remain alive for anyone who takes seriously a micro-theory of matter.

Recent historical studies have demonstrated the remarkable extent to which the epistemological problems of modern empiricism were a natural development from the "corpuscularian philosophy" of the seventeenth century.[4] This philosophy revived the speculative ideas of the atomists of ancient Greece, and it is illuminating to consider these ideas in their original form. For familiar reasons, the ancient atomists thought that the world must be composed of tiny particles jostling together in empty space. These tiny objects were considered to be colorless. If they had color individually, it would be difficult to understand how their mere movement, as in the churning of the surf, should bring about a change in the color one sees. Epicurus apparently thought that while individual atoms were colorless, the groups they composed were not. Color, for him, is something that clings to skins or membranes, filmy arrays of atoms that are shed from the surfaces of weighty aggregates and interact with the subtle atoms of the human mind. Color is not therefore a subjective phenomenon for Epicurus: it really exists "out there" on atomic aggregates and on their skins, which permeate the ambient air. Disregarding his theory of perception, one might characterize his view by saying that, according to him, color is an emergent property of groups of atoms, a feature that exists independently of actual and even potential perceivers: a thoroughly objective phenomenon.*

Leucippus and Democritus, on the other hand, although they taught before Epicurus, evidently had what scientists would call a more up-to-date theory. Relying on the obvious fact that the colors a man sees depend in part on the condition of his body, they apparently decided that colors and other sensible qualities are really aspects of the perceiver. One does of course think of physical objects as having color, not just of one's sense impressions of these objects as having it. But this fact has always been readily accommodated by the atomist: physical color, as opposed to phenomenal color, is just the power or disposition of an object to produce certain sense impressions in a sentient being. Thus, while physical objects, rainbows, and the like are properly said to have color, this means no more than that these public things have certain dispositions: the sensuous, colorful part of the world is really subjective, a feature, in some sense, of sentient beings.

It is well known by now that the relativity-of-perception arguments cannot themselves show that the sensuous part of the world is really subjective.[5] But these arguments are not necessary to the modern atomist. For him, the Epicurean idea of colors as emergent properties of atom clusters may be rejected on two grounds: first, that we have no good reason, theoretical or otherwise, to think that colors *are* emergent properties of atom clusters; and second, that we have good theoretical reasons for thinking that perceivers are not in intimate contact with the objects they claim to see. This latter conviction is justified by a complex psychophysical theory according to which the colors a man sees are the result of the bombardment of his retinas by radiation and of highly complicated changes in his nervous system. Visual fire does not accordingly

---

* The notion of an emergent property is discussed in Ch. IX; see pp. 251–252. My interpretation of Epicurus is supported by his interpreter Cyril Bailey: ". . . the compound body was to him [Epicurus] not a mere aggregate, but a new entity. . . . In the organism of the whole the atoms did collectively acquire new properties which as detached individuals they could never possess: no number of independent atoms could have color, but unite them in the new entity of the whole, and it acquired color," *The Greek Atomists* (New York: Russell and Russell, 1928), p. 293.

flow from a man's eyes, coalesce around an object, and return with a carbon copy. Vision is the result of stray radiation.

The atomist's theory, or a modern version of it, is naturally tempting to anyone who takes theoretical science seriously and interprets it in a straightforward way. And, for many scientifically minded thinkers, science ought to be taken seriously and interpreted in a straightforward way, since it is the peculiar task of science to tell us what our world is like, how it is put together—and to be straightforward about it. If in line with this attitude we too are moved to accept physical theory as giving us the best available picture of reality, writ both large and small, then the idea of sense impressions or sense data should strike us as both legitimate and extremely important, whether the terms are technical or not. In fact, it would appear that even if our everyday locutions concerning sense perception could be shown to commit us to nothing more than concrete physical objects and activities and dispositions of perceivers, reflection on the mechanism of perception as described by scientific theory would nevertheless warrant our using words like "sense impression" to refer to certain subjective occurrences or states which are not only always involved in normal perception but which differ radically from overt behavior and even polymorphous dispositions. The fashionable contention, therefore, that technical terms like "sense datum" or "sense impression" are legitimately used in philosophical discussion only when their meaning can be fully elucidated in everyday language appears to ignore the force of some very ancient considerations and to be, in addition, subject to very serious doubt. There is evidently no greater reason to think that these terms must be explainable in ordinary language than there is to think that technical terms like "electron" or "photon" must be so explainable.

3. DOES DIRECT REALISM CLASH WITH SCIENTIFIC THEORY?

Can one be a direct realist of the contemporary variety and also accept physical theory at its face value? This question is awkward to answer because contemporary realists tend not to develop their views in a systematic way. In light, however, of the foregoing discussion of atomism, we might approach this question by asking whether a direct realist could consistently accept the dispositional analysis of color that seems to be demanded by scientific theory. If he could not accept this analysis, or something like it, the presumption would be that he could not accept the theory that prompts it.

It goes without saying that anyone who can accept a dispositional analysis of color cannot consistently be a behaviorist. According to this analysis, "Physical object X is red" is defined to mean "X has the power or disposition to evoke *impressions* of red in normal observers when in standard conditions of visual perception." Obviously, anyone repudiating sense impressions must also repudiate this kind of dispositional analysis. But it is clear that even realists who are not behaviorists could not accept this analysis. To do so would be to commit oneself to the idea that the concept of a sense impression is more basic than the concept of a publicly observable property. And the realists of today would never accept this idea; to do so in their opinion would be to undermine the intersubjective character of talk about colors. A sense impression is, after all, a subjective state or occurrence; and although not all realists are behaviorists, they would nevertheless insist that we can make good sense of the subjective only by relating it in some way to what is intersubjective. Hence, for them, in attempting to analyze a public quality in terms of subjective impressions, the dispositional analysis given above puts the cart before the horse.

The really basic difficulty with the dispositional analysis is that it requires us to make sense of "standard conditions of visual perception" and "normal color observer" without any reference to "color" or to any other terms definable only in relation to "color." This requirement is needed to prevent the analysis from being circular. But how, in ordinary terms, can we possibly specify what we mean by "normal conditions of *visual* perception" except by reference to the whole range of colors that a standard observer can be expected, at certain times, to discern? And how, in ordinary terms, can we possibly specify what we mean by "normal color observers" except by reference to the variety of colors that are discriminable under certain conditions? The answer to both questions seems to be "We cannot"; and this suggests that from the standpoint of direct realism, where basic concepts apply to publicly observable phenomena, the dispositional analysis of color must be rejected as circular.

Actually, it is hardly necessary to provide complex arguments showing that the dispositional analysis is unacceptable to a direct realist. If a man really is a *direct* realist, then he is committed to the view that one can directly perceive public objects and directly perceive that they have this or that quality. And surely one of the most striking qualities of public things is their color. As Berkeley pointed out, you cannot actually see something that is totally colorless; it would be invisible. Dispositions, however, cannot be directly perceived; you can *infer* that something has a certain disposition by seeing what it does in certain circumstances, but you cannot see the disposition or "power" itself—any more than you can *see* the disposition of an unlit match to light *if* scratched.

To make this obvious point about direct realism is to recall the familiar claim of realists that color predicates are ostensively definable.[6] One is said to learn the meaning of basic color words by associating them with the colors that things can be directly seen to have. Color words such as "red" are thus commonly regarded as conceptually primitive, and not capable of any illuminating *verbal* definition. To know what redness is you really have to experience it; and if you are not color-blind you can expect to have this experience if you look at any fire-engine. The redness of a fire-engine, like the redness of a barn, is essentially a simple quality, which you can directly see but never explain to a blind man.

Although the realist's approach to the concept of color will be analyzed in considerable detail in Chapter VII, the foregoing remarks make it appear that he is firmly committed to something like an Epicurean view of color. As already seen, however, a view of this sort seems far out of line with the claims of physical theory. Not only does this theory evidently rule out the idea that a system of colorless particles could be totally enveloped in a sensuous redness, but it implies that all of the *sensible* qualities apparent in perception are in some sense subjective, belonging to perceivers rather than to bare, molecular reality. If physical theory is accepted at face-value, it then appears that the realist's view will have to be rejected as scientifically untenable.

In an effort to save direct realism and therefore common sense from this kind of objection, a number of escapes have been suggested. One of the most common explanations is that science and common sense ought not to be viewed as competing.[7] Ordinary discourse concerning colors and sounds involves a conceptual system distinct from that of theoretical science. These two conceptual systems actually represent alternative ways of viewing reality. Each is adequate in its own right, each has its own practical utility and its own criteria of application. But an attempt to unite them into a single view of the existing world involves some kind of category mistake. "Red," as a term of ordinary language, is incapable of informative verbal definition; yet it does have a legitimate application, and it is possible to correct people who misapply it. Physical theory, on the other hand, is utterly independent of ordinary language; it has its own criteria of application, its own standard of adequacy. Because it represents a distinct way of viewing reality, it cannot possibly be inconsistent with ordinary language. In fact, there are no logical relations whatever between such assertions as "That is red" and "That is a collection of largely FeO_2 molecules."

Although this interpretation of the relation between ordinary language and scientific theory is still defended by able thinkers, it is crucial to note that it is inconsistent with a major contention of many contemporary methodologists of science. According to these men, a physical theory is empirically significant only because of its coordination with ordinary discourse, which serves as the ultimate "observation language" for all theories treating of imperceptible entities.[8] Obviously, if these men are right—if theoretical discourse is factually significant only because it is related to ordinary language—then the logical independence of the language of science and the language of everyday life, claimed above, must be an illusion.

The idea that the language of theory is *not* conceptually independent of ordinary discourse does seem extremely plausible—and not just for the dubious reason that the so-called observation base for all rarefied theories must be formulated in the language of everyday life. After all, we normally employ physical theory in order to state just what physical conditions must obtain in order that such common things as rainbows can actually be seen. In fact, most of the explanations we are normally prepared to give of even the most humdrum occurrences involve both theoretical and ordinary conceptions. Take, for instance, the familiar example of the oar half-immersed in water. Who could explain its peculiar bent appearance without *some* reference to theoretical principles? Or again, who could explain why a man wearing a black suit in the tropics is likely to be uncomfortable, if reference to scientific theories were inadmissible or improper in such ordinary cases? Plainly, the yoking together of both ordinary and theoretical notions is as common as anything could possibly be; and the contention that these notions belong to utterly different conceptual schemes, each scheme having no logical connection with the other, *seems* as extravagant and far from fact as any contention of traditional philosophy.

Another explanation for possible conflict between theory and common sense is that we are far too literal-minded about the claims of contemporary physical theory. The standard manner of expositing this theory is actually very misleading, at least from a philosophical point of view; and like other misleading forms of exposition, it needs careful interpretation. In addition to the straightforward approach already considered, two alternative interpretations have been worked out by philosophers of science, and either one of these can quickly nullify the paradox in point.

Consider, first, the *operationalist* interpretation of theoretical concepts.[9] According to this view, alleged talk about theoretical entities is really just a shorthand way of talking about observable phenomena, the sort of thing that is adequately describable in the language of everyday life. Electrons, for example, are not really concrete or even highly tenuous objects; they are best understood as "logical constructions." We get into difficulty talking about them only because we fail to realize this. The term "electron" admittedly seems to refer to a unitary existing entity, but actually it is a kind of portmanteau word, which allows us to speak in a highly abbreviated way about a large class of observable phenomena, such as tracks in the Wilson cloud chamber, observable deflections in electrometers, and so on.

Another relevant interpretation is that of the *instrumentalist*.[10] In his view theoretical statements are not really statements; they do not, that is, speak about anything at all, not even classes of observable phenomena. They are rather calculating devices, tools of prediction. As tools, however, they are more like barometers than actual statements: we use them for the job of predicting observations, not for stating what we take to be basic truths about reality. The actual nature of reality is something that we know well enough by observation. We can simply see that reality is made up of shoes, ships, sealing wax; and any suggestion that it might be quite different from what our eyes and ears disclose can be nothing but irresponsible sophistry. What can we do but call a spade a spade? And what more can we reasonably demand of science than that it give us devices, tools, that will allow us to predict whether a given spade is sturdy enough for digging up the garden?

These two views, operationalism and instrumentalism, though to my mind completely wrong-headed, have nevertheless been associated with distinguished names, and have naturally proved attractive to direct realists eager to vindicate the claims of common sense and to defend the primacy of ordinary language. It is clear, however, that both views rest uneasy with a literal interpretation of the scientific method, and they obviously involve the idea that the nature of reality is to be discovered mainly by observation, not by the indirect confirmation of often highly rarefied theories. According to these philosophies of science, if an electron is not the kind of thing that could conceivably be *observed* by the senses, then we mislead ourselves and others if we speak of electrons as included among the furniture of the world. The concept of such a thing must rather be regarded as a "logical construction" out of observables, or else as a mere calculating device, aiding prediction but lacking all objective reference.

It is crucial to note that anyone who seriously accepts these assumptions is also committed to defend some form of philosophical behaviorism. As indicated at the beginning of this chapter, mental states are by no means *publicly* observable. Hence, philosophers with instrumentalist or operationalist leanings must regard even such expressions as "stinging pain" and "mild headache" as mere calculating devices, nonreferential expressions that merely allow us to predict observable behavior, or else as a kind of shorthand which enables us to refer to a wide variety of behavior in an extremely economical way. In either case their interpretation of these terms is bound to be highly unconvincing.

In general, it does not take much imagination to see that in an age of electron microscopes, Wilson cloud chambers, and worry about radioactive fallout, the general contentions of the operationalist or the instrumentalist are very hard to take seriously—all the more so when they imply that sinus or migraine headaches are either nothing at all (instrumentalism) or merely patterns of observable behavior (operationalism). One would surely think that the inner, occurrent, episodic character of a sinus headache is vastly more obvious than the cogency of any principle that would commit one to deny this.

4. A PROBLEM OF PERCEPTION

Since at least one of these doubtful construals of the molecular theory of matter seems necessary for a thoroughgoing defense of direct realism, the latter must be regarded as having at least a strong *prima facie* implausibility when the entire range of our knowledge is taken into account. On the other hand, the atomist's theory discussed earlier has special troubles of its own. Not only does it face a very serious difficulty in providing a sound dispositional analysis of sensible qualities such as color, but it appears to put one on a slippery slope that leads to all the puzzles of traditional epistemology.

The path of this slope can be sketched as follows. According to physical theory, the objects of our world do not really have the qualities they appear to have. Sensuous purples cannot strictly enclose the extremities of jostling micro-particles. This means that we do not see these objects as they actually are. Perception is rather concerned with the subjective appearance of things, not with the things themselves. Knowledge of the true nature of the world is thus a wholly theoretical affair; it is attained only by inference. But inference gives knowledge only if there is a secure basis for inference. This secure basis obviously cannot be purely theoretical, for theoretical matters are just the ones to be known by inference. Since matters of fact cannot be known *a priori*, the basis in question must be that of sense experience.

But how can sense experience provide a basis for claims about what is purely theoretical, that is, not directly observable? We cannot, after all, *observe* a correlation between what is observable and what is not. In fact, our experiential data might be as they are even if no external world existed. Lacking any experience of a correlation between our experiences and their alleged physical causes, we thus have no real assurance, and absolutely no right to assume, that there *is* an unobservable world lying behind those experiences. Hence we land in skepticism.

Skepticism is not, however, the worst consequence of this line of thought. Since our words can have referential meaning only if they are defined in terms of what we can experience, it appears that it is actually senseless to speak of a world of empirical objects from which we are, in principle, denied perceptual access. Berkeley made this last point very clearly when he argued that by "extension," as by "color," we mean something that can be perceived. Thus, by hypothesis, the alleged atomic world, as something distinct from the appearances we are said to perceive, cannot literally be extended or colored—in fact, none of our descriptive words can literally apply to it. This being so, any attempt to *say* something about such a world must be incoherent; indeed the very idea of such a world makes no sense at all.

But not only can we never directly observe and meaningfully describe the alleged world of the atomist; we can never even observe and describe the *selves* of such a world: we can observe and describe only the *appearances* of such selves. Hence even the idea of a scientific self is empty. This result is even worse than ordinary solipsism, for no self is strictly observable at all, not even a phenomenal one. As Hume put it in a famous passage:

> . . . when I enter most intimately into what I call *myself*, I always stumble on some perception or other. . . . I can never catch *myself* at any time without a perception, and never can observe anything but the perception. . . . The mind is a kind of theatre, where several perceptions successively make their appearance. . . . [But] the comparison of the theatre must not mislead us. They are the successive perceptions only, that constitute the mind; nor have we the most distant notion of the place, where these scenes are represented, or of the materials, of which it is composed.[11]

Although the preceding remarks are not entirely spelled out, they at least approximate the usual sketch of the slippery slope from atomism, classically conceived, to solipsism and utter intellectual disaster. This outcome is not perhaps forced on the atomist, for he might be able to refute one or more of the premises that define the slope's hideous shape. Still, as the philosophical infighting of two centuries makes abundantly clear, a mistake in the argument is very difficult to isolate and defend convincingly against all comers. So we seem to have a genuine problem. On the one hand, contemporary realism about perceptual objects, for all its sophistication and subtlety on matters of linguistic detail, apparently has crucial shortcomings. Not only does it lead, or give strong indications of leading, to such absurdities as philosophical behaviorism, but it evidently commits one to highly questionable interpretations of scientific theory. On the other hand, an attempt to do full justice to scientific theory in the way outlined above, which is the natural approach to take, apparently leads to disaster.

Since both contemporary realism and traditional, atomistic empiricism seem to involve fundamental difficulties, a thorough reappraisal of both would appear to be an obvious first step in working out an adequate philosophy of mind and nature. A reappraisal of this sort is perhaps best approached by a careful discussion of traditional empiricism, since the realism of today is in many ways an historically self-conscious position, owing a good share of its popularity to its critique of the older view. I have, besides, a special reason for beginning with this older view: I hope to show that its basic errors have not actually been brought to light by the realist's criticism. I shall argue, in fact, that today's realists have attacked traditional empiricism for the wrong reasons, and that the basic difficulties of direct realism are due entirely to old errors that the recent "revolution in thought" failed to identify and destroy.

5. A CLOSER LOOK AT
THE SOLIPSIST'S ARGUMENT

Any reappraisal of traditional empiricism can profitably begin with a close look at the solipsist's argument. Although this argument is painfully familiar to anyone with even the skimpiest knowledge of post-Renaissance thought, the linguistic turn of recent philosophy makes it important to emphasize the central role the argument assigns to scientific considerations. As I have stated it, the argument begins with a certain scientific claim about the world and proceeds to derive from this claim the skeptical conclusion that no knowledge of any real significance is possible. Anyone convinced, like most philosophers of the modern period, that this deduction is basically sound can expect to avoid its skeptical consequences only by arguing, in effect, that it provides a *reductio ad absurdum* of a literal interpretation of the scientific claim. To do this with any semblance of success, he must of course find some independent means of backing his idea that skepticism is unwarranted. One way of accomplishing this, especially effective in a tough-minded age, is to refuse to entertain any abstract doubts about the general reliability of sight and hearing, suggest some innocuous construal of theoretical science, and then hang like a bulldog to the common-sense idea that there is no reason why the world cannot be just as it normally *appears* to be. As is clear from the discussion at the beginning of this chapter, this approach is exactly what many recent realists seem to have taken.

There is no doubt something very admirable about the honesty and aggressiveness of a man who is in this way able to elude the marshes of theoretical perplexity and fasten himself so firmly to what the common man would regard as solid ground. Nevertheless, this stubborn procedure is far from imaginative and, everything considered, perhaps both hasty and ill-advised. The basic contention of the scientific atomist still seems to contain a profound truth, even though it is admittedly expressed in a misleading way. What is possibly not true are some of the philosophical assumptions that must be granted if the solipsist's argument is really going to succeed. One of these is the assumption that all matters of fact not directly amenable to observational check must be established inductively, by generalization from observed instances. But if there were things that by their very nature could not possibly be observed, such as neutrons, we might still know of them by their effects, even though we could not establish the generalizations that relate them to their effects by induction from *observed* instances. Another similarly doubtful assumption from the atomist's point of view is that it is senseless to speak of entities and processes not wholly specifiable in observation terms. But why, again, must we accept this idea? It would surely appear that there might be many things on heaven and earth not dreamed of in observation terms or not exactly describable in nontechnical discourse. Indeed, dozens of such things come immediately to mind: photons, electrons, and even radioactive fallout appear to be obvious examples.

Actually, the mere mention of the word "observation" recalls an important affinity between contemporary behaviorism and traditional phenomenalism.* Both of these views seem to be based partly on the assumption that any legitimate nondeductive inference must ultimately be based on instantial induction, that is, on some kind of generalization from *observed instances*. But whenever this assumption is accepted, the domain of empirical knowledge is largely determined by the kind of thing taken to be observable. Thus, the traditional empiricist, who holds that sense data or immediate experiences are the true observables, is inexorably led down the road to phenomenalism; for it is plainly impossible to establish by direct apprehension (his version of observation) any generalizations relating immediate experience to things not immediately experienced. If, accordingly, he wants to speak of other persons, physical objects, and the like, he seems forced into the position of having to regard them as logical constructions out of his immediate experiences. Similarly, then, for the direct realist, who takes public things such as chairs, ships, and rainbows as the true observables: if he, too, accepts the assumption in point, he will be led to an instrumentalist or operationalist interpretation of theories and he will find it natural to hold that sinus headaches and afterimages are logical constructions out of behavior, a position he might express by saying that these so-called inner phenomena are really either patterns of behavior or dispositions to behave in a distinctive way.

I am not suggesting that every direct realist writing today will be happy with behaviorism. My suggestion is rather that any direct realist who wishes to avoid both behaviorism and skepticism regarding the mental must reject a principle essential to the solipsist's argument—namely, that inductive inference is limited to forms of reasoning based on instantial induction. This principle must be rejected by such a realist because if some mental states are admittedly not publicly observable, then the generalizations relating them to overt behavior could not otherwise be defended empirically, which is needed if behaviorism is to be avoided. Since this inductive principle is essential to the solipsist's argument that is destructive to atomism, it appears that nonskeptical realists abjuring behaviorism will have to take atomism seriously. The basis for operationalist

* This view, which holds that physical things must be interpreted as constructs out of sense data, is discussed at length in Ch. III; see esp. pp. 74–78.

and instrumentalist contruals of molecular theory will have been rejected along with behaviorism.*

It might be objected at this point that I am being very naive in assuming that the generalizations relating inner episodes to behavior are empirical at all. Even though some mental states may be publicly unobservable, and not exactly and exhaustively describable in observation terms, they might nevertheless be *conceived* as X's that are related to observable behavior in a certain way. So conceived, the generalizations in point would presumably be analytic in some sense; they might in fact be said to state the "outward criteria" of the otherwise inaccessible inner states.

Although there is some plausibility to this suggestion, it is nevertheless highly problematic and actually does nothing to save the crucial principles of the solipsist's argument. Just consider the consequences of maintaining that *all* such generalizations are analytic. The first thing to strike the eye is that the door is immediately opened to a plethora of mysterious entities, the only restriction being that they are given objective criteria. Thus, gremlins might be specified in part by analytic statements concerning the behavior of apple trees, and it might be argued that we can be sure that the things called "gremlins" exist because ripe apples do fall from their trees in the autumn. Similarly with stinging pains: if as covert episodes they were known to exist *only because* they satisfied certain objective criteria, all relations between them and things observable being known analytically, then their existence would evidently be highly dubious. We could justifiably wonder, apparently, whether they were any more real than the gremlins just mentioned. In a word, if we could justifiably affirm the existence of unobservable entities on the sole ground that they are so conceived that familiar events like dropping leaves or moving water constitute their observable criteria, then we are evidently in danger of opening the door to all the demons and spirits of antiquity. We might just as well argue that because certain spirits were conceived as agencies that control the actual movement and growth of trees, the observed behavior of the latter leaves us no alternative but to maintain that these mysterious agencies really do exist. Obviously, we need some assurance that the unobservables for which we allegedly have ob-

---

* Note that any realist rejecting behaviorism will also have to reject the strong criterion of meaning mentioned above.

servable criteria do in fact exist, do in fact correspond to our conceptions of them—and this assurance plainly cannot be given by purely *a priori* reasoning.

In the light of these consequences it is perhaps surprising that I should have awarded any plausibility at all to the suggestion in point. But apart from the fact that some very forceful arguments have been given in its favor,[12] there is a common practice, influenced by Russell's work on definite descriptions,[13] of treating certain theoretical terms as referring to intrinsically unknown X's that uniquely occasion certain observable phenomena. It is in accordance with this practice that we might indirectly define the expression "Type A unfilterable virus" as referring to an as yet intrinsically unknown species of virus that is responsible for a certain kind of disease. Of course, in order to avoid the bizarre consequences of such a practice as were mentioned above, we must have some way of justifying definitions of this type. Exactly how we might do this is a very complicated matter, which will be discussed in later chapters. Here I shall only say that while such definitions certainly stretch their necks in the direction of the nearest chopping block, they can be justifiably advanced, apparently, *if* there is good reason to think that the theories to which they belong will be empirically confirmed and perhaps extended so that the skeletal conception of an unobservable X having certain causal properties will be rounded out by additional details. Most important, obviously, is the requirement that the theories to which such conceptions belong be subject to empirical confirmation. If they are not, if they fail to satisfy appropriate tests or are ruled out by more satisfactory theories (as the primitive theory of psychic demons was ruled out by the development of modern psychological theories), then the existential consequences of the definitions in point lose their tenability,* and the terms so defined should, like "impetus,"

* Since any definition of the form "$a = (\imath x)(Fx)$" immediately yields "$E!x(Fx)$" (at least on standard theories of descriptions), it is plain that such definitions are warranted only when the assumption that the latter statement is true is justifiable. This kind of justification cannot always be given, however, at the moment when such a definition is first introduced. But if the theory to which it belongs is capable of corroboration and extension, the justification can be given later. One might therefore compare such definitions to tools bought on credit: the propriety of using them depends on a reasonable confidence that their use will win a reward sufficient to pay their cost. (A

"aether," and "phlogiston," be dropped from the vocabulary of science.

In spite therefore of the admitted danger lurking in the contention that the generalizations relating covert mental states and observable behavior are analytic in some sense, we are not *ipso facto* in a position to brand it as absurd from the beginning—especially if it is held that the entire framework to which these generalizations belong is capable of some kind of empirical justification. Nevertheless, if a realist who abjures behaviorism is driven to defend this contention, he must obviously reject another principle necessary to the solipsist's argument, namely that all reference to what is not considered observable is illegitimate. But when this is rejected the atomist will still have a fighting chance to defend his claims; for he can then maintain, as against the realist's charges, that many of his generalizations relating molecular aggregates to their subjective appearances are analytic, that in his view many unobservable atom structures have phenomenal (or sensory) "criteria." And if, like the realist rejecting behaviorism, he can go on to show that his molecular theory as a whole is in some way capable of empirical justification, he is evidently in an excellent position to forestall the alleged solipsistic consequences of his general position.

It is fairly clear, then, that if a contemporary realist is to avoid an out-and-out behaviorism he must reject a principle essential to the argument traditionally considered a major barrier to a defensible scientific atomism. Of course, the realist has another line of attack: he will naturally want to dispute the subjective foundation on which this kind of atomism seems to be based. But because this line of attack raises very complicated problems of its own, I shall discuss it separately in the next chapter. For the moment, I simply want to emphasize that if a realist is to avoid the absurdity of a thoroughgoing behaviorism, he must reject at least one of the principles without which the solipsist's argument cannot possibly succeed.

While I have by no means demonstrated the untenability of the basic principles in point, which might be called "strong verification-

---

similar remark holds for definitions involving the more cautious Hilbert epsilon operator; on this see Rudolf Carnap, "On the Use of Hilbert's ε-operator in Scientific Theories," in Abraham Robinson, ed., *Essays on the Foundations of Mathematics* [Jerusalem: Manes Press, 1961], pp. 156–163.)

ism" and "narrow inductivism," I think I have made it clear that they are by no means obviously acceptable. Also, I have explained how, depending on whether one takes private sense data or public objects as the true basis of verification, they naturally lead either to phenomenalism or some kind of behaviorism—both positions being, at least to my mind, intuitively repugnant. In order, then, to avoid ruling out scientific atomism from the beginning, I shall begin my reevaluation of its traditional form by assuming that both strong verificationism and narrow inductivism are untenable. Although I shall make an extended effort to substantiate this assumption in later chapters,* my general approach gains plausibility from the work of certain methodologists of science who have taken pains to document "the tragic history of the verification criterion"[14] and have argued that the acceptance of narrow inductivism would make a shambles of the most impressive theoretical achievements of the scientific enterprise.[15]

6. A METAPHYSICAL RECONSTRUCTION
OF THE WORLD

Since my announced aim at this stage is to reevaluate the atomistic version of traditional empiricism, it will be instructive to start with the phenomenal (or sensory) basis of most older empiricisms and then, without at first quarreling with this starting point, see whether a defensible atomism can be built upon it. There are several reasons why this approach will prove especially fruitful. First, as I shall show in the next chapter, most of the standard objections currently urged against such a starting point do not hold up under close examination. Second, although a phenomenal basis for empirical knowledge has been out of favor for some time, there are signs that many thinkers are prepared to take it up again.[16] Finally, a stage will be reached in the argument of this book when the temptation will be very great to insist that our knowledge *must* be based on a phenomenal foundation.† In Chapter III, I shall try to show that this foundation of knowledge is ultimately untenable, though not for

---

* See Chs. V, esp. pp. 119–126, and X, esp. pp. 266 f.

† For many readers, this temptation will become acute when reading the last few sections of Ch. VII, pp. 168–176.

the reasons fashionably given. But in philosophy truth can be found and recognized for what it is only as the result of exploring many blind alleys with very great care. Accordingly, in order to gain the clearest understanding of the merits and defects of the traditional starting point of an empiricist epistemology, it is crucial to have some idea of what might be built upon it, granting that it is sound. If, as I hope to show, this phenomenal basis must ultimately be rejected, we shall at least have some understanding of what has to be rejected along with it.

Let us begin, then, with the phenomenal chaos envisaged by Hume* when, after ransacking his consciousness for traces of a unitary self, he was regretfully led to avow that his mind is nothing more than a kind of mock theater, which not only lacks evident continuity but whose momentary aspect is as protean as the shape of the phenomenal players it fleetingly houses. The most striking feature of this picture is that it grotesquely exaggerated, having about as much fidelity to fact as a surrealistic painting. For even if introspection discloses no unitary seat of consciousness, no self-contained spirit that thinks and acts, it does disclose considerable stability and coherence. In fact it patently discloses a coherent picture of what a direct realist would call objective reality—reality encountered from a unitary point of view. And this picture, far from lacking a visible self, features one prominently: it is a colored, bulky, sensitive thing, the back of which is generally turned away. Of course, critical reflection may prompt a thoroughgoing interpretation of this picture. Indeed, the idea that it actually contains one's self, one's fellows, and other furniture of the world, may have to be rejected in favor of the more considered opinion that it contains only appearances of these things. But if one's true self is not literally introspectable, it is perhaps inferrable: it might be grasped as *the* X that perceives the world in this unitary way.

Anyone engaging in the skeptical line of reasoning that generally leads to Humean disaster begins with the conception of a reasonably stable world composed of lawfully related, enduring physical things. He may, it is true, come to doubt whether a world of this sort actually exists, but he nevertheless retains his ideas—perhaps even his hopes and fears—concerning it. This holds not only for

* See above, p. 17.

his ideas of persons, trees, and mountains, but even for his conception of an objective, measurable space and time. He may come to agree, on reflection, that this space and time is not directly experienceable, but his ideas of them do not therefore evaporate. In fact, if he can be dissuaded from accepting the philosophical theses of strong verificationism and narrow inductivism, he may retain many of his old ideas as significant theoretical notions. If he does this, he can then attempt to reconstruct his common-sense knowledge by employing the scientific method of theory construction. On this approach, physical things, persons, and even his own self may be understood as "directly" unobservable X's that stand in objective spatio-temporal relations to one another—moving, interacting, changing, and producing the phenomenal effects that his introspection discloses.

The contentions he may be led to make in this spirit may also be rendered tenable, perhaps, by the use of the so-called hypothetico-deductive method. According to this method,* an hypothesis concerning unobservable entities can be satisfactorily confirmed by reference to the predictions it allows one to make about what will be observed under such and such conditions. Since for the thinker in question "observing" means "directly experiencing," he may proceed to test his newly developed theory of persons and a common world by attending to the experiences he has under certain conditions. If there is—as certain experiences together with his theory of common-sense objects imply—a solid, bulky object two feet from where he is standing, then if, theoretically speaking, he were actually to approach it, he should feel something heavy when, according to his theory and certain experiential data, he succeeds in putting his weight against it. If we assume, at least for the sake of argument, that test statements of this kind will regularly turn out to be successful, then his theory seems worthy of retention by anyone willing to endorse the essential soundness of the scientific method.

The assumption that the man's test statements are likely to be regularly satisfied is, of course, disputable. Yet the empiricist would maintain that their satisfaction is a condition of our having generated the idea of a common world in the first place. If, for example,

---

* This method will be discussed more fully in Chs. V. and IX.

my visual experience of touching a typewriter were not regularly
followed by appropriate tactile sensations, I would not possess the
notion of a typewriter as a visible, solid instrument of writing.
Thus, while regularities in one's subjective experience are not perhaps required for one's ideas about momentary experiences, such
regularities are positively demanded for one's possession of ideas
about persisting extended objects. Since it has already been granted
that anyone who begins to follow Hume into skepticism still retains
his ideas of a common world, it is thus implicitly granted (the empiricist would say) that the subjective experience of such a person
exhibits marked regularities. These regularities do not, of course,
guarantee that a common world exists—the skeptic is right about
this. But their presence is implied by one's initial possession of a
common-sense world-picture and, granting the scientific method,
they certainly add weight to a theory affirming the actual existence
of a world that produces predictable changes in our consciousness.

If such claims concerning the regularities of a man's experience
are granted, it would thus seem that the empiricist's basic strategy
in defending our empirical knowledge is not unreasonable. In fact,
his theory appears to have a decided advantage over the approach
of the direct realist. Unlike the common-sense realist, the empiricist
encounters no conflict with the claims of theoretical science. Since
the objective entities he initially postulates are conceived as bare
X's with distinctive causal properties, their subsequent interpretation in scientific terms could not possibly lead to an inconsistency.
As bare X's they do not, in other words, possess the kind of sensible
quality (such as occurrent color) that seems incompatible with a
gappy system of colorless particles. If the character of the world is
interpreted, in itself, in purely theoretical terms, then both conditions of perception and normal perceivers might be so describable
that the empiricist could avoid the circularity that most dispositional analyses of sensible qualities seem to face (see p. 11).

Consider the man's conception of his self. Initially, his self is
regarded as an unobservable unity that possesses a coherent field
of experience. Yet subsequent theorizing may lead him to conceive it as a complicated molecular structure. It is granted that a
self, as distinct from inanimate things like chairs, stones, and spin-
ning wheels, is able to think, feel, and act. But these features of the
self can be reinterpreted as aspects of a molecular structure. Thus,

it may be held that certain molecular structures contain elaborate systems of neurological circuits and gates; and the thinking done, the actions performed, and the pains felt, may be viewed as the "products" of neurological activity. On this approach the elements of the Humean bundle turn out to be aspects of a molecular structure, only the roots of which are tangled about with a less theoretical picture of man and nature. Yet it is the success of this sophisticated view that fully justifies the sketchy and somewhat risky notions that ultimately led to its birth.

If selves and sensible qualities can indeed be understood in the way suggested, the entire world picture of the scientific atomist seems to fit together in a way that the picture favored by most direct realists does not. This surely counts very high in its favor. Nevertheless, apart from the alleged difficulties with a basic phenomenal language, which will be discussed in the next chapter, the position as just outlined might appear to have the implausible implication that every child begins life in his own solitary phenomenal cell and then, by a highly sophisticated process of reasoning, develops a conception of himself and the world that is largely theoretical. But this is clearly an unacceptable consequence of any theory that purports to do justice to all our knowledge and that avowedly views with suspicion all elaborate attempts, like that of the instrumentalist, to reinterpret even the humdrum things we think we know.

In fact, however, this implication is not essential to the theory. Fully developed, the theory does not in any way deny the existence of a community of persons, nor does it deny that children learn to think and speak by interacting with their elders. What it purports to do is reconstruct the knowledge we actually have, to show the evidential basis on which it ultimately rests. Few people ever really bother about the foundation of their knowledge, but when they do they are naturally led down the historic path that ends in solipsism —a path that can be traced back to solid ground, according to the atomist in question, only if one is able to make use of the kind of map sketched above. Thus, it is only the person who has worried about the traditional puzzles of perceptual epistemology who would feel secure in thinking of his friends as swirls of particles known only because of their phenomenal effects. But thinking of them in this way need not occupy his daily activities; in fact, like

Hume at the billiard table, he can share the idiom of his friends in his nonphilosophical moments, speaking of them, like other so-called molar objects, as paradigms of observability. Yet it is only because he can envisage at least the general outlines of the kind of epistemological reconstruction sketched above—a reconstruction in which his friends appear as theoretical as electrons—that he will be assured of his place in a community of persons living on what he can safely call a stable planet. The intellectual horrors of a Humean exile are thus banished, for him, by an intricate fabric of logical reconstruction.

II

Does Knowledge Have an Indubitable Foundation?

The position outlined at the end of the last chapter was built on the assumption that a man's subjective sensory experience can provide a satisfactory foundation for the body of his empirical knowledge. Although this assumption has been a key tenet of traditional empiricism, most contemporary philosophers regard it as extremely questionable. In fact, it is now commonly believed that subjective experience, taken by itself, cannot possibly provide an adequate basis for any kind of knowledge at all. The main task of this chapter will be to examine the credentials of this current opinion.

1. THE RELIABILITY OF INTROSPECTION

Anyone who thinks it possible to develop his conception of himself and an external world solely by reference to his immediate experience is generally presupposing that the nature and interrelations of his sensory experiences can be classified and known independently of anything else. Although it will actually be shown only in later chapters that knowing and classifying are essentially linguistic and require some kind of conceptual scheme, I shall here assume that the presupposition can be expressed by the claim that one might possibly possess a primitive phenomenal language. Such a language or conceptual scheme may of course be used only in silent soliloquy. It will be considered primitive in the sense that its expressions will not be derivative from those of some other language, and it will be phenomenal in the sense that its basic use will be to classify the phenomena of immediate experience.

The point in expressing the above presupposition by reference to a language is to come directly to terms with Wittgenstein's influential critique of private languages,[1] which is commonly regarded as ruling out the possibility of a subjective basis for empirical knowledge. Since Wittgenstein's critique raises numerous questions of a highly controversial sort, I shall develop it dialectically as the chapter proceeds. As an introduction to the general strategy of his approach, the following remarks will be helpful.

If a man is to defend an assertion or proposition, he plainly needs some kind of argument. Arguments, however, need premises. Hence if there is to be a fundamental basis of empirical knowledge —something by which the truth of ordinary claims is to be defended—this basis must be propositional in character: it must be the kind of thing that can have a place in an argument. This being so, any adequate basis of knowledge will be radically different from raw experience. Pains, tickles, and itches are neither true nor false, and they cannot appear as premises in arguments. If, accordingly, the true basis of knowledge is regarded as phenomenal, it can at best consist of *propositions* about immediate experiences. Since these propositions are presumed to be true, they must themselves be capable of some kind of defense. If they cannot be defended, if no good reason can be given for supposing them true, then their claim to provide a secure basis of knowledge can be nothing but a sham.

Although traditional empiricists have notoriously regarded the truth of basic phenomenal premises as far too obvious to require an explicit defense, this is exactly what Wittgenstein demanded. If the very foundation of our knowledge is to rest on truths about our sense experiences, then, considering the enormous stakes involved, we must surely have *some* guarantee that our knowledge does not rest on sand. We may indeed have no haunting doubts about the reliability of our beliefs concerning our immediate experiences, but this does not allow us, as philosophers, to assume without question that all such doubts are strictly unjustifiable, that they must be mad or wild. Admittedly, it is exceedingly difficult to imagine that we might chronically misidentify our own experiences. But this is merely a psychological matter: some people cannot imagine a lifeless universe. It will be of no use here to appeal to intuition, since the intuitions of one man may easily conflict with those of another. What is needed, plainly, is an argument, something showing just why the products of our awareness may justifiably be held to be reliable. Unfortunately, nothing but the flabbiest arguments have ever been given in defense of this basic empiricist idea. Empiricists have for the most part simply taken it for granted that our knowledge of our sense experiences is both noninferential *and* absolutely reliable. Yet taking things for granted is the mark of the dogmatist—not the free, critical spirit that the empiricist has taken himself to be.

Contrary to what one might expect, it happens that good reasons can actually be given for doubting the allegedly infallible character of immediate awareness, though these reasons were not advanced by Wittgenstein. Consider, first, the verbal behavior of hebephrenic schizophrenics. These people frequently utter what are graphically called "word salads"; they pour out chaotic jumbles of words, which often appear to be utterly unrelated. Verbally, at least, these people are totally confused. Is there any reason to think that their thoughts are less chaotic than their words? Evidently not. In fact even psychoanalysts would have to admit that, consciously at least, such patients are totally confused: their conscious thinking, if indeed it merits the name of thinking, seems to be every bit as flightful and disconnected as the words they utter. Yet if these patients really are intellectually deranged, thoroughly befuddled, there is obviously good reason to think that this derangement also extends to their awareness of their feelings.

It might be objected at this point that the kind of intellectual befuddlement just mentioned can occur only in psychotics, never in an ordinary perceiver. This may be granted, though it would appear that less dramatic forms of intellectual befuddlement could occasionally exist in almost anybody. The philosophically important fact has, nevertheless, been established. It is simply that serious intellectual confusion is a possibility, and that identifications of even feelings and mental images are not logically incapable of error. I myself have no reason, of course, to think that I am as befuddled as a hospitalized schizophrenic, and my confidence in the truth of what I say about my feelings is extremely high. But this confidence is something that requires some kind of justification; it cannot stand by itself as the basis of all my knowledge. If I cannot justify my conviction that I am *not* a walking whirl of confusion, I plainly cannot justify the idea that I have any knowledge at all, let alone a substantial stock of infallible knowledge about my momentary states of mind.

Actually, the possibility of being mistaken about the character of one's momentary experience can be illustrated by reference to the behavior of perfectly sane adults. Consider, for instance, the following experiment.[2] We have a man, noted for his integrity, who reports having extremely vivid imagery. His imagery is so vivid, he tells us, that he can generally read off from it all sorts of facts about objects he has recently seen. We present him with the following letter-square, and let him scrutinize it for a few seconds:

e m f
r z a
o w p

We then take the square away and ask him whether he has a clear image of it. He says that he does. We then ask him to read off the letters from left to right, starting from the top and working down. He does so, and makes no mistakes. We then ask him to read them off in the opposite direction. Suppose that, contrary to his likely behavior,[3] he reads them off without hesitation, though he makes several mistakes. We have him do the same thing again—that is, read off the letters in both directions—and he gives the same answers. Without mentioning his error, we then ask him whether his image changed during the experiment. He says, "No; it remained the same throughout the experiment, vivid and sharp." In fact, he emphatically endorses all of the following claims, not even considering, so great is his confidence, that they might not be entirely consistent:

1. The image did not change during the experiment.
2. From left to right, top to bottom, the letters were: e, m, f, r, z, a, o, w, p.

3. From right to left, bottom to top, the letters were: p, w, o, *r*, *a*, *s*, f, m, e. (He was evidently wrong about the italicized letters.)

Now, if he has the image he claims to have, not all three of these assertions can be true of it; at least one must be mistaken. Whichever it is, we know that he has made a mistake about the character of his experience. Presented with this example, about the only thing the traditional empiricist can say, apart from questioning the honesty of the subject (which we have implicitly ruled out), is that the man's memory about the continuity of the image was erroneous— and memory, as anyone will admit, is by no means infallible. We could, however, vary the experiment indefinitely, using either a very small square or even just a short sequence of letters. If we have more than one letter, error will always be theoretically possible: the statements the agent will make could always turn out to be inconsistent. To blame the error in every case on the weakness of memory seems *ad hoc* and theoretically desperate. Besides, what experimental sense could we give to the assertion that it is always memory that is at fault?

The admission that memory is intrinsically fallible is, however, extremely damaging to the idea that phenomenal identifications could not possibly go wrong. There is plainly a sense in which memory is involved in all judgments of identification. To judge that a phenomenal occurrence has the property *F* is to assert that it belongs to the class of *F*'s, that the property it has is just the property that is possessed by other *F*'s. But how could one know this infallibly, if one's memory is intrinsically fallible?—if one may well misremember the peculiarities, the distinguishing features, of *F*'s generally? If it is replied that every assertion of the form "This is an *F*" is really an immediate matter, involving no reference whatever to other *F*'s or to their distinguishing features, then the assertion evidently amounts to no more than "I shall call this '*F*'." But if all phenomenal identifications have this import, and only this import, then it would be impossible to establish any generalizations, let alone infallible ones, relating different phenomenal items. Indeed, there would be no *bona fide* identifications at all; each so-called identification would turn out to be nothing more than a kind of ceremonial announcement or verbal baptism, something very different from an out-and-out claim to knowledge.

In view of this it appears that anyone wanting to regard all phenomenal identifications as invariably true is forced to admit that
memories, too, are sometimes infallible. If so, he must advance
criteria to distinguish fallible from infallible memories, for he must
be able to handle the puzzle raised by the example of the letter-
square. It happens, however, that no such criteria have ever been
advanced—and it is extremely difficult to imagine what such criteria
would be like. Yet until we have such criteria, the conclusion to be
drawn from the case of the letter-square seems inescapable, namely,
that it is quite possible for even a sane man to make mistakes about
the character of his immediate experience.

The temptation to regard sense experience as yielding infallible
knowledge seems to arise from the historic confusion of knowledge
with a kind of intellectual gazing: a sense impression has nothing
hidden about it, nothing not presented to the eye of the soul, so it
involves nothing about which one could be mistaken. But it is easy
to see, again by considering examples familiar to psychologists, that
knowledge, which is a matter of having true, defensible opinions,
is extremely different from intellectual gazing—and not just on
the ground that there really is no eye of the soul. Consider, for
instance, some of the experiments performed on congenitally blind
adults whose vision has been restored by surgery. While these
people learn to discriminate colors rather quickly, they often have
an extremely difficult time with visual shapes. Senden found, for
instance, that patients trained over a period of thirteen days to
discriminate squares from triangles sometimes learned so little that
they could not make these discriminations without methodically
counting corners one after another.[4] In fact some of these patients
were quite unable visually to distinguish spheres from cubes!
Though the shapes in point were physical ones, an empiricist could
scarcely deny that the patients had the appropriate visual impressions. Yet if they were familiar with the idea of a sense impression,
and were asked whether their current impressions were of spherical
or of cubical objects, they would no doubt have had to reply that
they could not tell. If so, we would have had the spectacle of men
intellectually wallowing in their immediate experience who nevertheless lacked the ability to appreciate the complex variety of what
they were actually sensing.

The point here, though troublesome to traditional empiricists, is actually well known in the history of philosophy. And if, like Plato, Kant, and others, we make the indispensable distinction between having an impression or experience and thinking about it, attempting to classify it, and the like, we should find it very natural to admit the possibility that persons whose vision has been restored by medical treatment may very well be unable to make accurate discriminations among the visual impressions that are novel to them. Indeed, the spectacle just mentioned, of men having sensory experiences they cannot distinguish or identify, is nothing but memorable illustration of the Kantian point that percepts without concepts are blind.

In spite of all this I am fully prepared to admit that given sufficient training, it is extremely unlikely that a normal person could fail to distinguish surfaces so palpably different as circles and squares. But this concession is of little help to the traditional empiricist. The point seems to be securely established that judgments of phenomenal identification are not, in fact, infallible. We may come to have enormous confidence that, after a protracted period of training, a man's opinions about the character of his own experiences are never really wrong. But our confidence here is based on empirical considerations. There is no longer any reason to think that such opinions *cannot* be erroneous; rather, we have fairly good, though not infallible, reasons to think that they are normally reliable. But these reasons are neither wholly phenomenal, derived from introspection, nor purely logical, semantical, or *a priori* in some other subtle way.

There is, of course, a familiar defensive move that empiricists are generally anxious to make at this point. They often contend that error here implies misunderstanding of the language in which the identifications are made, so that if a man is not linguistically or perhaps conceptually befuddled in some way, what he says or thinks about his immediate experience is always true. Unfortunately, though there is often point to this contention, it is wholly useless in the present context. When introduced here, it simply redirects the challenge in question, allowing it to be focused on the matter of whether a man's confidence that he actually understands what he is saying is ever justified. Linguistic or conceptual befuddlement is, after all, just as serious an intellectual defect as out-and-out error, for confusion and error are both cases of ignorance, which is failure to appreciate the truth. It may well be a necessary truth that *if* one is not conceptually befuddled, one's judgments of phenomenal identification are always true. But because of the possibility of improper coordination between thought and sensation, illustrated by the above experiments, this alleged necessity does not support the traditional contention that immediate apprehension is an infallible source of knowledge.

The foregoing discussion illustrates the position I shall take in this book: subjective experiences, or introspective knowledge of them, are not sufficient to constitute the foundation of anything, let alone all our empirical knowledge. This is not to say, however, that introspective knowledge is an illusion; in fact, I shall take special pains to defend the legitimacy of such knowledge against its behavioristic critics. The defense I give will nevertheless be far out of line with the contentions of traditional empiricism. Not only shall I insist that subjective experience cannot provide the true foundation of our knowledge, but I shall insist that our knowledge *has no foundations* in the traditional sense. By this I do not mean that it is unfounded or baseless, in the sense that it is subject to every shift in the uncertain winds of custom or fancy. I simply mean that there is no such thing as an indubitable foundation, on which knowledge of any sort can rest.

2. WITTGENSTEIN'S ATTACK

Although Wittgenstein's attack on a subjective basis for empirical knowledge is presumably consistent with the main lines of my argument against the infallibility of introspective claims, it involves further, more serious criticisms; in fact some philosophers see it as constituting a critique of introspective knowledge generally.[5] The fundamental point of the critique seems to be this. Anyone restricted merely to the domain of private experience has no possible way of checking up on, or even adding credibility to, his momentary apprehensions about his immediate experiences. Such a person could not, in fact, distinguish between knowing that an experience has, say, the property F and merely thinking or being under the impression that it has F. But if he could not make this distinction, and so justify the truth of his introspective claims, the very idea of introspective knowledge turns to dust and has, consequently, no significant place in serious epistemological deliberation.

In view of the far-reaching, indeed revolutionary, consequences of this contention, it is obviously important to scrutinize its credentials with exceptional care. As just presented, Wittgenstein's argument seems to rest heavily on the necessity of making a clear distinction between knowing that one has a certain experience and merely thinking that one has it.[6] But this distinction is actually not of crucial importance. The contradictory of "He knows that *p*" is "He does not know that *p*"; and if one can make sense of the latter, one can give sense to the former—even if, for some reason, "He merely thinks that *p*" remains unintelligible.* Assuming that Wittgenstein was correct in insisting on the necessity of finding some kind of significant contrast for the claim that a man knows he has a certain experience, we may thus regard this contrast as adequately given by the claim that the man does *not* possess this knowledge.

An obvious first step in coming to terms with Wittgenstein's evident attack on the possibility of basic introspective knowledge is to ask how, in his opinion, one is *ever* able to distinguish knowledge from ignorance. His general answer to this question, if I understand him correctly, is that an assertion may be regarded as an expression of knowledge only if it is made in accordance with some appropriate rule, one by which the propriety of applying the relevant words or concepts is to be appraised.[7] If this is indeed his opinion, it appears that if the empiricist of the last chapter can show that his application of a phenomenal term or concept is in accordance with some appropriate rule, then his contention that he actually does possess basic introspective knowledge stands a good chance of being justified even according to Wittgenstein's principles.

3. KNOWLEDGE, RULES, AND DUBITABILITY

If we are to make sense of the kind of knowledge in question by reference to rules, we must be clear about the *kind* of rule involved. Wittgenstein, unfortunately, was not entirely explicit about this.

---

* The importance of this reservation to Wittgenstein's argument is brought out in Ch. IV; see esp. pp. 95–98.

Yet if we consider his general assumption that the use of a word is governed by "criteria," which are in some sense based on the word's definition, a natural interpretation of his doctrine is not difficult to formulate.[8] Although his use of the term "criterion" is not without its puzzles,[9] we can surely agree that the question whether a thing is correctly described as, say, a "lemon" would normally be answered by at least a tacit or indirect reference to the defining characteristics of lemons—and Wittgenstein would presumably call these characteristics "criteria." Thus, if I am assured that the term "lemon" properly applies to yellow, sour fruit of a certain characteristic size and shape, I can justify my use of this term to describe or identify something by showing that the thing in point possesses these defining characteristics. In doing so, I may be said to be relying on a rule, one to the effect, roughly, that fruit of such and such characteristics are *correctly* called "lemons." The general connection between knowledge and rules suggested by this example is that one can ultimately determine whether a thing actually is a *K*—whether the word "*K*" properly applies to it— only by reference to rules that specify the criteria for *being a K.**

It is crucially important to note that the rules involved here strictly authorize what might be called "intra-language" moves.[10] This label highlights the special character of these rules, which is to authorize *inferences*. Thus, to continue with the same example, if one knows or has good reason to think that a thing is yellow, sour, of the appropriate size and shape, then the rule in point allows one to *infer* that the object is a lemon. And if, conversely, one knows that it is a lemon, then the rule presumably allows one to *infer* that it is probably yellow, sour, and the like.[11] (The utility of this latter rule is that it tells one what to expect when lemons are said to be in the vicinity.)

The idea that the rules with reference to which empirical claims are justified are *all* of this intra-language sort immediately leads to a very serious problem. In order to justify a claim by an intra-language rule one has to know that some other claim is justifiable, the claim, namely, that serves as the premise for the inference. Yet if this latter claim can be justified only by a rule of in-

---

* I am here using the word "criterion" in an informal sense, which is slightly different from the technical sense I introduce in Ch. V, pp. 114 f.

ference, one must know that still another claim is justifiable, and so on without end. This, however, seems to make it impossible to justify anything. To put it in another way, since intra-language rules merely authorize inferences, they cannot themselves justify any basic premises. Yet without such premises, we could never obtain justified conclusions; and without justified conclusions we could never have knowledge of the actual character of the world.

This kind of puzzle takes us immediately to the basis of traditional empiricism and partially accounts for the tenacity of the idea that empirical knowledge must be built on a phenomenal foundation. It is precisely phenomenal awareness, whose infallibility is so difficult to doubt, that is supposed to justify the basic premises of empirical knowledge. One justifiably makes these basic claims as the result of one's awareness of a certain experience—an occurrence or datum which, unlike physical things, is entirely open to view. Once these primitive claims are made, rules of inference allow one to move on and construct a warranted picture of the world.

Although I have already advanced arguments against the idea that immediate experience provides an indubitable basis of knowledge, the assumption that knowledge requires some such basis is still very much alive. Since this assumption seems to rule out the plausibility of Wittgenstein's general approach by sustaining the problem mentioned above, a brief resolution of that problem must be attempted before proceeding any further with Wittgenstein's argument. I shall attempt to do this by showing that the assumption in point is untenable and that the problem it poses for Wittgenstein's approach is actually misconceived.

The line of reasoning behind the empiricist's assumption is, again, that while intra-language rules may validly take us from premise to conclusion, they cannot themselves establish empirical truth. If the premises you start with are false, you will have no guarantee that the conclusions you reach are not false either. Hence, to attain knowledge of the actual world, you must ultimately have premises whose truth is acceptable independently of any inference and whose status is accordingly indubitable. Only by having such premises can you gain a starting point that would make inference worthwhile. For convenience, these indispensable basic premises may be called "intrinsically acceptable." The possibility of empirical knowledge may then be said to depend on the availability of intrinsically acceptable premises.

If this line of thought is sound, it follows that utter skepticism can be ruled out only if one can locate basic empirical premises that are intrinsically acceptable. Although philosophers who attack skepticism in accordance with this approach generally think they are defending common sense, it is crucial to observe that they cannot actually be doing so. The reason for this is that, from the point of view of common experience, there is no plausibility at all in the idea that intrinsically acceptable premises, as so defined, ever exist. Philosophers defending such premises fail to see this because they always ignore the complexity of the situation in which an empirical claim is evaluated.

I have already given arguments to show that introspective claims are not, in themselves, intrinsically infallible; they may be regarded as virtually certain if produced by a reliable (sane, clear-headed) observer, but their truth is not a consequence of the mere fact that they are confidently made.* To establish a similar conclusion regarding the observation claims of everyday life only the sketchiest arguments are needed. Obviously, the mere fact that such a claim is made does not assure us of its truth. If we know that the observer is reliable, made his observation in good light, was reasonably close to the object, and so on, then we may immediately regard it as acceptable. But its acceptability is not intrinsic to the claim itself. Thus, philosophers who, like G. E. Moore,[12] attempt to prove by direct inspection that they have hands do *not* proceed just by taking a quick look at their hands; they rather turn them over, look at both sides, pinch them, and the like. The certainty they arrive at is thus based on a whole group of observations, as well as on numerous tacit assumptions concerning the general reliability of their senses, the accuracy of their memories, the sort of things hands are supposed to be, and so on. I would venture to say that any spontaneous claim, observational or introspective, carries almost *no presumption* of truth when considered entirely by itself. If we accept such a claim as true, it is only because of our confidence that a complex

---

* Some philosophers argue that the truth of certain statements is a consequence of the fact that they are made with maximum understanding. I attacked this argument briefly on p. 37, and I shall attack it in detail in Ch. IV; esp. pp. 102–105.

body of background assumptions—concerning observers, standing conditions, the kind of object in question—and, often, a complex mass of further observations all point to the *conclusion* that it is true.

Given these prosaic considerations, it is not necessary to cite experimental evidence illustrating the delusions easily brought about by, for example, hypnosis to see that no spontaneous claim is acceptable wholly on its own merits.[13] On the contrary, common experience is entirely adequate to show that clear-headed men never accept a claim merely because it is made, without regard to the peculiarities of the agent and of the conditions under which it is produced. For such men, the acceptability of *every* claim is always determined by inference.* If we are prepared to take these standards of acceptability seriously, we must accordingly admit that the traditional search for intrinsically acceptable empirical premises is completely misguided.

To rule out intrinsically acceptable claims on the grounds of common experience is to presuppose two things: first, that common experience *can* somehow provide an acceptable basis for knowledge and, second, that utter skepticism is untenable. If these presuppositions can be defended, it will therefore follow that the argument purporting to establish the need for intrinsically acceptable empirical claims must contain some crucial flaw. Although I shall attempt a justification of these presuppositions only in later chapters,† I can say now that the basic flaw in the empiricist's argument arises from a grossly oversimplified conception of the structure of empirical reasoning. In assuming that we must have unalterable and incontestable truth in order to infer something on which we can reasonably depend, it overlooks the important fact that successful empirical reasoning can proceed only against a background of general assumptions (many of them empirical‡) in terms of which

---

* To say this is not to imply that one always does infer, or actually come to a reasoned conclusion, that a given observation claim is acceptable. It is rather to say that the acceptability of such a claim is to be justified by inference; that its acceptability is not intrinsic to it. This is entirely compatible with the obvious fact that human beings constantly accept claims as true without thinking about them at all.

† See esp. Ch. V, pp. 123–126, and Ch. VI, p. 137, footnote.

‡ As indicated above, some of these assumptions will concern the reliability of the observer (*whoever* he is), the character of the standing conditions, and so on. For further discussion of this, see Ch. V, pp. 123–126.

we interpret our experience and assess the truth of what we say about it. The empiricist's basic error is thus his presumption that we could actually start out with a fistful of merely inferential rules and then, as innocent of the world as the youngest child, cast about for some self-justifying premise that will permit us to draw an inference. The error of this presumption is patent, because even though a premise may come to mind that is actually certain, we must have good reason to believe it is certain if we are to use it in an inference. Even if it were to bring with it the strongest feeling of confidence, or even wear a little label saying "I am true," we would plainly require some rational means of deciding whether the confidence or the label can be safely trusted.

If it is granted that no empirical claim is strictly justifiable on its own merits but requires some kind of support from a body of other claims, we may accordingly infer that Wittgenstein's conception of knowledge as something requiring justification by reference to rules is not basically unacceptable. In fact, we may note that his insistence on the necessity for rules in this connection brings out the important fact that both confirmation and disconfirmation (or proof and disproof) involve relations between claims, between statements or propositions. To show that a statement is false, you have to establish some other claim with which the first one is inconsistent; and to show that a statement is true, or probably true, you have to show that it is rendered so by certain statements that formulate the relevant evidence. The basic point here is that confirmation and disconfirmation are *logical* relations; and such relations hold between items belonging to the conceptual, rather than the natural, order.

Once it is seen that there are no intrinsically acceptable empirical claims and that confirmation as well as disconfirmation can be rendered only by other claims that also lack intrinsic acceptability, it becomes apparent that the process of firmly establishing an empirical claim can be, in principle, almost endless. Suppose, for instance, that I happen to be in some doubt as to whether the fruit I am holding is actually a lemon. In order to remove this doubt and confirm my tentative belief, I might appeal to my neighbors. If they agree that it is a lemon, and if I have no reason to doubt the honesty of their testimony, then I would ordinarily be considered justified in taking it to be a lemon. But I might, of course, be mistaken in trusting them. Should I later become aware of this mistake, I might consult still other persons, or perhaps do some research in a library. What I learn from these sources would normally settle my doubt, but it need not insure the truth of my belief. In fact, if I began to suspect that I had recently been hypnotized, and told to misinterpret any direct evidence bearing on the kind of fruit I am carrying, I might fall into an utter quandary.* To work my way out of this quandary I could appeal to other considerations and make further tests. This kind of appeal could, however, go on indefinitely, with a theoretical possibility of mistake at every turn. It is, of course, granted that in most cases I would not have to make many such appeals in order to establish my claim beyond any reasonable doubt. But the important fact remains that the confidence I attain need never be logically immune to a rational challenge.

4. A REJOINDER TO WITTGENSTEIN

Assuming that the sort of rule to which Wittgenstein requires one to appeal for purposes of justifying an empirical claim is of the intra-language sort so far discussed, we may now consider whether a defender of phenomenal languages could possibly establish his claims to knowledge. In view of the foregoing discussion, we may pose our question as follows: "Could such a thinker justify a basic phenomenal claim, 'This is an A,' by relating it to some intra-language rule that he possesses?" The answer to this particular question seems to be "Yes."[14] In order to justify his claim he might have recourse to a rule that relates the expression "A" to another expression "B." He could then argue that he knows that the item is an A because it is also a B and because it is a rule of his language that anything that is a B may properly be called "an A." Admittedly, the

* In the paper referred to in note 13 of this chapter, an actual case of such a quandary was demonstrated experimentally. A man had been given a post-hypnotic suggestion that, after writing on some sheets of paper before him, he would forget having written on them and be unable to see that they were written on at all. During the experiment, he was subjected to close examination regarding what was written on the papers and, when his denial that anything was written on them met with constant objection by his interlocutors, he became both angry and confused, showing all the signs of a man whose perception of an obvious matter of fact meets with universal disbelief. A case of this sort should carefully be kept in mind by any philosopher who thinks that obvious matters of fact are always easy to settle.

question whether it is indeed a *B* can also arise, and this question would have to be settled by further appeals. *But the possibility of such constant queries and appeals is not peculiar to phenomenal language.* As already indicated, it holds generally. To assume otherwise is simply to accept the immediately infallible in another form, and in so doing to reject the spirit of Wittgenstein's attack.

It might be thought that I am simply begging the question here by assuming that the phenomenal thinker may indeed have rules. How, for instance, is he to distinguish between his actually having rules and his merely thinking that he has them? This question may, however, be attacked in all sorts of ways. For one thing, the thinker may employ a variation on Wittgenstein's own "This language-game is played" theme,[15] arguing that he is fully confident that his language-game is under way, that he has absolutely no reason, concrete or otherwise, to think that he is not employing rules, and that he cannot, in point of fact, even conceive the possibility that he is not operating with rules, since conceiving such a thing would require him to have them already. (He could not, therefore, "merely think" that he has rules; for thinking this, rather than that, is a rule-governed activity, which may involve inconsistency and error.) Another approach to the question would be to declare that it is fundamentally misconceived. The thinker might, that is, reject the whole question, arguing that one's linguistic rules are not the sort of thing whose existence one must prove (such a proof would require rules anyway) but something one simply uses. Rules are not factual contentions, and to accept a rule is to adopt a procedure— a specific way of thinking, of organizing one's ideas. If the thinker actually has rules, his use of them will be *shown* by the inferences he draws concerning the character of his phenomenal data. If he draws inferences at all, he is thereby operating with rules, whether he is articulate in formulating them or not.

5. WITTGENSTEIN'S CHALLENGE AND ANOTHER KIND OF RULE

So far, I have taken the term "rule" in a fairly strict sense; I have regarded linguistic rules as the sort of thing that may justify an inference. There is, however, another sense of "rule" lurking in

Wittgenstein's discussion. This sense concerns linguistic regularity, and it is brought into the picture as soon as it is asked whether a word or concept is, "as a rule," applied to the same kind of object, or whether a particular inference is regularly drawn from the same type of premise. This sense of the word "rule" is nothing like what has been called the "regulation" sense,[16] for it is essentially descriptive and cannot itself justify an inference or establish some claim. It is nevertheless of central importance to the issue of phenomenal languages, since the empiricist who wants to defend the legitimacy of such languages must be assured that he is at least consistent in the use of his phenomenal terms.

Such "rules" can exist, then, only when there is a certain linguistic practice. The question is, Could a solitary thinker have a consistent practice of applying his phenomenal terms? Could he, that is to say, be consistent in his application of certain concepts to elements of his immediate experience? Although one would think that the answer to this is an obvious "Yes"—that the interesting question is not whether he *can* be consistent but whether he can defend his conviction that he *is* consistent—it is perhaps wise to consider two general lines of argument that might be urged against the very meaningfulness of the contention that a practice of this kind might exist, let alone be known to exist by the agent involved. The first objection concerns the meaning of the word "same" in the context of "applying a concept to the same phenomenal items," and the second concerns the identity of the thinker who is supposed to use a phenomenal language.

Beginning with the first objection, we might ask what the word "same" is supposed to mean in a special phenomenal language. This term plainly belongs to ordinary English, and when it is applied to purely phenomenal objects, where familiar criteria are not involved, it appears to lose whatever sense it had. Yet if it does lose its familiar sense in this new context, it is obviously misused; for it is employed as though it had its usual sense—in fact, it is used in this context just because it has a very familiar but crucial job to perform. If it had an utterly different meaning as used here, it would prevent the present issue from even being formulated.

Actually, this kind of objection concerning the meaning of "sameness in kind"—for that is what is presently involved—is not so troublesome to the phenomenal theorist in this context as it appears to be elsewhere.* As used here, the expression has a purely formal significance, which is quite independent of any specific subject matter. Thus, the theorist can easily advance the following definition:

"*a* and *b* are the same kind of thing" means "there is a kind of thing, *A*, of which both *a* and *b* are instances."

Since this definition is wholly general, mentioning no specific kind of thing, the peculiarities of a phenomenal subject-matter are logically immaterial to the meaning of "the same" as it appears here. Whether one is speaking of furniture, phenomenal data, or even sporting events, the expression "the same" as so defined retains precisely the same meaning.

Given, however, that "the same" has a purely formal significance, there is still the question of how the sameness of two or more things is to be determined. The answer to this immediately brings us back to the ancient puzzle about the relation between words and the world. Are *a* and *b* both lemons? Are they both instances of Lemonkind? Well, do they both satisfy the criteria for being lemons? Are they perhaps yellow, sour, of ovoid shape? As already indicated, to answer these questions is to establish the truth of other factual contentions, which may require justification as well. Questions of this kind can no doubt be answered to the satisfaction of a reasonable man, but the answers given will by no means be immune to critical examination.

Similar considerations naturally apply to the contentions of the silent thinker. If he is to justify his contention that two phenomenal items are the same in kind—both instances, that is, of some kind-concept—he need only appeal to certain other contentions, about which he is reasonably confident. There is simply no way of getting outside all conceptual schemes in order to see whether one's concepts are consistently and accurately applied to reality. Tests for semantic regularities must necessarily be carried out within the framework of some conceptual scheme, and the question whether a thoroughly intersubjective framework is consistently applied can be raised in just the embarrassing way that it is raised in connection with phenomenal languages—given, that is, that questions of this

* Its importance in another context is discussed in Ch. III, sect. 2.

type are legitimate ones. The silent thinker cannot, it is true, assuage such doubts by an appeal to the testimony of other persons. But a wide variety of appeals is still open to him, at least as regards any particular doubts he might have; and even if he could make an appeal to other persons, this would do nothing to settle any *general* doubt he might have concerning the consistent application of his language as a whole, for he would have to interpret their testimony within the framework of the scheme he happens to have.

Assuming, then, that a defender of phenomenal languages faces no greater obstacle in making sense of "same in kind" than anyone else, we have to consider the other line of objection mentioned above: Just who, or what, is this thinker that is supposed to have the solitary practice of applying phenomenal terms? The answer to this has already been given: the thinker in question is the X that has the phenomenal items in point, the person who, according to the empiricist reconstruction of the last chapter, has a certain body, a certain position in the world, and so on (see pp. 25–29). Of course, this answer cannot be given by the thinker himself at this stage of his deliberations. As already explained, his conception of his self is something he will proceed to construct on the basis of an ascertained "coherence" among a certain field of phenomenal items. It is not, therefore, binding on him to identify and describe himself at this stage of his argument. He will attempt to do this later on, when his phenomenal language is enriched by what are for him theoretical notions. At the present stage, he could conceive the general question regarding semantic regularities only along lines similar to this: "Might *certain* thoughts or conceptual episodes, such as 'This is a K' or 'The item that is a G is also a K,' consistently occur in connection with, and only with, K-kind phenomenal items?" If he can answer this question in the affirmative, and if, after forming his conception of his self, he can show that these regularities are simply manifestations of *his* practice, then the objection in point could evidently be met.

But an argument can be quickly advanced against this procedure, too. Just what admittedly subjectless thoughts and phenomena are supposed to be involved here? Since the answer "Mine!" cannot possibly be given at this stage, must the class not include any phenomena whatever? Yet if it does so—if it includes even those which, if the thinker's language were fully developed, he would ascribe to other persons—then the existence of the appropriate regularities could never possibly be established without reference to nonphenomenal considerations, a reference that is explicitly excluded from the present context.

A defender of the traditional theory of awareness would naturally be tempted to reply to this question by contending that the phenomena in point are simply the objects of direct awareness. But this reply would obviously misfire in the present connection, and not just for the reason that no reference to subject of awareness is presently allowable. The main difficulty is rather that an appeal to "awareness" solves nothing whatever. Any identification must be made within the framework of some conceptual system, not outside such a system by a conceptually neutral act of direct awareness.*

It is possible, however, for the thinker to approach this question in a way that ought, by now, to be familiar. He need only ask: "How are identifications ever made? How is a domain of objects *ever* identified and circumscribed?" The answer to this, plainly, is that they are described in some way; they are picked out as the things falling under certain concepts. But if the private thinker has, as he claims, a phenomenal language including such terms as "K-kind," "A," and "B," then he would have no trouble specifying the objects in question: they are simply the things falling under these terms or their corresponding concepts. It is surely not binding on him to specify these objects in some language different from his own; and although we, who do not understand his language, will not know just what things he is talking about when he uses such terms as "K-kind," it does not follow from this that they are really meaningless, or really not terms at all.

All of this may sound very naive to a philosopher immersed in the intricacies of contemporary semantical theory. Such a philosopher might immediately wish to reply: "If we are serious in setting out an interpretation of a given language structure by specifying a domain of objects to which its various terms refer, we shall have to proceed in what is strictly a metalanguage.[17] When we do this, we can then formulate semantical rules by which to determine the application of expressions in the object language. We will not therefore be limited to saying that a domain of objects is simply the class

---

* The limitations of direct awareness will be further explored in Ch. III, sect. 4, where the doctrine of "logically proper names" is discussed.

of things falling under certain concepts; we can rather identify the domain independently of these concepts by using the expression of the metalanguage. Thus, if we were using English as a metalanguage in order to outline the semantics of French, we might say that '*les chiens*' denotes the class of dogs. It would then be by reference to this rule that we could determine whether a given Frenchman consistently applies '*chien*' to the right things."

Although this argument is very familiar, it is clearly useless. Even if we actually had a hierarchy of metalanguages in which to specify the objects referred to by the terms of each sublanguage, we would still have to have one language the semantics of which is just "understood." It would be understood, moreover, without the aid of semantical rules. And if this understanding is not *really* understanding, if we could not strictly understand what we are talking about when we use this language, then, since each sublanguage can be ultimately understood only in terms of this one—the semantics of the first sublanguage being expressed in it, and so on down to the lowest level—we could not really understand any language at all. Hence, if the reference of words is ever to be understood, it must be possible to understand it without the apparatus of semantical rules.

Another difficulty with the semanticist's argument is that when we are concerned with natural languages, we are not free to lay down just any semantical rules; we must rather be able to justify every such rule that we advance. Yet when we consider how this justification is to be given, we see at once that knowledge of the reference of a term must be in hand before we are in a position to advance the appropriate semantical rule. Suppose, for instance, that we are concerned to justify the rule concerning "*les chiens*" given in the last paragraph. How might we proceed? Surely by showing that the French expression applies to just those things, actual and possible, that we call "dogs." We have to consider possibilities as well as actualities because not all of the things to which an expression may legitimately apply need actually exist. To take a well-worn example, if there were no plucked chickens, the animals to which "featherless bipeds" might actually apply would be restricted to human beings, though the expression could also apply to a plucked bird should one exist. Because possible as well as actual applications of a given expression must be considered in establishing its distinctive reference, it becomes clear that in order to be fully justified in advancing the semantical rule concerning "*les chiens*" we must have some access to the criteria on the basis of which Frenchmen determine whether something describable in a certain way is or is not *un chien*. What we have to determine, in fact, is whether the things that are dogs, according to our criteria, are the same as the things that are *chiens*, according to the criteria of Frenchmen. And to determine this, we would have to be able to establish the extension of "*les chiens*" without reference to the English language.

The basic point here, to which even the private thinker can appeal, is simply this: a *kind* of thing, such as *Chien*, Dog, or *K*, is definable only within some conceptual scheme or other, and it is only by reference to the criteria involved in the *appropriate* scheme that the decision whether a given thing belongs to a certain kind can possibly be reached. (Of course, once these criteria are ascertained, we may express them in other languages and so state semantical rules of the sort just considered.) The question, then, whether a given thing belongs to the domain of objects about which the silent thinker's phenomenal idiom allows him to speak, can properly be said to be answerable according to the criteria he happens to have, not to the criteria appropriate to some other conceptual scheme, whether public or not.*

6. THE SIGNIFICANCE

OF OSTENSIVE DEFINITION

It might naturally be objected at this point that I have badly underestimated the importance of ostensive definition. If our language is actually to be applied to reality, it must surely be possible to indicate the reference of our basic descriptive terms by pointing out, grasping, or sometimes even manipulating, instances of the things to which they apply. This pointing, grasping, or manipulating is more primitive than language, does not require the apparatus of a conceptual scheme,[18] and is therefore a logically fundamental means

---

* Since the silent thinker's domain of discourse is initially restricted to phenomenal items and does not allow him to speak of conscious agents, his linguistic rules can initially be formulated only as modal conditionals or equivalences: for example, "*A*'s are necessarily *B*'s."

of indicating which objects are denoted by various basic terms. Since this pointing, grasping, and so on cannot be utilized by a private thinker, he labors under an irremedial handicap, and it is exactly this handicap that renders his theoretical labors futile.

Familiar as this argument is, it is not difficult to see that it cannot possibly succeed. Collingwood pointed out years ago[19] that a gesture of the kind in question is a linguistic act itself, whose reference is in no way more obvious than that of audible speech. When a man points, one must not just look at his finger, as dogs naturally do; one must look *away* from his finger, and then try to decide what he is attempting to draw one's attention to. Doing even this requires considerable sophistication, but it takes far more to appreciate the particular intent of the man's gesture, which must be understood if his so-called ostensive definition is going to succeed. The foregoing discussion has proved, however, that this intent—which is to indicate that the object of the gesture is an example of something or other—could never be entirely given by a group of *actual* gestures, no matter how many might be made. The reason for this is that the meaning or denotation of a term can be determined only by reference to possible applications, and these cannot be surveyed by a process of pointing. Whatever is merely pointed out or manipulated can be classified in an indefinite variety of ways, and a condition of understanding a certain classification is that one know just what is encompassed by it. To know the meaning, or conventional application, of an expression "K" we must accordingly have a grasp of the criteria for being a K, for it is only with reference to these criteria that we could possibly delimit the variety of things that, should they exist or come to our attention, would be correctly classifiable as K's. Since these criteria cannot possibly be given by a mere gesture of pointing, it is clear that a so-called ostensive *definition* is a misnomer. The most that ostension can do is direct our attention to a vaguely delimited region of space and time; if we are to understand *what* is being pointed out, we must understand the relevant principles of classification.

Although these remarks make it plain that pointing is in no way sufficient to establish the meaning of any term, it might nevertheless be thought that it is necessary for the purpose of learning certain words. This view has at any rate been expressed by philosophers who attempt to draw philosophical conclusions about meaning from their conception of how a child might be taught certain words. The idea here is, however, false; there are no words whose meaning can be taught only with the aid of pointing gestures. As already indicated, the most that pointing can do is direct one's attention to a vaguely defined region of space,* and this can be accomplished by verbal signals just as well. The gesture of pointing is in no sense easier to understand than familiar verbal directions such as "Over there!"

It is important to observe in this connection that a child's first words are not really *taught*. As every parent knows, such words are learned "naturally" in a way that seems wholly mysterious. It may be granted that when a child is old enough to benefit from his parent's untutored and clumsy attempts to teach him words, he can best learn such nouns as "ball" when the appropriate things are in his view. But a gesture of pointing has no special utility in the learning situation. If a child hears the word "ball" when he is playing with one, his attention will already be directed to the appropriate object, and a gesture of pointing would only distract it. The actual process of learning language is really far more complicated than philosophers seem to think; and those who believe that the gesture of pointing has some special utility for language-learning should note that psychologists hardly ever mention pointing when discussing the subject of how people learn words.† Pointing is neither necessary nor sufficient for learning language, and the private thinker's inability to rely on gestures of pointing is thus of no significance at all.

This reference to language-learning prompts a further comment. It might be thought that the inability of an alleged private thinker to be taught his language by some other agent shows that the idea of his actually having a language is senseless. But this view is clearly false, because it is certainly possible, logically, for a child to be

---

* I speak of a "vaguely defined region of space" because a mere gesture of pointing does not pick out a circumscribed thing or region. In pointing at a man I may be interpreted as pointing at his head, his eye, his pupil or eyelash, or even to the spatial area through which his head is moving.

† If a gesture of pointing is understood as a linguistic act, comparable in significance to, say, "Look at that!," it would be considered a "mand" by the psychologist B. F. Skinner. Yet in Skinner's discussion of learning in his *Verbal Behavior* (New York: Appleton-Century-Crofts, 1957), Ch. 3, pointing is never even mentioned. In his view words are learned by the progressive reinforcement of appropriate "operant" behavior.

born with the ability to speak his parent's language.[20] Of course, if such a child does indeed possess a language at the hour of his birth, he must then be able to apply its terms correctly and consistently. In ordinary life this is something that we would determine by observing the child's verbal behavior. In the present case this is admittedly ruled out. Here we are concerned with the possibility of a phenomenal language, the correctness and consistency of whose use can be determined only by phenomenal considerations. They are the only legitimate considerations because, as already shown, the question whether a particular expression is correctly applied can be determined only by reference to criteria *internal* to the language in point. For the private thinker, these criteria are phenomenal, not public; and it would thus be logically inappropriate to demand that his phenomenal claims be assessed by criteria of any other kind.

7. A BASIC PUZZLE
ABOUT SEMANTIC REGULARITIES

The argument of the last section was built around one basic question: How, ultimately, can one ever justify the contention that the concepts of a given conceptual system are in fact consistently applied to the same kind of object? The topic of ostension was introduced because it is difficult to see how a justification of this sort could possibly be given by a mere appeal to intra-language rules. If, in order to assure oneself that "*A*" is correctly applied to *X*, one could only appeal to such rules as "Anything having an identifying feature *B* may be properly called 'an *A*,' " then one would have to know that *X* has in fact the feature *B*, which means that "*B*" properly applies to it. But if there is a general doubt about whether the conceptual system in point is correctly and consistently applied, then an appeal to this kind of rule is question-begging, for the doubt about the application of "*A*" accrues *also* to the application of "*B*." Hence, if we are to take seriously a general doubt of this kind, it would seem that we must ultimately make an appeal to extra-conceptual considerations, perhaps to immediate awareness, pointing, or something similar.

Having argued that any question whether a given concept is

correctly and consistently applied to the same *kind* of object can
be answered only by reference to the criteria distinctive of that
kind of thing, I am obviously committed to reject any extra-conceptual means of ruling out such a doubt. But this does not mean
that I am committed to take a general doubt of this sort seriously.
On the contrary, if the preceding argument is sound, such general
doubts are completely idle, baseless, and logically incapable of
casting any real suspicion on anything at all.

To see this, note that any serious doubt requires some kind of
basis. In involving the claim that some alleged matter of fact is indeed doubtful, a justification is obviously in order. This justification
can actually be given, however, only within the framework of some
conceptual system. Consequently, if a man has only one conceptual
system, one "language," he will not be able to formulate a serious
doubt about the correct application of that system as a whole—for
he would have to use the system in order both to formulate his
doubt and to establish a justification for it. This does not mean that
he will be unable to question the propriety of particular claims that
are made in its terms, or even to revise large segments of the system
while hanging by his bootstraps to the part that remains. But a
general doubt about the correct and consistent application of his
system as a whole will not be open to him—and this will be true
of the private thinker too, if he has only one conceptual scheme
with which to work.

It might be thought, however, that such general doubts could
justifiably be made within the framework of *some other* conceptual
system. Wittgenstein at any rate purported to do just this when he
attacked the possibility of private languages. And on the face of it
at least, an external attack of this sort seems entirely reasonable.
Suppose, for example, that members of a native tribe were observed
to apply a given expression to a very large, highly disconnected
group of objects—to things that we would call "cows," "trees,"
"rocks," "manure," and so on. Would not this scattered sort of
application show that their expression was not consistently applied?
The answer, of course, is "No." To appreciate this answer, we have
only to consider more closely the question at issue: Are certain
expressions consistently applied to the same *kind* of object? The
crucial word here is "kind," for kinds are determined only with
reference to some conceptual scheme. And while it may be true

that the expression in point is not consistently applied to anything that we, or indeed any other civilized person, would regard as a single kind, this may not be true for the natives. In fact there is no theoretical limit to the variety of ways in which they may happen to carve reality.

Admittedly, if we knew something about the general structure of the natives' language, or even about their chief interests and beliefs,* the number of these alternatives could perhaps be cut down to manageable size. But we would in any case have to determine the extension of the terms they use by reference to the ways they use them; and to the extent that their usage is puzzling, or seemingly inconsistent when measured by our way of viewing things, their conception of things is simply beyond our ken— which means that we are yet in no position to say whether they consistently apply their terms to what they consider the same *kind* of thing. In order to settle doubts about the semantic regularities involved in their verbal behavior, we must in fact approach the question from within, by learning their language and solving our problem by an appeal to the considerations they themselves invoke in appraising the success of their own verbal performances. Only in this way is it possible to discover whether they conceive the world in a manner even remotely analogous to the way we conceive it, and whether our language even has the resources to permit a definition of the *kinds* of thing to which many of their crucial terms apply.[21]

If a wholly general doubt about semantic regularity cannot legitimately be raised within the framework of the system to which it applies, and any other doubt raised within the framework of some other conceptual system is similarly self-stultifying—in that any specification of the kind of thing to which the terms in question are supposed to apply must be justified with reference to what are considered the semantical regularities governing their use—it then follows that a general doubt about the consistent application of an entire language cannot possibly be justified. Such a doubt must remain absolutely idle and pointless, with no possibility whatever of

---

* The relevance of both interests and beliefs in this connection can be illustrated by reference to the word "carbon." A man with suitable interests might apply this word to precious diamonds, industrial diamonds (which may appear to be gravel), and ordinary chimney soot.

gaining empirical support. Since a doubt of this kind is no less idle when directed to phenomenal languages, we must conclude that an external attack on such languages cannot succeed. This, however, seems to be the approach Wittgenstein took in attacking them.

Granting that general doubts about whether a phenomenal thinker does "as a rule" apply his terms consistently are, in this way, illegitimate, one might nevertheless insist that the foregoing argument renders particular doubts both unavoidable and irresoluble. If there is indeed no ultimate foundation of empirical knowledge, will not any attempt to answer a particular doubt inexorably lead to an infinite regress? As before, the answer to this question must be "No." While it is assuredly possible to raise doubt after doubt, any particular doubt that is worth heeding must be justifiable—which means that it, too, must be supported by contentions that are themselves subject to challenge and, potentially at least, in need of justification. I say "potentially in need of justification" because if we could never take something as not requiring justification *for the moment*, no doubts and no contentions could ever reasonably be advanced. Justification must therefore, as Wittgenstein said, come to an end somewhere—if only for the time being. True, we can in principle challenge the credentials advanced in favor of any *bona fide* contention. But in doing so we must base our challenge on reasonable considerations and we must be willing to waive our doubts in the face of appropriate evidence. The idea that a justification may be self-justifying is nothing but a myth, and a reasonable man can expect nothing more than favorable results from the tests he is willing to make in support of some contention on which he bases his confidence. If he is sufficiently critical, sufficiently suspicious of dogma in all its guises, he can scarcely be accused of intellectual levity or gullibility.

8. PHENOMENAL LANGUAGES AGAIN

The question that led to the foregoing discussion was whether a solitary thinker might in fact be consistent in applying basic phenomenal terms to elements of his immediate experience.* So far, I

* See p. 47.

have argued that any positive reason for doubting the consistency of such a practice cannot, by the very nature of the case, be formulated. The question arises, however, whether the idea of semantical regularities in a wholly phenomenal language actually makes sense. I think that it does. If, in line with the anti-behaviorist assumptions on which we have been operating since Chapter I, one is prepared to grant that one's own feelings and sense impressions are covert occurrences or states, then the suggestion that one might attempt to identify them in thought by devising a special language for them does not appear to be incomprehensible, nor does it seem unlikely that the judgments of identification one might proceed to make in the new idiom would consistently correspond to the appropriate phenomenal occurrences. If one is prepared to admit, moreover, that other people also have covert feelings and sense impressions, and are also capable of silent thought, then it should not be excessively difficult to imagine another person employing such a language either.

It is not necessary, after all, that these phenomenal occurrences be intrinsically private in the sense that no one but the private thinker could *conceivably* know that they occurred or existed. Although Wittgenstein apparently did attack the intelligibility of utterly private objects,* there is nothing in the contentions of the solitary thinker presently in question that would commit him to the existence of these peculiar things. Not only does his skimpy, basic conceptual apparatus lack the resources necessary to speak of other persons, but when it is enriched by nonphenomenal terms, so that discourse about selves and a public time and space can be carried out within it, he will endeavor to show that other persons *can* understand him when he speaks—in that language—of the feelings, thoughts, and sense impressions that he happens to have. Hence, since there is no initial presumption that the phenomenal items in question are intrinsically private in some profound epistemological sense, only a radical behaviorist should have special diffi-

---

* It is important to recall that I am presently concerned with the question whether Wittgenstein's argument refutes the view outlined at the end of Ch. I (see pp. 24–29). Whether his argument succeeds against the view he actually had in mind, which I take to be a form of logical atomism (see p. 67, footnote), is a very different question, not at issue here. Many philosophers apparently think that his argument rules out *any kind* of basic phenomenal language, and it is this opinion that I wish to refute here.

culty in understanding the idea that a practice of applying phenomenal terms might in fact be quite consistent.

It should be observed in this connection that even if, as is often
claimed, we ordinarily describe our experience in relation to patterns of behavior with which it is correlated, it does not follow
that no other mode of describing our experience is possible. Thus,
while itches are commonly distinguished from other feelings partly
by reference to their tendency to bring about scratching, it is not
inconceivable that a solitary thinker might classify those of his
feelings that happen to be itches in a less indirect way. If the phenomenal theorist's strategy of enriching his basic language were
accomplished in any significant degree, he might in fact reach the
point of *identifying* the referent of one of his phenomenal terms
"*A*" with what he later learns to call "an itch that I feel." The
identity-statement he may later affirm, "*A*'s *are* itches that I feel,"
would of course be a contingent one, since *A*'s, unlike itches, are
not definitionally tied to the tendency to scratch. But the merely
contingent character of this statement will not prevent us from
saying that the items he initially identifies as *A*'s may be nothing
more mysterious than what *we* might call "itches that he feels."

If the idea of identifying what are in fact one's sensory experiences in a special language so meagerly constructed as to have no
room for describing persons or public objects does make sense, and
if, further, no serious doubt about the consistent use of such a language can legitimately be raised, it seems clear that the phenomenal
theorist's claim to a primitive phenomenal language cannot be dis-
missed on *a priori* grounds. This means that his initial steps toward
constructing the position described in the last chapter eludes the
kind of objection we have been considering. It may be that this
initial step leads into a blind alley, but the step itself seems entirely
coherent. It is *not* absurd in principle.

9. SOME LIMITATIONS
OF PHENOMENAL LANGUAGES

Although the Wittgensteinian arguments sketched in this chapter
do not abolish the possibility of all phenomenal languages, my discussion of them has disclosed two points that should minimize the

attractiveness of any appeal to subjective experience as the basis of all empirical knowledge. The first is that subjective experience cannot really provide the logically unshakable foundation of knowledge that empiricists have traditionally sought. In fact the very idea that there can be an ultimate foundation for knowledge has been thoroughly undermined. As I have argued at length, *any* empirical claim, phenomenal or not, is subject to possible correction by other claims. This means that although we may justifiably advance claims that concern nothing more than the momentary character of our immediate experience, we have not thereby reached the bedrock of unalterably certain knowledge that empiricists have tried to find in their subjective experience.

The second point disclosed by the foregoing discussion is perhaps more exciting: phenomenal claims are not intrinsically more reliable than claims of other kinds, such as those concerning persons and physical objects. Thus, as I have shown by describing a number of psychological experiments, it is quite possible for a person's introspective claims to be flatly erroneous. Not only might one be deficient in conceptual ability, but one might be drugged, dazed, insane, or hypnotized. In order to rule out such contingencies, one must have some way of defending the reliability of one's introspective claims. This is most easily done if an appeal to others is taken seriously: their corroboration of my claims adds significant credibility to them. Of course, the fact that their corroborative remarks are likely to be true is itself open to doubt. But to doubt it justifiably one must have some *reason* to think it is perhaps false. To have this reason is obviously to have access to a far wider range of considerations than is available to one whose theorizing is carried out wholly in a phenomenal language. Yet this wider range of considerations in no way lessens one's chances of finding the truth. On the contrary, as I shall argue in subsequent chapters, the wider the range of considerations to which one can appeal, the sounder one's opinions are likely to be.

My view on this matter is almost the opposite to that of traditional empiricists. For them, the accuracy of a man's outlook varied inversely as its scope: the more it encompassed, the more it risked; and the more it risked, the less reliable it was. I prefer to argue that the possibility of error is not the same as the likelihood of error, and that in demonstrating error one is also demonstrating truth.

If you can show that a statement is false, or likely to be false, you have thereby shown that its negation is true or likely to be true. Hence for me any theory that increases the possibility of demonstrating error is far preferable to one that minimizes this possibility. As every gambler knows, when the stakes are low, so are the winnings.[22]

III

Meaning and Immediate Experience

If claims about the character of one's immediate sensory experience cannot provide an absolutely secure foundation for empirical knowledge—if, indeed, they are not necessarily more reliable than claims about less transient things such as trees and windmills—then the basic motive for attempting to construct a primitive phenomenal language seems to evaporate. It would appear that we might just as well proceed to found our knowledge on the equally fallible but far more convenient basis of public observability, which would allow us to employ the familiar idiom of everyday speech.

It happens, however, that there are other reasons why certain traditional minds would want to cling to basic phenomenal languages even when they are purged of their assumed infallibility. These reasons spring mainly from a familiar theory of meaning, which traces the reference of empirical terms to some kind of association with elements of immediate experience. Since some of the fundamental assumptions of this theory are held even by vociferous critics of traditional empiricism who in effect transpose these assumptions into a new philosophical key, it will prove highly instructive to spend a little more time probing the intricacies of phenomenal languages.

1. ASSOCIATION, ABSTRACTION, AND MEANING

The essential claim of the theory in point can be set down somewhat as follows. Even though one might be able to construct a complicated conceptual system whose basic verbal elements are bound together by rules of inference, the system as a whole must be securely tied down to the world of experience if it is to be a proper descriptive language. Many terms of the language may of course have meaning because they inherit it from others as the result of definition. But at least some terms, the empirically basic ones, must have a kind of meaning that cannot possibly consist in their mere syntactical relations with others. This special kind of meaning must be extra-linguistic in character, for it concerns a word's relation to the world.

For many traditional empiricists eager, like John Locke, to repudiate the faintest trace of an innate idea, this kind of meaning was thought to arise from a process of abstraction or sensuous differentiation involving the immediate data of sense. I say "abstraction *or* sensuous differentiation" because in attempting to explain the origin of abstract ideas—which become, by association, the meanings of general terms—two quite different theories were generally tangled together, one for determinate abstract ideas such as mauve or scarlet, and one for determinable abstract ideas such as triangularity or color.[1] According to the first theory, one gains ideas of determinates merely by sorting out one's experiences. In eating an apple, for instance, one is presented with an intertwined complex of impressions—of red, sweetness, apple-shape. In order to conceive this particular redness in the abstract, one has only to isolate out the appropriate impression (or "idea") from the other elements of the complex. This is generally, but not necessarily, brought about by the presence of other impressions of red, in other complexes. When a certain kind of impression is multiply present, in imagination if not in sense, it is generally recognized as a unitary sort—and this recognition is what yields an abstract idea or concept. The process by which these concepts are formed might, then, be called one of "sensuous differentiation"; for to the extent that one can simplify the blooming, buzzing confusion of immediate experience, and so distinguish resembling items, one has a concept of a determinate item of experience.

The other account, the one concerned with determinable ideas, was the familiar abstraction theory. According to this account, after a number of similar items have been experienced and perhaps retained by the imagination as a sort of composite memory image, their common nature or essence is abstracted out and brought before the mind as a unitary concept. This kind of abstraction is plainly very different from what I have called sensuous differentiation. The result of abstraction is something general rather than specific—the idea, for instance, of a polygon, with no determinate number of angles. Of course, starting with Berkeley, a good many empiricists had extreme difficulty with the doctrine of abstractionism. Tending to confuse ideas (or concepts) with images, they could not imagine how one could actually have an abstract idea: surely an *image* of a polygon must have a determinate number of angles! Accordingly, they tended to merge their account of determinates, which in the hands of Berkeley and Hume had led to the view that ideas of determinates are just less vivid counterparts of actual experiences, with a dispositional analysis of abstract ideas (that is, determinables), according to which having such an idea is essentially a disposition to image concrete, individual things "of a certain sort," with for instance a determinate number of edges.

But while many empiricists went back to abstractionism, arguing that concepts are not to be confused with images, a fundamental motivation of the old theory seems to have been lost. In spite of its patent errors, the older view made an energetic attempt to account for the intentionality or reference of thought. If a man's thoughts are actually occurrent mental episodes, the question always arises as to how they can be *about* other things, how they can refer to them. On the older theory this was tacitly explained by their similarity to their objects. A thought of scarlet was, as an experience, similar to a sensation of scarlet—it was a less vivacious, less vivid counterpart—and so could be *of* or *about* that sensation. Thus, in thinking about scarlet, scarlet was literally present to the mind; it was *there*—though not, of course, in its full, sensuous splendor.

This attempt to account for the reference of thought may seem very naive, but it has the undeniable merit of coming squarely to terms with a very serious problem. This problem arises for anyone who regards thinking as involving covert episodes and who is tempted to brood about the various media—words, images, and the like—in which thinking is generally carried on. When a man thinks, he necessarily thinks about something, and if his activity of thinking is episodic, the particular objects he is thinking about are presumably determined by the special "reference" that his thoughts possess. The suggestion that a man's thoughts involve fleeting pictures is thus not utterly stupid, at least in connection with traditional concerns. Not only does it explain the mechanism of mental reference by assimilating a thought of X to a picture of X, but it fits in nicely with the persistent tendency to regard thinking as an inner process that necessarily requires a sensuous medium.

Unfortunately, it is easy to see that even if we are eager to disavow behaviorism and insist that thinking is, or at least may be, a wholly silent process involving introspectively accessible episodes, the imagistic theory of thinking does not warrant our assent. This is not just because thought is essentially "judgmental," possessing the categorical, hypothetical, or modal forms discussed by Kant.* It is also because we can think of countless things we cannot possibly image (such as million-sided polygons) and because we can have images that picture things exactly and yet not be thinking of the things pictured. Suppose an image comes to mind which I can render quite accurately on canvas. This image might constitute a very good likeness of a certain person, say Socrates. But in having this image I need not be thinking of Socrates. Indeed, I could have this image without thinking of anything whatever—except, perhaps, how odd it is that I should have such a strange image. To insist that I must be thinking of Socrates in this case is tantamount, one might say, to insisting that one who sees stars when hit on the head must be thinking of astronomy.

Once the shortcomings of an out-and-out imagistic theory of meaning were fully recognized, it was natural for empiricists to regard thinking as essentially linguistic. Thinking then becomes a kind of covert monologue, the basic elements of which are bound to experience by association. Certain sensuous qualities recur in experience, and one comes to associate particular words with them.

* These forms of thought are discussed carefully in Ch. VIII; see esp. pp. 178 f. and 187 f.

If this association is well established, one then has a concept of the appropriate quality; for on this view a concept is essentially an ability—an ability to apply the right names to the right things. Unfortunately, this view is not able, when pressed, to dispense entirely with images; in order to explain how a person can think about something he is not experiencing, and to explain why he will always apply the same word to the same kind of object, images are always dragged back into the theory. Thus, on most accounts it is only because one can imagine the sort of thing to which a basic word applies that one is successful in using it, and it is only because basic words are associated with images that one can think about experiences one is not currently having. According to this view, when one uses a basic word an image of the thing to which it applies is brought before the mind; and it is exactly because the word's referent is thus imaginatively in mind that its use in silent soliloquy can fulfill the requirements of being a thought of the appropriate object.

As I have presented it, this theory of the mental word obviously requires amendment if it is to be consistent with what was established about the structure of admissible phenomenal languages in Chapter II. For one thing, even the basic descriptive terms of the language cannot be *mere* names or labels; their logic is too complex for this. If logical atomism is untenable,* then even basic assertions must have conceptual connections with others; and this requires intra-language rules that relate the basic expressions so that the system as a whole may reflect a coherent conceptual scheme. Consequently, the role of imagery in the total picture could at best carry the added requirement that one be able to imagine the kind of thing to which the basic terms apply.[2] This latter requirement is just what a man blind from birth cannot satisfy in connection with color-words, and so he is said to lack an understanding of such basic words as "red."

---

* Logical atomism was ruled out by the argument of the last chapter. Logical atomism, as opposed to the sort of scientific atomism described in Ch. I, is a philosophical theory concerning the logical structure of language and reality. The atoms it concerns are not physical particles but "states of affairs" that are incapable of being analyzed into simpler ones. A useful discussion of this position can be found in J. O. Urmson, *Philosophical Analysis* (Oxford: Clarendon Press, 1956), Parts I and II.

2. CONSEQUENCES OF AN ASSOCIATION
THEORY OF REFERENCE

Assuming for the sake of argument that the theory, so qualified, provides at least an initially plausible account of thought and reference, what are its consequences? Does it allow one to make sense of a world of persons and physical things located in a common space and time? Does it, in particular, bring aid or disaster to the metaphysical construction of the world envisaged at the end of Chapter I?

According to some contemporary writers, the theory fails in all these purposes; in their opinion, anyone accepting it is simply treading the path to solipsism.[3] To see their point, notice that anyone holding the theory is faced with a very serious problem of justifying the application of phenomenal terms to the experience of other persons. If such terms actually gain their referential meaning by association with the elements of one man's subjective experience, then their reference will evidently be *restricted* to the elements of his experience. To put it in another way, since the theory in question construes basic word-world connections as associational, basic phenomenal terms will apply only to those objects with which they may be associated. Since other persons presumably cannot have the particular experiences belonging to this class, the phenomenal terms in question cannot truly apply to them. If this is indeed so —if the class term "experience" must apply to a particular, personal domain of items—then it cannot be truly applied to another domain of items; and this means that, given the relevant sense of the term "experience," other persons presumably cannot actually have experiences.

To this it might be replied, "Just why must the experiences in point belong to a single agent? Why couldn't some of them be shared, for example?" But this reply simply ignores the manner in which the concept of a self is defined by the reconstruction in Chapter I.* If, in accordance with that reconstruction, we think of the self that establishes the meaning of certain terms mainly by association as *the* X that has the experiences $E_1, \ldots, E_n$, then $E_1, \ldots, E_n$ are necessarily the experiences of that self. Thus, let K

* See Ch. I, p. 25.

be the class of these experiences. Then, from the definition of the relevant self (namely, that self = the X that apprehends the elements of K), it follows that there is one, and only one, X that has K-elements. Hence, the idea that other selves might also have K-elements is clearly contradictory.

It may be very tempting at this point to reject this way of defining a basic self. But doing so involves very serious consequences for anyone defending an associationist theory of referential meaning. For one thing, since no phenomenal self is introspectively apparent, as Hume and others have insisted,* the only other alternative seems to be a conception of the self as a bundle of experiences. Yet this conception is not only untenable, for reasons I shall mention a little later, but it is clearly out of line with the general strategy of the empiricist construction we have been considering. The main point of that strategy was to resist all attempts to reduce things to their appearances, and the bundle theory of the self simply reduces the self to its subjective or phenomenal appearances.

Assume, then, that we may cling to the "Kantian" conception of the self just defined, at least for the time being. Is there any other way, given this definition, of saving the theory from the above objections? One way suggests itself immediately; it is connected with the idea of resemblance. The argument is this: if a certain phenomenal item, P, is taken as the paradigm of a certain phenomenal *kind*, then the class of all items resembling P can be taken as the extension of the appropriate phenomenal term, say "A." If, accordingly, there is reason to think that other persons have items resembling P, then the term "A" could reasonably, and perhaps truly, be applied to the experiences of others. P itself would of course be one's own experience; the experiences of others would simply be items which, though not observable to oneself, are nevertheless similar to P.

The trouble with this approach, as Wittgenstein clearly saw, is that the sense of "resemblance" in point here is exceedingly obscure.[4] In what sense—given our present assumptions—could the experiences of others possibly resemble P? Surely not in an immediately perceptible respect; it would obviously be impossible to have both one's own and others' experiences at the same time, and so be able to appraise their similarity by direct inspection. Ac-

* See Ch. I, p. 17.

cording to most traditional theories, any experience of which one is immediately aware is necessarily one's own, not someone else's; so on these theories it would be a contradiction to suppose that such inspection is possible.

One does not, of course, have to be wholly traditional in these matters. One might maintain, for instance, that phenomenal items may be conceived as ownerless, and so grouped in classes without reference to any self at all. And if this were done, it might then be possible to develop a very general concept of *having an experience*, which having is not necessarily tied to the notion of a particular self. But the drawback here—and indeed with other, more bizarre attempts, which might try to splinter a self into cognitive and sensitive parts, and then discuss the possibility of joining the cognitive part of one self with the sensitive part of another, so that the inspection of one self's sensory data by another becomes a logical possibility—is that a very complicated, indeed highly theoretical account of selves and their relation to their experiences must be in hand—and must, moreover, have something in its favor.* But because the central concepts of this account would be theoretical, not phenomenal, they could have no direct ostensive component and must, accordingly, gain their application entirely by their relation to purely phenomenal concepts. How this is to be done is, however, extremely unclear and problematic.

Let me expand on this theme for a moment. If *having* were an ostensively definable relation, its relata would presumably have to be ostensively definable as well. Since one of the relata is to be a self, the self, too, would have to be introspectively apparent. But every staunch empiricist since Hume has failed to find such a self: all they find are bundles of experiences. It would not, in any case, really help matters if such a self could be found. Anyone regarding the concept of a self as a purely ostensive one would have exactly the same difficulty justifying its application to "others" as he would have with any of the more familiar phenomenal concepts already discussed. On the other hand, if *having* and *selfhood* were not ostensive concepts, or were not wholly analyzable in terms of such concepts, they could legitimately be employed only if one has a theory in hand which has a strong possibility of being confirmed and which would justify their use. A theory of this kind would,

* See Ch. I, pp. 21 f.

however, be related to phenomenal items only indirectly, as is presumably the case with the relation between any theory and its so-called observation base.

It is, of course, possible that a philosopher with a strong empiricist spirit would accept this latter approach and attempt to introduce the notion of another's experience only at a very high level of theory. In fact an attempt to do just this would be entirely consistent with another stratagem dear to empiricist hearts, namely, the analogical argument for the existence and nature of other minds. Since the spirit of this argument is still haunting philosophical periodicals, it is worth spending a moment to consider how it might be developed from a phenomenal base.

Suppose, to begin with, that a man has a well-developed phenomenal language of the kind already considered. In accordance with the strategy outlined at the end of Chapter I, he might then posit a world of physical structures in space and time, and define "having an experience" as a relation between a physical structure of a certain kind and a covert, nonphysical thing or occurrence. His self would then be just one of these posited physical structures. Assume that his theory is reasonably confirmed, and that his enriched vocabulary is sufficient for the description of the behavior of these physical structures, which he calls "human bodies." He might then proceed to deal with the experiences of others as follows.[5] He notices, first, that he (body M_1) has a certain experience, A, whenever he is in certain circumstances, C, and that whenever he has A he is disposed to exhibit a certain kind of behavior, K. He then notices that other bodies similar to his also exhibit K-ish behavior in C-ish circumstances. He then defines "A_0" (a term for another's experience) in this way: A_0 is that unobservable condition of another M-kind body that is expressed or accompanied by behavior of kind K in circumstances of kind C. Since his own experience, A, is also accompanied by K in C (an inductively established regularity), he finally concludes, by analogy, that his and others' experiences are sometimes of precisely the same kind, that is, they are all instances of *A-in-general*.

But such an account is obviously impossible. Given the definition of "A_0," it is logically impossible for a person (a "body") to have A_0 and not at least be disposed to exhibit K-ish behavior in C-ish circumstances. Hence his concept of another's A is not the concept of a mere phenomenal item; it is rather the concept of something that, of logical necessity, is connected with a certain kind of behavior and circumstance. Thus A and A_0 are really quite different; they are not in any sense the same sort of thing—at least by definition. The meaning of "A," which was established by a private ostensive procedure, has logically no connection with that of "A_0"; the necessary and perhaps even inductively sufficient conditions for the truth of "M_2 has A_0" are the existence of certain dispositions, namely to exhibit K in C; but for the occurrence of A the fact that K in C obtains is logically irrelevant. Hence there is strictly no justification for calling A_0 just a case of "another A"; by definition they are utterly different.

It might be replied that although A and A_0 are not similar by definition, they are similar nevertheless: they are "accidentally" similar in view of their causal properties. This may be so—indeed, it seems to be so, if the relation of having is understood as a causal relation between a body and something that is not publicly discernible, such as A's or A_0's. But while this accidental resemblance might well exist, "A_0" has no ostensive component; and if, accordingly, the resemblance they do have were crystalized into a definition, so that "A" and "A_0" became synonymous terms, the phenomenal content of "A" would be cut away, leaving only a reference to causal properties. This, however, would be far from the intentions of the man who wants a phenomenal foundation for all his empirical knowledge; in fact it would destroy such a foundation completely.

In view of this consequence, a philosopher might be tempted to fall back on the old idea of Schlick,[6] namely that terms like "pain" or "afterimage" really have two senses, a public and a private sense. In the latter sense these words are used mainly in introspection, in labeling sensuous qualities which are strictly indescribable so far as other persons are concerned; but in the former sense these words function in a publicly understandable way, where their force can be captured by a general description such as "that unobservable occurrence which results from a certain kind of stimulation and in turn disposes one to behave in a particular manner." In this latter use a psychological term plainly conveys nothing of what is known immediately and intuitively, and nothing of what is captured by private ostension.

Although this view is no doubt highly repugnant to common sense, it has been defended by subtle thinkers, and its air of contrivance and implausibility is not therefore a demonstration of its error. But anyone who commits himself to it is nevertheless going far beyond the phenomenal foundation on which the most secure empirical knowledge is alleged to rest. In fact, in order to speak of a subject of experience—indeed, to speak of *his own* experience and the reliability of *his own* contentions—he must abandon the phenomenal foundation altogether.

To see this, recall again that the concept of one's self is to be introduced by definite description. Assuming that $E_1, \ldots, E_n$ are the elements of the phenomenal field about which one is brooding, the *self* in point is thus to be defined as *the X*—or *the body*, which from the point of view of the empiricist's reconstruction turns out to be an *X* anyway—that is related by *having* to $E_1, \ldots, E_n$.* Now, as was explained in Chapter I,† such definitions are legitimate only when there is a good chance that they will be backed up by a well-confirmed theory, which will tell us just what the *X* is and will show us, in fact, that there really is such an *X*. When developed, however, this theory would require such concepts as those of public space and public time—and therefore such concepts as those of persisting external bodies and objective periodicities. But from the point of view of the phenomenalist all these notions are highly theoretical, lacking any direct ostensive component: the things to which they apply are *in principle* cut off from direct phenomenal scrutiny. Consequently, the very possibility of using the idiom of a nonphenomenal self depends on the availability of nonphenomenal knowledge—knowledge of an independent, persisting, publicly detectable world. Yet if all of this knowledge is required in order to substantiate one's claims about *one's own* experience, the phenomenal foundation is clearly abandoned.

In view of these very serious consequences of talking about a trans-phenomenal self or subject of experiences, anyone wanting to hold fast to a phenomenal basis must retreat to an out-and-out

---

* Recall from Ch. I that the motivation for a definition of this kind is the Kantian one that a phenomenal field is coherent rather than chaotic, that it discloses a unitary point of view toward what one would ordinarily regard as the physical world.

† See again pp. 22 f.

phenomenalism of the translational variety. Anything he can legitimately say will have to be expressed entirely in phenomenal terms, and anything he wants to talk about—a public world, other persons, even his own self—will have to be understood as some kind of construction out of phenomena. Phenomenalism thus conceived is, however, completely untenable; in fact when consistently developed, it turns out to be a weakly disguised form of solipsism— something that any seeker for truth would naturally want to avoid.

3. THE SOLIPSISTIC CHARACTER OF RADICAL PHENOMENALISM

Radical phenomenalism can be fairly characterized as an attempt to interpret the world without reference to anything essentially nonphenomenal; and if it is to succeed, anything not directly apprehensible, or not specifiable wholly in phenomenal terms, cannot meaningfully be mentioned. In my view the usual statements of this position are intrinsically self-contradictory, since in attempting to reconstruct our world of public things in a purely phenomenal manner, the phenomenalist nearly always tacitly assumes the existence of nonphenomenal, public things—and is, for that reason, inconsistent with his presuppositions.

One of the public things tacitly smuggled into the phenomenalist's austere picture is an objective time, a kind of time not definable wholly on a phenomenal basis. That the kind of time he *can* define is not adequate to the needs of his general program of translating talk about public things into a phenomenal idiom may be seen as follows. Any kind of time, physical or phenomenal, is necessarily an order, one which is presumably transitive, symmetric, and irreflexive. This is just a topological feature of time, which phenomenalists seem to think is quite independent of the sort of metric ordinarily provided by clocks.* Assuming that *later* could be taken as a basic temporal relation, the phenomenalist would have to regard it as having, for his purposes, a private ostensive component. According to the argument given earlier, this means that the rela-

* But the argument is untenable, since this toplogical property is true only of metrically homogeneous intervals—for example, for seconds or minutes or hours, but not all together.

tion can strictly hold only between occurrences of which the man who defined it is, or could be, aware. Yet to give an account of other minds, and to express such facts as *He felt sorrow before I did,* or anything else concerning what others felt or did before one existed, some other conception of time is necessary—a time in which others live and move and have their being. This other time is not, however, definable on the basis of the phenomenal predicate "later," which, because it is fundamentally a term of private ostension, relates only the occurrences of one's own peculiar history.

It might be thought that this last difficulty can at least be partly avoided by claiming that others, and their experiences, do exist in one's phenomenal time because they are to be understood as logical constructions out of one's own phenomenal data. But one can hold this position only if, among other things, one is prepared to ignore the *private* data of others. Their data is obviously not one's own; and if a place for such data is to be honestly made, it must be in their own phenomenal time, or in a common time, not definable by the phenomenal predicate "later," in which all phenomenal series are located. Both of these alternatives are, of course, unacceptable to a consistent phenomenalist. If he cannot allude to items not definable by reference to those *he* directly apprehends, he plainly cannot discourse or even conceive of another person's private time; and a common time is out of the question because in regarding other persons as logical constructions out of his data, he must strictly regard their so-called phenomenal data as logical constructions out of the logical constructions (from his data) which he might term "their behaving in such and such a way in such and such circumstances." Thus, a consistent radical phenomenalist is necessarily a peculiar sort of behaviorist with respect to the experience of others, and he cannot, therefore, speak of a common time in which both his experiences and the experiences of others might coexist as occurrent phenomenal items.

This brings me to a second fundamental criticism. Phenomenalists generally want to find translations (in phenomenal terms) for such truths as "That table not only looks to be, but actually is, brown." In order to provide a translation for this, however, the notion of a possible or conditional sense content must be introduced, since things are not, generally, all and only what they seem to be at a certain moment. Roughly speaking, a conditional sense content (or phenomenon, as I have been using the term) is usually defined as the sense content one would have if. . . . Clearly, if phenomenalism is to succeed, everything following the "if" must be explicated wholly in phenomenal terms, which means that no ineliminable reference can be made to objective conditions, such as the dentist's office on a certain blue Monday, in which the appropriate phenomena would be experienced. This latter requirement, that all reference to objective conditions be expressed wholly in phenomenal terms, is notoriously bothersome to the phenomenalist, since to make even an initially plausible case for the translation of such pedestrian descriptions as "the office on Fifth and Main" and "Two o'clock, next Monday," endlessly long phenomenal screeds would be required.[7] These screeds would be endless because in order to insure that an objective situation is uniquely described in phenomenal terms, an account must be given which, presumably by relating the phenomena appropriate to each stage of the route through space and time from the given situation to that of the present moment, will distinguish it from the countless situations that might superficially resemble it.[8]

Instead of dwelling on difficulties of this sort, serious as they are, I want to call attention to a fatal confusion in the description of a conditional phenomenon.[9] These phenomena are defined as the phenomena *one* would have if . . ., not as the phenomena *I* would have if. . . . Yet, unless the fundamental principle of phenomenalism is tacitly abandoned, I cannot admit, as phenomenalist, that others could have their own phenomenal data in their own subjective time, nor could I know anything about the private phenomena of people generally: in fact, I can strictly make no sense of the idea of such things. The notion of *one's* data (impersonal "one") is presumably an abstraction, like the average plumber; but unlike my knowledge of the average plumber, which is based on knowledge of many individual plumbers, my knowledge of what phenomenal data *one* would have if this or that cannot be based on knowledge of what phenomenal data various individual persons have when this or that. Accordingly, *the only conditional phenomena I can strictly make sense of are my own.* As a consistent radical phenomenalist, I simply cannot make sense of the subjective data of others, whether these data be actual *or* conditional. All that I can strictly know is this: that there is a system of phenomenal data, some of which are *here*, directly known as they occur; that others would occur if certain others happened to occur; that these occurrences take place according to certain patterns; and that various elements of these patterns can be divided up into classes, some of which may be called "aspects of myself," others of which may be called "aspects (or awarenesses) of dogs, trees, other people." For me, this is all there is or can be. Given my principles, I cannot even make sense of the idea that there might be other series of phenomena, which do not overlap this series. The limits of my experience are the limits of my world.

In the light of these inescapable restrictions it is obvious that if I want to make sense of such familiar facts as that my own phenomenal history reflects the contingencies of my own nature and surroundings, and the peculiarities of my particular sense organs, I am in a thoroughly hopeless position. Assuming that I am color-blind, I must conceive a red object as merely a class of largely gray phenomena, some of which are connected with phenomena representing other persons' behavior, in particular their saying "It really is red." Aside from this, the gray series with the sound-phenomena classifiable as "the voices of others" is all that the expression "a red object" can mean to me. The idea that there is literally a sensuous feature, an occurrent redness, which I cannot see but which others can, thus makes no sense to me at all. The same holds true, of course, for *all* so-called sensible properties—for odors, noises, shapes, and even perceptible resistance. This being so, the very idea of a *public* physical object, one having occurrent sensible properties that, due to my own peculiarities as a perceiver, I may fail to appreciate or accurately apprehend, is something that I cannot strictly have. My conception of a persisting physical body amounts to no more, in other words, than what a common-sense realist would call "a physical thing's subjective appearance to a solitary, and perhaps extremely peculiar, observer." Since my entire view of the world is to be understood along similar lines, it follows that I am not only wedded to a theory that is essentially solipsistic, but that I cannot, strictly speaking, even conceive the possibility that I have a view of things that is limited, peculiar, or perhaps, from an objective standpoint, entirely accurate and complete.

Few phenomenalists have ever been happy with this meager picture. Instead, they have cheerfully talked about the phenomena (or

sense data) of others, feeling that so long as they were only talking
about phenomena, and clusters or classes of them, all is well—no
matter whose phenomena they are. But all is not well with this conception. To speak of the phenomena of others in any nonsolipsistic
way, in particular to talk about the phenomena *one* would have
if . . . (where "one" is not interchangeable with "oneself"), involves
a tacit but entirely clear rejection of the fundamental principle
of phenomenalism, namely, that nothing strictly unobservable,
nothing nonphenomenal to the speaker, can meaningfully be described and referred to. Without the forbidden impersonal "one,"
however, there is absolutely no plausibility to the idea that a world
of public things can be characterized wholly in phenomenal terms.

4. PRACTICAL CONSEQUENCES OF THE PHENOMENALIST'S APPROACH

Suppose, however, that someone is willing to accept the meager
kind of phenomenalism just mentioned. What would be the practical consequences of adopting such a position? Would it actually
increase, or might it not severely delimit, the range of what we can
know even about our own sensory histories? And might it not
carry other, perhaps logical, difficulties along with it?

The basic assumption of the whole phenomenalist program, as
I have indicated, is that one can ascertain the truth of statements
about phenomenal regularities independently of all reference to
nonphenomenal things and occurrences. If, therefore, a phenomenalist is to refer to, and assert something of, a particular phenomenal
object, he must have some immediate means of distinguishing that
item from the hordes of phenomenal occurrences that constitute
his sensory history. But just what means are available for this purpose? How, that is, is he to make this distinction without in some
way alluding to such nonphenomenal matters as the objective time,
place, and situation in which the occurrence was experienced?

A favorite answer to these questions, one characteristic of logical
atomism, may be drawn from the well-known doctrine of "logically proper names." According to this doctrine, one simply bap-
tizes phenomenal items with a name, and is thereafter able to refer
to them by the use of these names. For the time being I shall not

quarrel with this doctrine as applied to items in one's present phenomenal field; I shall agree, for the moment, that present items can be named and referred to in the manner described. What I question now is whether this doctrine serves to account for one's ability to refer to things experienced some time ago.

Suppose that I once baptized a phenomenal occurrence with the name "Tom." Would it follow from this that whenever I use the word "Tom" I am referring to that particular item? Obviously not, for I might accidentally use it in connection with some other item, for instance one that I am perceiving now. But suppose that I do remember calling a thing "Tom" in the past and now want to say something about that particular object. Can I not do this at once by using the word "Tom"? The answer, of course, is "Yes," but it does not tell us what makes my use of the word an act of *referring* to (or naming) something, especially something in the past. To this other question one is tempted to say, at least if one holds the theory of reference described at the beginning of this chapter, that one can use a name to refer to something only when its use brings a referent to mind by way of image or idea: the name must be *associated* with an object.

It is easy to see, however, that this conception of a name is completely inadequate. For one thing, the mere fact that one associates something with a word is absolutely no guarantee that the word names (or refers to) anything at all, let alone that with which it is associated. I might associate a bad smell with the word "barn" or even the word "fallacy"—and I might imagine that smell whenever I hear either of these words—but it would in no way follow that either or both of them must be my name for, or my means of referring to, that particular smell. The fact is, I may associate all sorts of things with various words I use, and the significance of this association, far from implying that something or other is a name, may in most cases remain entirely mysterious—being either a subject for amusing speculation or else, possibly, for a grim foray into the jungles of psychiatry.

If an expression is actually to be the name of an object, far more is thus required than a blind association. Naming is clearly a conscious process, and the object named must be conceived rather than merely reacted to, indeed it must be conceived as an instance of a particular *kind* of thing. This latter point, which is an obvious consequence of the argument of Chapter II (see especially sections 5 and 7), is crucially important, because if I am actually to know what I am talking or thinking about when I use a familiar name, I must surely be able to decide whether the thing before me—the thing I now imagine, picture to myself, or in some other way have in mind—is *the same thing* as that to which I formerly applied the name. The expression "the same K" lacks determinate sense, however, until the kind of thing represented by "K" is spelled out. Thus, if one were merely to point to a body of water moving between two banks and ask "Is that the same as what you fished in yesterday?" a true answer could be either "Yes" or "No" depending on how the body of water is conceived. If it is taken as a river, the answer could be "Yes," since rivers are the kind of thing that can be fished in twice. But if it is taken as a mere volume of churning water, the answer could easily be "No; the water molecules are not the same." The point here is that the identity of an individual is always determined by reference to the criteria appropriate to the kind of thing of which it is conceived as an instance. If the thing in question is a phenomenal item, conceived as a type of "momentary particular," then the criteria appropriate to the kind will dictate that any qualitative alteration in one's phenomenal field will imply the existence of a different phenomenal item. If, on the other hand, the thing in question is conceived as a persisting thing, then, like a chameleon crawling on a wall, its qualitative alterations are entirely consistent with its being the same thing (for instance the same chameleon) as before.

Since to name a thing requires that one conceive it as a particular kind of thing, it is clear that two types of criteria are crucial to its identification. The first type will be the criteria for belonging to a kind that were discussed in the last chapter. The second type will be the criteria that distinguish this instance of the kind from other instances. These two types of criteria may be brought together by saying that an expression A can actually be the name of an object X only if X satisfies some description, or family of descriptions, that are in some way associated with A.* To say this is not to say that

---

* To speak of *the* descriptions associated with a name is to generalize from the descriptions that individual speakers associate with it. These various descriptions may be quite different. The question whether two men use a name such as "Smith" to refer to the same man is answered by reference to the criteria associated with the expression "the same man."

names are mere shorthand for descriptions; it is rather to indicate that names gain their peculiar significance only against a background of descriptions, the latter providing basic criteria by which the bearer of the name is to be distinguished from other possible objects.[10] The significance of this is that far from being the simple labels that logical atomists have taken them to be, names are actually every bit as complicated, conceptually, as the kind-expressions discussed in Chapter II. For something to be a name, as opposed to a mere noise or fragment of verbal imagery, it must be connected with other expressions of a language in a suitable way.

If we take this conception of names seriously, we run into several practical problems in any attempt to apply a purely phenomenal conceptual scheme. Given that the bearers of names are to be distinguished from one another by various principles or criteria, a phenomenalist can then be sure of the reference of a term "Tom"—especially if the referent is not in his present phenomenal field—only if he is aware of a description that distinguishes Tom from all the other phenomenal items constituting his sensory history. But this runs into a problem similar to that prompted by the phenomenalist's interpretation of situations in an allegedly public time and space. If phenomenal items, being the sort of thing that falls into familiar classes, cannot be expected to be descriptively unique, there is always the possibility that countless items will satisfy any description that one could advance. Hence, assuming that one can make sense of reference to present items without difficulty, as in "Tom is the unique red thing now," the objects of all other reference must be uniquely determined not just by their intrinsic features but by their relations to the present phenomenal field. Because the character of one's immediate experience is continually fluctuating, it follows that overwhelmingly long "maps" will be needed—not only to make sense of the reference to such constructions as other bodies, public space and time, but even for *particular* phenomenal occurrences. Hence, to talk about most things less closely tied to the present than a current phenomenal particular, one would have to be the master of a virtual wilderness of phenomenal maps, many of which are unimaginably long. And this means that if, as is usual, phenomenal particulars are to be individuated by changes, however slight, in a phenomenal field, no one who ever lived could have the power of memory to think about, let alone know facts about, occurrences in his phenomenal history which happened more than just five minutes ago. But if this is true, it makes a curious joke of the phenomenalist's idea that one can put empirical knowledge on a secure foundation, and give a true account of how we think and why our judgments are true, only by rejecting all references to what one cannot immediately experience.

5. EXPERIENCE AND KNOWLEDGE:
THE BASIC CONNECTION

In the light of these consequences, we might ask just what could ever tempt a man to take phenomenalism seriously. In part, no doubt, it is the ancient idea, aired earlier, that perceiving or sensing or experiencing is knowing properly so-called. But this idea is plainly false, as was shown in Chapter II: men may wallow in novel experiences without knowing anything about them at all; for not only may they be speechless, but they may be thoughtless and conceptless as well. Knowledge is a matter of having true, defensible opinions—and it is not true *a priori* that one's opinions about one's current feelings or mental imagery are necessarily immune from error. The specter of personal instability and confusion must always be faced, and this cannot be ruled out by *a priori* means.

But it is not just the question of truth or knowledge that tempts one to engage in the phenomenal quest; it is also an inveterate tendency to think that *meaning* must, in the end, be reduced to an association between coexperienced items. Yet association of this sort cannot itself account for meaning; in fact, it is not even essential to meaning. A term or string of terms has meaning because it has a place in a conceptual scheme, a system of expressions that allows one to describe reality. And reality need not be reached at some special grass-roots level. What is essential to an empirical statement is not that it can be reduced to something basic but that it be capable of being refuted or corroborated by other statements, which are considered empirical and true. The question whether a statement is empirical is determined, moreover, by the conceptual scheme of which it is a part. Reality may be conceptualized in many ways and at many levels of generality; and as we shall see in later

chapters,* statements about mental states are in no sense more basic
and more empirical than a nonanalytic statement about a positron.
Statements about the latter are empirical for the same reason that
any other statement is empirical, namely, because the objects they
concern are so conceived that they have a theoretically ascertaina-
ble place among the furniture of the world.

Many things now regarded as mythical or even nonsensical have
admittedly been regarded as legitimate furniture of the world. Obvious examples are demons, devils, and phlogiston. Yet conceptions
of these things are not objectionable because they cannot be specified in terms of actual and possible sensations or observations—as
phenomenalists and positivists often allege. They are rather objectionable either because they are conceived in too indefinite and
too uncritical a way, or because the conceptual system to which
they belong has been superseded by a better, more comprehensive,
and more highly confirmed way of viewing reality. To say that
sensation or observation does not itself provide the ultimate measure
of a theory's worth is not, of course, to suggest that experience is
somehow irrelevant to the vindication or rejection of a conceptual
system—for it surely is relevant. But experience, as was shown
in Chapter II, always requires interpretation; and it is always some
conceptual scheme, however rudimentary, and not virgin reality,
that supplies the criteria by which an interpretation of experience
is to be appraised. Hence the vindication or rejection of a conceptual scheme must always, paradoxically, come from within that
scheme—from its ability to accommodate novel situations in a
critical way and to permit a coherent picture of reality; or from its
inability to do these things. Our predicament here is, in short, the
one described by Neurath when he compared us to sailors who are
forced to rebuild their ship on the open sea, without the chance of
dismantling it on a dock and constructing it anew from better
materials.[11]

* See esp. Ch. X.

IV
Language
and Avowals

Once the theoretical shortcomings of egocentric empiricism are brought squarely into view, less rarefied considerations are sufficient to show that our knowledge of the world is not something inferred from facts about subjective experience. Most of us actually pay very scant attention to our current sensory experience, and we are remarkably imperceptive about its peculiarities. Our constant concern is rather with the threats and promises of the world around us. We commonly lack the discrimination of the painter, the poet, and the wine-taster, and we lack their interests as well. For most of us, immediate sensory experience (with certain exceptions such as pain) is far too tenuous and evanescent to attract much attention—let alone provide ready premises for an easy inference. On the contrary, sensory experience is generally but a spur that drives us into action.[1] Of course, when our action is frustrated, or when our spontaneous claims are met with disbelief, we may indeed volunteer a description of our subjective experience. But when we do this, the words we use are typically parasitic on our public idiom, and they reflect our knowledge of a common world.

To many contemporary philosophers, the patent intersubjectivity of existing modes of speech requires more than the admissions just made; it requires us to acknowledge that the mental states we speak of must have public, behavioral criteria. According to the current view, a man can gain a conception of himself as a sentient, intelligent creature—a living being that feels, thinks, and acts— only by realizing that he belongs to a community of such creatures. His concepts of thinking, feeling, and acting will thus have a general application from the very beginning; he will not initially apply them just to himself and then, as the result of some analogical form of inference, extend their application to his fellows. Learning their application is rather a unitary process, one that is not completed until the full range of their possible application is appreciated and the public criteria they presuppose are fully understood.

The idea that psychological concepts such as *thinking* and *feeling* have behavioral criteria is not only fascinating in itself—especially since it turns the traditional view of mentalistic concepts entirely on its head—but it requires a radically new approach to language-learning and concept-formation. The object of this chapter is to map out the distinctive features of this new approach by discussing its application to a man's avowals about his current feelings.

I. ON UNDERSTANDING THE SENTENCE "I AM IN PAIN."

In an influential discussion of how one learns to use a public language, Norman Malcolm made the following claim:

> There is . . . a criterion for determining whether someone uses the sentence "I am in pain" *correctly*—and this makes it an intelligible sentence. The behavior and circumstances of an infant are the original criterion of his being in pain. As he grows older and begins to talk it will normally come about that often when his behavior and circumstances are those of a person in pain he will say the words "It hurts," or some synonymous ones; and hardly ever will he say them when either his behavior or circumstances do not satisfy the original criterion of pain. This development fulfills our criterion of his *understanding* those words.[2]

Although it is unclear just how much qualification Malcolm is prepared to give the statement just cited, it is obvious that a good deal of qualification is actually needed. Suppose that a certain child merely satisfied the criterion Malcolm mentioned. Suppose, that is, that a particular child could say nothing other than "It hurts" or "I am in pain"; that he had absolutely no idea of the effect his words are likely to have on those around him; that he were completely unable to recognize a denial or misinterpretation of his words; and that he could follow none of the usual talk concerned with pains, such as words of advice and warning. Under these conditions the child's linguistic sophistication would not differ appreciably from that of a Skinnerian parrot carefully conditioned to squawk out the sounds *ai am in pein* when and only when a painful stimulus is applied. But this itself is obviously not sufficient to constitute an understanding of words in a common language.

To understand the conventional significance of a group of words is at least to understand what one who uses them is saying or doing. Yet merely to exercise a habit of responding with special noises in certain circumstances is not, by itself, to use language at all. One typically *uses* something for a purpose or end. And so with a sentence: one uses it to inform, to amuse, to deceive, and so on. To say this is not to imply that one who uses a sentence must have some end in mind before he utters the words, or that one must know exactly what one wants to say before a means of saying it is found. On the contrary, one often becomes clear about one's intentions in the act of trying to speak.[3] But in order to use a sentence to make an assertion, tell a lie or relate a joke, one must at least utter it in a certain frame of mind—in a certain state of readiness to reexpress or attempt to clarify what one has said, to follow it up with further remarks, to handle obvious objections, appreciate comments, and the like. Actually, it is largely this frame of mind, which is so far beyond the powers of a parrot to attain, that determines exactly what one is doing when one utters a string of familiar noises.

Important as these considerations are for a thorough account of intelligent speech, it is not necessary to dwell on them to see the crucial drawback of Malcolm's simplified picture. In order to understand the *sentence* "I am in pain" you must understand it whenever and wherever it is properly used—and this means understanding it when it is uttered by another person. But this latter understanding is not given by the trained disposition on *your* part to utter the words "I am in pain" when you are in pain. Hence, if you can understand the sentence "I am in pain" you must understand another person who uses it as saying that *he* is in pain. Since his being in pain has (if Malcolm is right) an essential relation to some kind of behavior he is at least inclined to exhibit, your understanding of "I am in pain" presumably requires an understanding of something about behavior, something describable by some behavior words or other. Yet most of this required understanding was not even tacitly suggested in Malcolm's account.

Actually, once it is noticed that understanding a sentence is a matter of understanding it whenever and wherever it is properly used, it becomes apparent that "I am in pain" and "He is in pain" are so related that an understanding of either requires an understanding of the other. To see this, note that when another person uses "I am in pain" he uses it to talk about himself, not about me. Yet if I did not know something about the logic of pronouns, I could not possibly appreciate this. The logic of pronouns turns, moreover, on a fundamental contrast between "I" and "he": anyone calling himself "I" is a *he* (or *she*) to others. When others talk about me, when they relate what I have said, they use "he" or perhaps even "you" in reference to me, and I must accordingly know something about these words to know how my remarks about myself are taken. Similarly, when I react to their first-person utterances, I can show my understanding of what each of them says only if, for the most part, I am able to connect their remarks with statements about *them*—and I can do this, generally, only by taking them as the referents of certain uses of "he" or "you." Hence, the grammars of "I" and "he" are intimately related, and to understand the *full* force of one, you must understand the force of the other. Since the meaningfulness of saying "We are in pain" implies that "pain" has the same meaning in "I am in pain" as it has in "He is in pain," it follows, almost as a matter of grammar, that a person can fully understand the former sentence only if he can understand the latter.*

* Actually, this is an oversimplification, holding only for persons who understand no other language comparable to English. Obviously a Frenchman could understand the sentence "I am in pain" if its French translation, and only this, were made available to him. He could do this, however, only because the French "*je*" plays the role of a first-person pronoun, having an essential contrast with "*il*" and "*vous*." Hence, my point here is more accurately stated thus: in order to understand the full force of "I," and therefore of "I am in pain," one must understand *the role that is played* by other-person pronouns

Although I regard the argument just given as entirely successful, it will nevertheless provoke the reply that there is something so immediate and personal about what a man wants to convey in saying "I am in pain" that it is absurd to suppose that his special use of the sentence presupposes a familiarity with pain-talk generally. An honest avowal of being in pain is normally considered infallible or "incorrigible," and if the purport of a man's avowal were strictly similar to the purport of saying "He is in pain," facts about the man's subsequent behavior could presumably cast serious suspicion on its truth. This being so, the "incorrigible" character of what one says in using "I am in pain" seems adequate by itself to show that knowledge of behavior-patterns is strictly irrelevant to an understanding of one's own avowal use of the first-person sentence.

2. AN APPROACH TO
THE INCORRIGIBILITY OF AVOWALS

In order to evaluate the above objection it is obviously necessary to appreciate the grounds on which avowal uses of "I am in pain" may be said to be incorrigible. Traditional philosophers rarely argued for this kind of incorrigibility; they merely took it for granted. Recently, however, two arguments have become popular in this connection, and both of them have been discussed by Professor Malcolm.[4] According to the first argument, a person's words about his present feelings have the same logical status as his cries and facial expressions,[5] so that a mistaken use of "I am in pain" is just as senseless as a mistaken groan. As Malcolm puts it:

> A man cannot be in *error* as to whether he is in pain; he cannot say, "My leg hurts," by mistake, any more than he can groan by mistake. It is senseless to suppose that he has wrongly identified a tickle as pain. . . . True, he may be undecided as to whether it is best described as an "ache" or a "pain". . . , but his very indecision *shows* us what his sensation is, *i.e.*, something between an ache and a pain.[6]

The idea here is that after suitable training, saying "I am in pain" becomes learned pain-behavior. As such, it attains the expressive

in some language or other, such as "he" in English or "*vous*" in French. The importance of the notion of a linguistic role will be discussed in some detail in Ch. VIII.

function of crying or groaning, and it is therefore incorrigible.

Although this argument is highly suggestive, it is far from sufficient to fulfill Malcolm's purpose. Unlike cries and groans, an utterance of "I am in pain" is normally a self-conscious use of language. Malcolm, of course, recognizes this difference,* but his manner of avoiding it is unsatisfactory. His remark that even groans may be used to inform others of how one feels actually suggests that one might even groan by mistake on special occasions. Groans are certainly under our voluntary control much of the time; and although a man may have agreed to answer a certain signal of his dishonest bridge-partner by uttering a short cough, he might momentarily forget this at a crucial point in the game and respond with a groan instead. If we assume that the man is just as anxious to cheat as his scheming partner, he might actually curse himself for making this mistake—and it would be a mistake, because he deliberately made a noise that he recognized, a little later, as inappropriate for the task at hand.

This objection may appear excessively contrived, but actually it undermines the basis of Malcolm's argument. When it makes no sense to speak of a groan's being mistaken, there will be no question of a person's groaning for a purpose. When a person just groans—when the groan just escapes him—there is never any question of his making a mistake: he is not trying to do anything. Similarly with verbal behavior: if a man merely emits certain noises—if the noises merely escape from his lips—there is no question of his making a mistake. But such an emission of noises does not count as an identification or description of anything either. To identify in words the feeling that you have, it is not sufficient that the words just escape from your lips. Others may, it is true, know from this emission what your feeling happens to be (as they might know what a parrot feels from the sound of its squawk). But your utterance will not count as a verbal identification of anything unless, among other things, you produce your utterance while in a suitable frame of mind (see p. 87).

* In fact, he registers an inclination to object: "The natural expressions . . . are not used to inform others; they are not 'used' at all; they have no purpose, no function, they escape from me." See p. 109 of Norman Malcolm, *Knowledge and Certainty: Essays and Lectures.* © 1963. Reprinted by permission of Prentice-Hall, Inc., Englewood Cliffs, N.J. Permission is also granted for the passage cited on p. 89.

The point is, we do sometimes identify our feelings in words; our words do not always just escape from our lips. Yet if Malcolm's incorrigibility thesis extends to our words when they represent a self-conscious attempt to communicate with others, then his thesis is not established by the above argument. If our utterances are just expressions of feeling (as moaning *in order* to gain attention is not) they are not *uses* of language. To use language, you have to do more than merely parrot a sound. Of course, if your training in producing a certain sound has been very carefully given, it is perhaps unlikely that you will produce it at the wrong time. But this fact is useless for the purposes of Malcolm's argument. Even if we were to grant that making a mistake about one's feelings might be nothing other than uttering the wrong noises, it would not follow that the idea of such a mistake is in any way senseless. Malcolm's contention that indecision about whether to say (= utter after training) "It hurts" or "It itches" *shows* that the feeling one has is "an indefinite, ambiguous one,"[7] is thus slightly inaccurate. Another possibility has to be ruled out, namely that this wavering between responses is simply irregular—something that is merely unlikely in view of one's previous training. Since unlikely responses are nevertheless possible responses, even the most charitable interpretation of Malcolm's argument cannot therefore support the claim that there is something "senseless" about the idea of a man's making a mistake about his current feelings.

3. AVOWALS AND EXPRESSIVE BEHAVIOR

If Malcolm's attempt to account for the presumed incorrigibility of avowals by assimilating them to cries and groans fails, the question arises whether there is any value to this assimilation. In my view there is some value to it, though it is less significant than Malcolm would have us believe. If avowals cannot themselves be assimilated to spontaneous grunts and groans, the noises one produces in making an avowal sometimes can. This is not a paradox, because the noises one makes can be viewed in more than one way. Some of these noises, such as *ai am in pein*, may occasionally be interpreted as mere behavior, as a conditioned response that indicates the state of the animal that produces them. In order to interpret such noises in this way, we need not raise any questions about whether the creature understands the conventional significance of his responses. Once the response pattern is firmly established, we can immediately take these responses as reliable indicators of the state in question.

But we can also interpret these noises as a person's attempt to communicate with his fellows. Such an interpretation is possible, of course, only under special conditions. These conditions consist largely in the person's readiness to manifest a whole battery of habits—habits of responding to noises (words) with other noises (other words), of behaving in special ways when certain noises are directed to him, and so on. In a word: just as one can make a move in chess—as opposed to merely changing the location of an ivory piece on a checkered board—only when one is prepared to proceed in accordance with the strategy of the game, so one can make a move in language—avow that one feels pain rather than merely parrot a noise—only when one is able to proceed in accordance with the moves and counter-moves distinctive of the language one is speaking.[8]

4. ANOTHER APPROACH TO THE INCORRIGIBILITY OF AVOWALS

I remarked earlier that Malcolm provides another argument for the incorrigibility of first-person reports. According to this argument, inappropriate utterances of "I am in pain" do not count as proper assertive uses. To say, honestly and affirmatively, "I am in pain" when one is not in pain is to show that one has not mastered the use of the words one utters. This might be expressed by saying that the conditions under which one makes a true statement in uttering the words "I am in pain" are just those conditions under which one demonstrates full understanding of the words one uses. If a person not in pain uttered the words "I am in pain" with no intent to deceive, make a joke, or anything similar, then he shows us that he does not possess a complete mastery of the words he is using. In uttering these words under these conditions he is not actually making the assertion he seems to be making—and he is not, *a fortiori*, making the false assertion he seems to be making. Hence, any genuinely honest assertion that one is in pain is incorrigible; its truth conditions are identical with its being the *bona fide* assertion it seems to be.*

Although this argument may sound plausible, I believe it rests on a serious misconception, which exaggerates the requirements for making legitimate assertive uses of such sentences as "I am in pain." I shall try to destroy this misconception later, when several important distinctions are conveniently at hand. Here I want to plunge more deeply into the perplexities concerning avowals by raising some questions about the concept of awareness. Even if, like Malcolm or myself, one throws aside the traditional idea that awareness is what confers infallibility on a man's honest avowals, it remains true that *awareness* is not an entirely empty notion. In some sense or other it surely has something to do with the making of avowals. The essential question to investigate is: just what is this something?

5. ON BEING AWARE OF ONE'S PAINS

In his book *Dreaming* Malcolm made a tantalizing remark about awareness, which seems entirely in the spirit of traditional empiricism. He said: ". . . it makes no sense to speak of *finding out* that one is in pain, where this would imply that one was previously in pain but not aware of it."[9] This remark is tantalizing because in the light of his well-known critique of introspection,[10] it is unlikely that he would actually wish to defend the traditional *esse est percipi* doctrine of pains. Yet if he is not prepared to defend this doctrine, what could he have meant by the remark? What, indeed, could he have meant by the expression "being *aware* of one's pain"?

* This argument seems implicit in the passage from Wittgenstein, which Malcolm cites in his review: "If anyone said 'I do not know if what I have got is a pain or something else,' we should think something like, he does not know what the English word 'pain' means, and we should explain it to him. . . . If he now said, for example: 'Oh, I know what "pain" means; what I don't know is whether *this*, that I have now, is "pain" '—we should merely shake our heads and be forced to regard his words as a queer reaction which we have no idea what to do with." See Ludwig Wittgenstein, *Philosophical Investigations*, trans. G. E. M. Anscombe (Oxford: Blackwell, 1953), Pt. I, sect. 228; also Malcolm's review, p. 555 in *Phil. Rev.* (LXIII), and *Knowledge and Certainty*, p. 126.

The answer to these questions is simply not clear. But notice that the senselessness of speaking of finding out in connection with one's pains can scarcely be defended by resorting to the traditional idea that feeling pain is a mode of awareness and that "being aware of one's pain" just means "feeling one's pain." If feeling is to count as awareness, the connection between being aware and finding out is then left entirely obscure. After all, what one finds out is always the truth of some proposition; yet what one feels, and what one is allegedly aware of in this traditional sense, is not a proposition at all. Yet if the thing felt is quite different from the thing found out —as a feeling is different from a proposition—just why should the two be inseparable? Why should it be impossible to feel pain and yet not know, and so later come to find out, that pain is what one feels?

One reason for believing that the two are inseparable arises from the historical tendency to run together two different kinds of awareness. One of these is the kind already mentioned, of which feeling is a determinate form. (Whether this sense of "awareness" is a philosopher's invention, I shall not say.) The other differs from the first in having a very obvious connection with the matter of finding out. Here one is aware *that* such and such is the case, which is to say that what one is aware of here is *the same* as what one might find out, namely, the truth of some proposition. It is easy to see that once these distinct kinds of awareness are confused, it becomes natural to assume that finding out could not possibly occur in connection with what is felt; for one can find out that p only if one was previously unaware that p, and this would be impossible in the case of feeling pain, *if* feeling were just a determinate form of being aware that. . . .

There is, however, a more recent line of argument purporting to show that it makes no sense to speak of finding out in connection with one's feelings. This argument, which springs from Wittgenstein,[11] begins by emphasizing that "finding out that p" implies "coming to know that p," and then goes on to argue that "He knows that he is in pain" is actually senseless. If the latter contention were true, then of course "He found out that he is in pain" would have to be senseless as well.

Although this argument is extremely weak, its consequences are sufficiently important to render it worthy of consideration. Essentially, it is based on the following line of thought. It is only sensible to speak of knowing in situations where there is room for doubt, where there is a meaningful contrast between "He knows that p" and "He merely thinks, or doubts, that p." But one cannot merely think, or doubt, that one is in pain. To doubt or merely think something is to exercise some concept; hence to doubt or merely think that one is in pain is to employ the concept of pain. A criterion of having this concept, however, is that one has gained the tendency to say "I am in pain" *confidently* on the appropriate occasions, to say it, namely, when one is indeed in pain. If, on a given occasion, one hesitates to say "I am in pain" for fear of saying the wrong thing, this shows not that one really doubts whether one is in pain but only that one is none to clear about what pain is. But if doubting requires concepts, and if having the concept of pain demands confidence about one's feelings—demands in fact that one is never wrong about being in pain—it then follows that doubting and merely thinking that one is in pain are impossibilities, and hence that "knowing" has no place here.

Notice that this argument hinges on the undefended contention that "He knows that p" makes sense only if "He doubts, or merely thinks, that p" makes sense. But this contention is dubious on at least two counts. First, if every meaningful sentence must have an intelligible contrast, a contrast for "He knows that p" can be supplied by its contradictory, "He does not know that p"; and when its contradictory, rather than one of its contraries, is used as contrast, then "He knows that he is in pain" *is* meaningful by the contrast test. Although a suitably trained person may be presumed incapable (in some sense) of being mistaken about being in pain, it is always possible that he either lacks this training or has lost his hold on the concept of pain—in which case he would not know the answer to the question "Are you in pain?" and hence would not know *that* he is in pain (he would simply have no idea of what pain is).[12] Secondly, the universal applicability of the contrast between knowing and doubting is also dubious on the ground that if there were knowledge resting entirely on the analysis of concepts, then it would be natural to suppose that there would be many cases in which the criteria for understanding a statement are the same as those for recognizing its truth. Thus if a person did not know that one plus one equals two, it would probably be held that he did not know what addition is, or that he did not know what is meant by "one," "two," or "equals." Under these conditions it could be argued that a person could not possibly doubt whether one plus one equals two, since to doubt this would require the exercise of these primitive arithmetical concepts. If it were true, however, that knowing implies the possibility of doubt, we would then have to conclude that "One plus one equals two" states something that could not be said to be known—which is absurd, considering the normal usage of the word "know."

There is still another kind of argument that might be raised against me here. Although I have elucidated a use for the sentence "He knows that he is in pain" by contrasting it with "He does not know, or he is ignorant of the fact, that he is in pain," I have done nothing to show that "I know that I am in pain" is significant. Yet if this latter sentence has no intelligible use—or at any rate has no use that differs from that of "I *am* in pain"—then it is still senseless to insist that one might, oneself, know that one is in pain, and so be capable of finding out that pain is what one feels. That is, while "knowing" and "finding out" may well be applied to other persons in this connection, one could not in this way apply them to oneself.

This sort of objection is unfortunately very weak. If "He knows that he is in pain" is meaningful, and capable of being used to make true statements, then others might use it to make true statements about *me*, to state that *I* know that I am in pain. There might of course be something peculiar with *my* using the words "I know that I am in pain" by themselves—something pragmatically peculiar perhaps—but it would not follow that they *could not* be used to make the statement that others might make by using the words "He knows that he is in pain."[13]

This trivial retort will no doubt immediately prompt Wittgenstein's well-known challenge: what is "I know that I am in pain" supposed to mean, except perhaps that I *am* in pain?[14] Fortunately, an answer to this challenge is not hard to find. "I know that I am in pain," unlike the mere "I am in pain," says that I have *knowledge* of a particular matter of fact. It may be granted that if a man says that he is in pain, he conveys the information that he is not ignorant of what he feels. But it is essential to see that this "conveying of information" is not asserting. Strictly, in saying "I am in pain," a man says nothing whatever about not being ignorant, nor does *his statement* imply that he is not ignorant. What, in the strict sense, a man says about himself in using the words "I am in pain" could be said of him by someone else by using the words "He is in pain"— and *what is said* here does not imply anything about the conceptual abilities of the subject, since it could truly characterize a child, dog, or idiot, as well as a sophisticated adult.

The reason the man who says "I am in pain" conveys the information that he is not ignorant of his state is that he could not say what he does say unless he had a language, had concepts, and thus presumably knew what he felt when he uttered his words. The temptation to think that he would be saying the same thing by uttering "I know that I am in pain" as he would by uttering "I am in pain" thus rests on a simple confusion over the sense in which something is communicated when certain words are uttered. The man would not be making the same statement or assertion in both cases, but the total information indirectly conveyed might indeed be the same.

6. AWARENESS AND CONSCIOUSNESS

I have been arguing that because "He knows that he is in pain" may be contrasted with "He does not know, or he is ignorant of the fact, that he is in pain," the former is a perfectly legitimate, entirely meaningful sentence, which could be used to make a true statement. My grounds for this contrast were not, of course, novel; they were simply an application of the Kantian idea, defended at length in Chapter II, that factual knowledge always presupposes a conceptual scheme. Since a man's mastery of a certain conceptual scheme is at best a contingent fact about him, there is thus nothing absurd in saying that he might lack the concept of pain, and all similar concepts, and so not know that he is in pain when pain is what he feels. To insist that it is senseless to deny such a man knowledge of his own pains—and hence senseless, rather than perhaps mistaken, to credit him with such knowledge—is just to coast on the momentum of the old idea that knowing, in at least one of its forms, is *not* sharply distinguishable from feeling, from experiencing something that is "given."

As this allusion to Kant indicates, my purpose in defending the propriety of such locutions as "He knows that he is in pain" was thus not just the grammatical one of correcting what I take to be an unjustifiable restriction of the possible contexts in which the little word "know" can reasonably appear. On the contrary, apart from wanting to expose some obvious weaknesses in certain well-known arguments, I was mainly concerned to *reverse* the current idea that there is something philosophically dangerous about such locutions, that their use is likely to involve one in serious philosophical errors. For the fact is, to think that there is something dangerous about these locutions is to overlook the immense difference that exists between actually knowing something and merely having a certain feeling. Indeed, even to deny that it can ever be illuminating to use the word "know" in relation to a man's awareness of his feelings is to give the erroneous impression that this difference hardly exists at all.

This last point brings out another of my concerns in the previous argument. By emphasizing the legitimacy of saying that a man may know that he feels pain, that he may be fully aware of the truth of this proposition, I wanted to take at least a small step toward elucidating a persistently neglected sense of "awareness," a sense that involves the possession of concepts, of some sort of language. This sense needs elucidation because it is only too easily confused with the traditional sense which, although lacking any obvious connection with "thinking" and "finding out," has historically been taken to describe the true basis for first-person reports or avowals. When this confusion is made by contemporary philosophers, who are struck by the uselessness of trying to treat a feeling, taken as a "mode of awareness," as a basis that guarantees the truth of first-person reports, they are very naturally tempted to junk the idea of awareness altogether.

To yield to this temptation is, of course, to make a mistake. Although one may, without blundering, cast aside the sense of "awareness" that counts feeling as one of its determinate forms, one cannot do this with every sense of the term. It makes perfectly good sense to speak of a man's being consciously aware of his aches and pains; and as the word "consciously" implies, this kind of awareness is a *cognitive* one, which resists being lumped together with brute feeling. To be aware of an ache or pain in this sense—to be aware of it as only a language-user can be aware of it—is not just a matter of having or feeling it. It is rather a matter of being able to recognize it for what it is: of being able to describe it, think about it, worry about it, and perhaps, if moral philosophers are right, appreciate its basic significance in at least the ethical life of man. All this plainly cannot be done naturally, preconceptually, without any learning whatever.

If there is, then, an important sense of "awareness" that applies only to the experience of a concept-possessing animal, can we say that it is this awareness that serves as the basis for a man's honest avowals? To raise this question is to see how confused and unnecessary the notion of a basis is in this connection. To be aware that one is in pain is just to be in pain and either think of oneself as being in this condition or to be in a frame of mind to do so. In either case the question of having a basis for one's avowals makes very little sense. If I think of myself as being in pain, I do not have to arrive at this thought by inference: I have it already. And if I were to put my thought in words, by avowing that pain is what I feel, my thought itself would not justify the truth of what I say, for the authority of my thought would be no greater than the authority of my ingenuous speech.* If, on the other hand, I do not actually think of myself as being in pain but am merely in a frame of mind to do so, then, again, the question of a basis for my avowal is entirely empty, since a frame of mind is not a peculiar kind of premise, which can warrant inferences or justify spontaneous claims. In general, then, although a suitably trained person is in the best imaginable position to make true statements about the aches and pains he currently feels, these statements are not founded on, in any quasi-logical sense, either the feeling or his awareness. On the contrary, if he is suitably trained, then the mere fact that he has certain feelings disposes him to make any number of spontaneous claims about them: no "basis" is required. What justifies the leaps into language one makes here is the fact, emphasized by Wittgenstein and others, that one has been trained in such a way that the words one utters (and the thoughts one naturally has†) have a *prima facie* claim to truth.

* This point will be discussed fully in Ch. VIII.

† That one's linguistic training accounts for the *prima facie* truth of certain thoughts that one naturally has is a theme emphasized especially by Wilfrid Sellars. For an extended discussion of this theme, see Ch. VIII.

An avowal, as opposed to a typical grunt or groan, is thus the product of consciousness. But consciousness cannot be conceived in the traditional way. It is not, for instance, a bundle of feelings and thoughts, nor is it a sort of generalized awareness. To be conscious in the sense suggested above is to be prepared to make moves, largely linguistic,* that are appropriate to one's condition and circumstances. If one is prepared to do this, if one's nature has been properly shaped by training and experience, one is then a conscious agent capable of taking part in the basically normative activity of thinking and speaking.

7. CONCEPT-FORMATION WITHOUT STEPPINGSTONES

In emphasizing the complex variety of linguistic and other abilities involved in an awareness that something is the case, I have simply been reaffirming my conviction, defended since Chapter II, that knowledge of any sort presupposes a conceptual scheme, a *system* of concepts. In order to prepare the way for a satisfactory treatment of certain residual problems concerning psychological concepts, I want now to make some specific comments on a view of language-learning or concept-formation that runs counter to the position I have been defending. For convenience, I shall refer to this contrary view as "the steppingstone theory."

According to the steppingstone theory, one comes to understand a language by coming to understand its constituent parts: the words, phrases, and sentential forms of which it is composed. On this view many sentences, such as "He is asleep" or "I am in pain," are understandable as isolated units; and the mastery of such units provides the steppingstones that lead to a mastery of the language as a whole. If what I have been arguing is correct, the essential connections between the elements of a language plainly rule out this sort of linguistic atomism. If one cannot fully understand "I am in pain" without understanding "He is in pain," and vice versa, then, obviously, neither of these sentences can serve as independent steppingstones to the mastery of English. Unless one

---

* The precise sense in which thinking is linguistic in character is explained in Ch. VIII, where the various modes of consciousness—thought, belief, emotion, intention—are discussed.

knew a great deal of English already, such as the use of the English pronouns, the forms of the verb "to be," the grammar of the word "to feel," the full significance of these sentences would be far beyond one's ken.

All this may have the air of paradox, for it is perhaps hard to see how, if I am right, one could understand anything at all. Thus, if one must understand "He is in pain" in order to appreciate the full force of saying "I am in pain," *and vice versa*, it would appear that an understanding of either sentence is impossible. One would then have to understand a sentence before one understood it, which is obviously no easier than swallowing the moon.

Actually, there is no paradox here. In order to see why the above circularity does not arise, one need only consider what understanding a sentence amounts to. As explained above, this understanding is a matter of having a particular battery of abilities—to utter certain sounds when one has certain feelings, to respond to questions with appropriate words, to act appropriately when particular sounds are heard, and so on. One of course gains these *abilities* piecemeal: as one grows up, one is gradually trained to make responses of the appropriate sort—and this training, along with attendant learning of a very complicated sort, normally extends over a period of many years. But no one of these abilities, such as that of uttering the words "I am in pain" chiefly when and only when one is in pain, is itself sufficient to constitute an understanding of the words in question. To say, therefore, that one does not fully understand one sentence until one understands another and vice versa is only to say that verbal and other abilities (tendencies, and the like), the having of which constitutes an understanding of one sentence, are so wide-ranging and various that one could not have them without thereby satisfying the criteria for understanding the other sentence as well. There is thus no circularity in my account of understanding: a whole battery of abilities and tendencies is gradually attained as one grows older, and when it is sufficiently complex so that one satisfies the criteria for understanding one sentence it is *ipso facto* complex enough so that one satisfies the criteria for the other, related sentences.

To say all of this is not to imply that it is entirely false to speak of children understanding words and phrases when their grasp of language as a whole is still extremely tenuous. Obviously, there are degrees of understanding, and an agent's grasp of the conventional sense of an expression may be more or less adequate. When a child begins to make appropriate verbal responses when he feels pain, he shows us that he is beginning to get the hang of the words he is using—even though his parents, being proud and incautious, may immediately proclaim that he understands those words. Nevertheless, full understanding comes only with a whole battery of verbal skills; and the more of these the child has, the greater and more sophisticated is his understanding. Thus, the child who knows nothing of comas, unconsciousness, total anesthesia, or feigned sleeping, but whose practice of uttering "He is asleep" is, in point of fact, normally successful has indeed grasped the meaning of the sentence in a rough-and-ready way. But until he knows a good deal more about the tricky contrasts that "He is asleep" has with other sentences of English, he will not fully understand it.

8. EXPERIENCE, AND DEGREES OF UNDERSTANDING

This talk about degrees of understanding leads back immediately to the contrast between "He is in pain" and "I am in pain." Would a person who had never felt pain really understand the meaning of the word "pain"? Would he, in fact, understand the force of either "He is in pain" *or* "I am in pain"? To both of these questions I should say "Yes, to a very large degree." It is true, of course, that anyone who had never felt pain would presumably lack the ability to recognize such a feeling in the normal way; his "pain-reporting mechanism" (as the psychologists would say) would evidently not be developed. But if his other training in the use of English had been of the usual kind, he would still be able to tell when others are in pain. He would know the sort of question to which "I am in pain" is an appropriate answer; he would know how to act, what to say, if another cried "I am in pain," and so on. In fact it does not appear unreasonable to suppose that he could have most of those abilities (to speak, to act, to infer) in which the full understanding of "I am in pain" consists. It is true that he could not imagine, at least very well, what it is like to feel pain—though if he had experienced a wide range of tickles, itches, and pangs, he would perhaps not be entirely in the dark. But he would know enough so that if he were to be in pain for the first time he would probably be able to give an accurate description of his condition by attending to his own behavior. All of this, I should say, would count for a very high degree of understanding.

My view here, that someone who had never felt pain could use the sentence "I am in pain" with understanding, is evidently contrary to that of Malcolm, according to whom an utterance of this sentence can be a use of language only if a "connection" has been established between being in pain and uttering the sounds *ai am in pein.** It is also, obviously, contrary to the Wittgenstein-Malcolm contention that a condition of having the concept of pain is that one be able to recognize one's pains for what they are without hesitation. The present issue makes it necessary, therefore, to come to grips with the "criteriological" argument for the incorrigibility of first-person reports that was mentioned on p. 92f.

If there is any force to the argument Wittgenstein used in support of the idea that a person who could not say whether he is in pain or not would thereby exhibit his ignorance of what "pain" means (see p. 93, footnote), it can only be due to the tacit assumption that if a man could not tell when he is in pain, he could not tell when others are in pain either. I say this because if a man's acquired ability to respond correctly without thinking became disorganized, he could nevertheless proceed to identify his state (assuming, that is, that it is sufficiently distinctive to be recognized by others) by relying on his own behavior, thus using the linguistic abilities normally concerned with the case of the other person. Consequently, if he really did not know how to describe his condition, he would presumably not understand the significance of his own behavior —which shows not only that his pain-reporting mechanism has broken down (or has not been developed) but that he has lost (or never gained) the ability to interpret the significance of pain-behavior generally.

Malcolm, of course, has gone on record as saying that one cannot use "I am in pain" to state a conclusion,[15] but this assertion strikes me as unwarranted. "I am in pain" is perhaps normally used in avowals—that is, when used by itself it is normally uttered spon-

---

* *Dreaming*, p. 16: "His saying 'I am in pain' can be a use of language only because a connection has been established between the words and the outward phenomena that are the original criteria of pain."

taneously, without prior inference—and anyone who understands it must know what this normal use is. But this does not imply that it cannot be used in a less spontaneous way, or that anyone who finds it necessary to conclude that he is in pain is doing something linguistically illegitimate. For one thing, it would be senseless to correct someone who concludes, rather than simply avows, that pain is what he feels. For another, the only thing strictly unusual about concluding that one is in pain, at least so far as language is concerned, is the manner in which the words are produced, not the content of what is said. Whether one concludes that one is in pain or simply avows it, one is saying the same thing about one's condition—and is, therefore, in a crucially important sense, using the sentence "I am in pain" *in the normal way*. Finally, the fact that a person is unable to use "I am in pain" in making spontaneous avowals does not show that he does not know what avowals are or that he does not understand what the normal, avowal use of "I am in pain" is. He understands this, presumably, if he can make sense of the avowals of others.

It is important to see in this connection that being able to avow or say without reflection that one is in pain does not require an understanding of something that could not be understood merely by reference to the linguistic behavior of others. It is true, of course, that one must learn to make spontaneous avowals, but this only means that one's ability to say certain words spontaneously and reliably results from a kind of conditioning. And although one gains a distinctive ability in this way, it does not follow that the ability alone carries with it a special kind of understanding. The only form of understanding peculiarly connected with avowals is an understanding of their conventional significance—and this can be gained by attending to the behavior of others. We must not suppose that we begin our lives with a wholly natural, built-in understanding of what pain is, and then, after linguistic training, come to understand that *this* and *that* are to be called "pain," that the time to say "I am in pain" is when I experience something like *this*. To suppose such a thing is plainly to fall back on the erroneous empiricist idea that the classification of experience is not dependent on the use of some kind of conceptual scheme.

To advance these criticisms is not to deny that a person who has to conclude that he is in pain lacks a very important ability that people normally have. It is only to say that if such a person's other linguistic abilities are sufficiently varied and complicated, there is an ample basis for crediting him with some understanding of what he says when he does conclude that he must be feeling pain. To assume that he necessarily gibbers or misuses language is tantamount to saying that Helen Keller gibbered or misused language when she wrote and spoke of the observable world around her.

It is clear, then, that the Malcolm-Wittgenstein "criteriological" argument for the "incorrigibility" of first-person psychological utterances requires considerable revision. Like their "pain-behavior" argument, it clearly fails to show that there is anything intrinsically incorrigible about such utterances. If we allow that a person who has never felt pain, or whose pain-avowing mechanism is not fully developed, may still have a high degree of understanding of the sentence "I am in pain" if he has most of the abilities in which a completely unqualified understanding of the sentence consists, then it would be possible for him honestly to assert that he is in pain and yet be wrong: for in relying, as he must, on behavior that is accessible to all, his statement faces the same risks that are faced by the statements other people might make about him, or by the statements he might make about the feelings of others. A person in his position is, of course, rare, for man's lot is not a dumb one; and it is natural, therefore, to assume that a living person in his position is unlikely to be found. But the possibility of such a man is still relevant to the philosophical task of testing the bounds of our concepts, for it shows that our criteria for an assertion that one is in pain are not so strict or definite that a mistake about being in pain is a conceptual impossibility, something it is "senseless" to talk about.

9. SUMMARY

I have tried to bring out the considerable complexity involved in simple avowals of being in pain. My general point in doing this has been to show that even the simplest sentences are very deeply embedded in the web of language, and that understanding their meaning is never just a matter of uttering them in circumstances in which they happen (considered as assertions) to be true. In the process of emphasizing this complexity, I tried to clarify the notion of awareness, and this led to a reaffirmation of the Kantian point that percepts without concepts are blind, a reaffirmation of the errors that infect the traditional conception of immediate awareness, and the still-defended steppingstone theory of language-learning. In connection with this latter theory I gave arguments in support of what might be called a modernized coherence theory of meaning—modernized in the sense that the mastery of a language is to be understood as a gradual attainment of a perfectly respectable set of abilities rather than as a growing intuitive awareness of an objective domain of interrelated concepts.

V

Inner States and Outer Criteria

 An important implication of my discussion of avowals is that our everyday psychological concepts involve a tacit reference to observable behavior. Although this implication is wholly in line with the contentions of the behaviorist, it does not in any way commit me to his general view. In this chapter I shall try to pinpoint the behaviorist's crucial errors and, in doing so, clarify the complicated structure of our reasoning about "inner" states such as pain.

I. THE BASIS OF BEHAVIORISM

In order to locate the root errors in analytical behaviorism it will be useful to consider the basic argument that makes the position seem attractive. The chief assumptions of this argument were developed but not criticized in previous chapters. They are the Wittgensteinian ones that there can be no such thing as an inner (or subjective) criterion, and that inner states such as pain must have criteria if they are to be identified or described in an intersubjective language.

Given these two assumptions, we might consider some allegedly covert mental state M and its behavioral criteria $C_1, \ldots, C_n$. A question that immediately arises then is this: just what rational confidence can one have that when $C_1, \ldots, C_n$ are present, M is present as well? It would seem completely unreasonable to suppose that this confidence could be entirely *a priori* and conventional.* Clearly, our confidence that something actually exists behind (as it were) the public play of behavior must have some *empirical* warrant if it is at all reasonable. The question is, though: is this sort of empirical warrant strictly possible, given Wittgenstein's assumptions? The answer seems to be "No." To insure that M actually does occur in connection with $C_1, \ldots, C_n$ we must be able to identify M in some way and then, independently of this, go on and ascertain its relation to $C_1, \ldots, C_n$. But by the very nature of the case this procedure is impossible. By hypothesis, the *only* available criteria by which M can be identified are $C_1, \ldots, C_n$. This means that an independent identification of M and thus the requisite *empirical* check on its relation to $C_1, \ldots, C_n$ is plainly out of the question. Consequently, since the idea of a purely conventional assurance for the existence of something belonging to the natural order is obviously untenable, the impossibility of giving an empirical backing to the assumed correlation implies that such a correlation cannot be rationally defended. Hence, if Wittgenstein was right about criteria, the only reasonable interpretation of mentalistic concepts must be behavioristic.

Since it is Wittgenstein's views about criteria that seem to lead to this behavioristic conclusion, anyone rejecting behaviorism would naturally be inclined to reject those views at once. A rejection on this basis might, however, be a little hasty; for when the above argument is carefully examined, as many as four crucial assumptions are involved, any one of which might be the troublemaker. These four assumptions might be expressed as follows:

1. All criteria, or criterion characteristics, are external or "outward."
2. Objects and processes can be identified and described only with reference, ultimately, to criteria; there is no such thing as a concept without criteria.

* See Ch. I, pp. 21 f.

3. If there were a *de facto* relation holding between something observable and something publicly unobservable, its existence could not be ascertained by convention but would require some kind of empirical investigation.

4. In order to give an empirical corroboration of any supposed lawful relation between a number of things, $A_1, \ldots, A_n$, one must be able to identify them independently of one another and then ascertain their actual relation by classical inductive means.

In my view, the real trouble-maker here is assumption (4). I think there is a sense in which (1) is perhaps false, for I believe that one can defend the idea that there are derivative criteria that are not "outer" in any obvious sense. I also think that assumption (2) is false as well.* Even so, the shortcomings with these first two assumptions do not seem to me to be crucial to the behaviorist's argument. I think they can be patched up in such a way that they hold good for the present case, since all that has to be held is that all mental states need outward criteria. My opinion on this matter can be sustained, of course, only by a detailed analysis of the notion of a criterion. So while I think that assumption (4) is really the root difficulty, I shall nevertheless begin with an examination of what might reasonably be meant by a criterion.

2. WHAT IS AN "OUTER" CRITERION?

Instead of approaching the problematic notion of a criterion by reference to psychological states, I want to begin by considering the application of a criterion to a very simple disposition concept, namely, water-solubility. I want to begin this way, not only because the very character of our psychological concepts is presently in question, but also because the sort of thing that counts as an outward criterion for such a concept has been discussed so often that it is almost impossible to get a fresh perspective on it. By starting with the examination of a disposition concept and endeavoring to identify what could reasonably count as its criteria, I hope to be

---

* My opinion on this point hinges on my conception of a criterion. As I define "criterion" it will turn out that primitive concepts such as *red* do not possess criteria. On this see especially p. 248, footnote.

able to isolate some of the principles that lie behind our intuitive reasoning about criteria, as well as to gain a clearer perspective on the sort of thing that a behaviorist, who is fascinated by such concepts, might naturally take a criterion to be.

A superficial look at the literature is sufficient to show that until very recently dispositions like water-solubility were regarded as mere conditional properties, definable by sentences in the subjunctive mood.[1] Thus, the following analysis of water-solubility has been offered countless times:

"X is water-soluble" means "X would dissolve were it put in water."

It is easy to see, however, that this simple definition is completely inadequate. Suppose we have what we have very good reason to think is a homogeneous substance, samples of which have repeatedly dissolved in water. This history of dissolving would give us, I take it, conclusive grounds for thinking the substance water-soluble. But suppose one day a sample failed to dissolve when put in water. Would this prove that the sample was not water-soluble? Hardly, for the water may have been cooler than usual, and we are surely not committed to the idea that a soluble thing will dissolve in water at any temperature whatever. One might of course think that difficulties of this sort should have been forestalled by including in the above definition a reference to the temperature of the water. But could we have framed a definition that made reference to *anything* that might frustrate the dissolving of what we know is a thoroughly soluble clump of matter? I think not. Suppose we tried the definition:

"X is water-soluble" means "X would dissolve if it were put in water *under standard conditions.*"

This definition looks all right until one considers how standard conditions are to be specified. If they are understood, for instance, as those conditions under which the object dissolves, then the definition becomes a tautology and everything is accordingly water-soluble, since "X is water-soluble" will then be true for every value of "X."

How, then, can we make sense of the notion of standard conditions? A natural approach to the problem is this. Standard conditions are those in which our usual expectations with respect to a *kind* of thing or substance can reasonably be depended upon.* Since the growth of our knowledge changes our expectations, our conception of standard conditions will accordingly change as well. Thus, as we discover things whose presence frustrates the expected course of affairs, we begin to regard them as constituting abnormal conditions. We can therefore say: "These conditions are clearly abnormal, since this substance—which is, say, sugar—normally dissolves at this temperature." Plainly, statements of this sort lead to such knowledge-enriching questions as: "Just what is peculiar about these conditions? What accounts for the failure of our normal expectations here?" As time goes on, we may come to recognize hundreds of occurrences which may, because they are unusual, frustrate our general expectations; and in this way our conception of standard or normal conditions, where these frustrating occurrences are absent, continues to grow.

It is because our knowledge can be expected to grow that we cannot define "X is water-soluble" as "If X were put in water under what are recognized as normal or standard conditions, it would certainly dissolve." There are, without doubt, unknown conditions which, if they occurred, would frustrate our expectations even here; at least we do not know that there are *no* such conditions. So the definiens of our definition, if it is to be reasonable, must have a probabilistic force; it must at least have the cautious character of "If X were put in water under what we take to be standard conditions, then, in all probability, it would dissolve." The probability-rider here would not involve reference to some numerical conception of probability, but would rather serve to make room for the possibility of unknown frustraters, and have the force of "virtually certain."

It might strike some readers that this last definition must certainly be unacceptable. How can we possibly know what solubility is and yet be unable to specify it without reference to the notion of "in all probability"? Does not our inability to give a more straight-

---

* In the following discussion it is to be understood that the standard (or normal) conditions I speak of hold only for a particular *kind* of thing or substance, not for every *kind* whatever. Because of the close tie-up between standard conditions and kinds of thing (or substance), it is best to define such dispositions as solubility in terms of kinds rather than instances. I ignore this complication in the text because it is not essential to the point I wish to make concerning criteria.

forward, necessary-and-sufficient-condition type definition show
that we do not really know what we are talking about when we use
the word "water-soluble"? The answer to this last question is "No."
We mean by "water-soluble" a relatively permanent feature of
something, a feature characterized indirectly by reference to a kind
of change a thing having this feature will exhibit under a certain
range of circumstances. That we are speaking of an intrinsic feature
here comes out from two facts, at least. First, you can, at least in
principle, make something soluble by doing something to it. For
instance, it is possible that there are substances that will dissolve
only after, say, heating. Thus, "It is now soluble" will indicate the
result of some actual change. It is natural to think of this result as
actual, rather than just hypothetical, even though it manifests itself
only after the thing in question is subjected to some appropriate
test-condition. Second, although with the growth of our knowledge
our conception of the conditions under which dissolving can be
expected changes, we do not necessarily regard this increased
knowledge as determining a change in the concept of solubility.
We can still say, "For X to be soluble is for X to *be such* that if it
were put in water under what we regard as standard conditions,
then it would, in all probability, dissolve."

Having set out some of the basic elements of a reasonable analysis
of a familiar disposition concept,* I can now turn to the question of
criteria. What are the criteria for water-solubility? Is dissolving
under standard conditions a criterion? This is certainly how we
discover whether something is soluble, and a criterion is generally
said to be that by which we ascertain whether a concept applies
to a particular case. But notice that if "dissolving under recogniz-
ably standard conditions" does state a criterion for solubility, the
satisfaction of this criterion does not strictly insure the solubility
of the object, and vice versa. Not only is it possible that the dissolving might result from some unknown and atypical cause (for instance some peculiar, hard-to-detect radiation), but there is an
essential "in all probability" clause in the definition, which leaves
open the possibility that a truly soluble object will not dissolve in
these conditions. Given our confidence, however, that the present

---

* It is essential to realize that the analysis I have given of water-solubility
is not intended to apply to every kind of disposition whatever, least of all
to the dispositions of fundamental particles, such as electrons.

conditions are not unusual—a confidence that is capable of inductive support—we have an extremely good basis for inferring solubility from dissolving and vice versa: for the very definition of "water-solubility" guarantees that in all probability our inferences will be successful. To put it another way, in normal circumstances dissolving provides us with a "logically adequate basis" for inferring that a substance is really soluble,[2] even though it is not a logical truth that a substance dissolving under what we regard as standard conditions is in fact soluble.

Because this last point, if sound, brings out an extremely important but frequently unnoticed feature of criteria, I want to nail it down with a little more discussion. The feature I have specially in mind is the surprising indirection of our reasoning when we deal with certain kinds of criteria. I have indicated that even when we are confident that the conditions are standard we cannot infer deductively that a thing that has dissolved is certainly soluble. The reason for this is that in order to infer the solubility of an object A we must be able to establish the truth of the statement:

1. A is such that if, in standard conditions, it were put in water, it would, in all probability, dissolve.

And this statement does not follow from the statement of the information at our disposal in the case described:

2. The conditions are standard, A is put in water, and A dissolves.

Statement (1) does not follow from (2) because (1) has a partially lawful force: it states something general and nonaccidental about A's behavior in certain circumstances. And there is nothing general or lawful about the statement (2). In spite of this, however, the inference from (2) to (1) is a very safe one, far superior to an arbitrary move from "B is F and B is G" to the partial law-statement, "If B were F, it would also be G."

But how, exactly, do we account for the strength of the inference from (2) to (1)? The answer, I think, is this: (2) includes the information that A is put in water *under standard conditions.* These conditions, however, are those from which all abnormal occurrences are probably (almost certainly) absent. This is a consequence of the very meaning of "standard conditions." But when abnormal occurrences are definitely (not just probably) absent, dissolving results from the mere immersion of soluble objects in water. Hence, to know that A is in standard conditions is to know (by definition) that abnormal occurrences are probably absent, and hence to know that it is *probable* that the dissolving was due to the solubility of the object, and nothing else. But to *know* that the latter is probable is to know that one may justifiably affirm it. Hence, the inference from (2) to (1) is justifiable by virtue of the very definition of "water-soluble." This does not mean, again, that the inference here is purely analytic, that (2) logically implies (1). All that (2) logically implies is that (1) is *probably* true. Yet if we know, given (2), that (1) is probably true, we have an excellent, in fact a "logically adequate," basis for affirming it.

Before comparing the criteria for water-solubility with the outer criteria for a specimen mental state, I want to introduce some terminology. Following Michael Scriven,[3] I shall distinguish two categories of criteria, or criterion characteristics.* I shall say that a criterion C is *analytic* for X just in case (a) C is at least a logically sufficient condition for the occurrence, presence, or existence of X and (b) the concept of C is in some sense more basic than the concept of X, that is, the expression "X" is in some way definable in relation to "C" but not vice versa. "Being trilateral" might thus state an analytic criterion for being triangular; and being universal and necessary might count as an analytic criterion for being *a priori*. A criterion is *normic for X*, on the other hand, if it is not analytic for X and if it is related to X in roughly the manner that dissolving is related to solubility, that is, as a probabilistic indicator that is definitionally (or conceptually) related to X in some appropriate way. Thus, if N is a normic criterion of X, then by virtue of the definition of "X," the occurrence of N in certain circumstances counts for, but does not strictly insure, the existence or occurrence of X. Since one may also find out whether X exists, is present, and the like, by reference to something empirically correlated with it but not mentioned in its definition (as being granular would allow one to determine solubility if it happened that everything granular were soluble), I shall speak of *synthetic indicators*

---

* In order to keep my conception of criteria in line with current discussion, I have fallen in with the common practice of running criteria together with criterion characteristics—the former being more accurately conceived as belonging to the conceptual rather than the natural order.

in addition to normic ones, which are criteria. Thus, as I shall speak, the categories of indicators and criteria overlap: there are two kinds of indicators, synthetic and normic, and two kinds of criteria, analytic and normic. The category of the normic is thus an intermediate one, since normic criteria, unlike analytic ones, are probabilistic indicators.

3. THE CRITERIA FOR PAIN

With the above terminology in hand, I am now in a position to consider how the criteria for solubility compare with the criteria for pain. The first thing to notice here is that Malcolm, a staunch defender of Wittgenstein's thesis that an inward process stands in need of outward criteria, makes the similarity seem very close.* With reference to the question "Do the propositions that describe the criteria of (a man's) . . . being in pain *logically imply* the proposition 'He is in pain'?" Malcolm says that the answer is "clearly in the negative. Pain-behavior is a criterion of pain only in *certain* circumstances."[4] His reasons for this are, moreover, similar to the reasons given above for the lack of implication between "X dissolves" and "X is water-soluble," namely, that the number of things, such as hypnosis, theatrical interest, or the wish to deceive, that could justify our refusal to apply "pain" even in the face of a typical pattern of pain-behavior is indefinite:

> . . . one would like to think that one can formulate a logical implication by taking a description of his pain-behavior and conjoining it with the negation of every proposition describing one of these circumstances that would count against saying he is in pain. . . . But this assumes that there is a totality of those circumstances such that if none of them were fulfilled, and he was also pain-behaving, then he *could not but* be in pain. . . . There is no totality that can be exhaustively enumerated, as can the letters of the alphabet. . . . The list of circumstances has no "all," in that sense; the list is, not infinite, but *indefinite*. Therefore entailment conditions cannot be formulated; there are none.[5]

* The quotations from Malcolm appearing in this section are taken from Norman Malcolm, *Knowledge and Certainty: Essays and Lectures.* © 1963. Reprinted by permission of Prentice-Hall, Inc., Englewood Cliffs, N.J.

Although there is, then, an interesting element of similarity between pain, conceived by Malcolm, and solubility, conceived by me, just how far can it be pressed? Can we conclude, for example, that pain-behavior is at best a normic indicator of pain? Malcolm, at least when he wrote his review of Wittgenstein's *Philosophical Investigations*, would seem to deny this. It was his opinion that the presence of criteria—that is, the presence of standard criterion characteristics in certain circumstances—settles the question beyond doubt. He says:

> . . . if it does not *follow* from the behavior and circumstances that he is in pain, then how could it be *certain* that he is in pain? . . . It *looks* as if the conclusion ought to be that we cannot "completely verify" that he is in pain. This conclusion is wrong, but it is not easy to see why.[6]

Admitting that he comprehends Wittgenstein's thought on this issue only dimly, Malcolm suggests that the presence of the man's behavior in certain circumstances does give us certainty, does allow us to verify that he is in pain, because "doubting has an end":

> Perhaps we can *imagine* a doubt; but we do not take it seriously. . . . Just as it becomes certain to us that there is a chair over there, although we can imagine a *possible* ground of doubt. There is a concept of certainty in these language-games only because we stop short of what is conceivable.[7]

In the last paragraph I said that Malcolm "would seem" to deny that pain-behavior, even in "certain circumstances," provides only a normic indicator of pain. I used these words because while he says that the criteria give certainty rather than probability, he does not deny the possibility of doubt, or even its legitimacy if one has grounds for it. This is something with which I heartily agree; I can even agree that, when the behavior is striking and one has no reason to suspect fakery and the like, one is entitled to feel certain and to claim that one is certain. There undoubtedly is a concept of being certain about particular matters of fact, and this concept may be applied even when all the evidence that might conceivably or theoretically bear on the issue is not in hand. Thus, although I speak of normic indicators giving only probability, I do not intend to imply that they never entitle one to speak of certainty, but only that they leave open the theoretical possibility of error in a way that analytic criteria, as I have defined them, do not.

4. THE PROBLEM OF ABNORMAL CONDITIONS

While Malcolm's words seem, except for a difference of emphasis, to be entirely in line with what I have been arguing, they nevertheless raise a problem, which I have done something to solve for solubility but which has not in any way been met for pain. The problem is this: what considerations are relevant for picking out what Malcolm calls "negative conditions"? How in general, that is, does one go about identifying the conditions in which pain-behavior does not insure the presence of pain? Malcolm does not tell us anything about this at all; he merely reminds us of some of the things, such as feigning, acting, or hypnosis, which we would all agree count against the presence of pain even when a person exhibits very striking pain-behavior. But while it is easy to see that these particular activities should be inconsistent with the presence of pain—since "feigning pain," "acting as if one were in pain," and the like, *logically imply* that one is not in pain—it is by no means clear how other patterns of behavior, or indeed anything else, could be shown to constitute such negative circumstances. In fact it is not even clear why Malcolm (or Wittgenstein) should think that the list of these circumstances is indefinite, rather than just very long and hard to complete.

The significance of this point can perhaps be drawn out by another look at the example of solubility. Recall the point made earlier that although a substance has actually dissolved in water, we might still refuse to take this as proving that the substance was actually soluble if we knew that there were impurities in the water or if, to take Scriven's example,[8] we detected the presence of ultrasonic standing waves. But why might we be hesitant to conclude that the substance was soluble under these conditions? The answer, I think, is that we might not be sure that the dissolving was due to the action of the water on the substance and not to the action of these waves or these impurities. Solubility is, after all, a specific feature of a substance, a feature that results in dissolving when the substance is put in water. Since it might have been the standing waves or the impurities that accounted for the dissolving, rather than the nature of the substance and its natural reaction to water, we could thus deny application of "water-solubility" even when dissolving occurs.

Consider the converse case. Why can we not say that if a substance fails to dissolve in warm, distilled water it is simply not soluble? The answer, again, is that we mean by "water-soluble" a specific feature of a substance that brings it about that the substance will *naturally* dissolve in water. And the number of things that might frustrate this natural reaction cannot be foreseen in advance: its "negative conditions" are therefore conceptually indefinite in character. Accordingly, if we have satisfied ourselves that a certain substance is soluble, then unless we have reason to think that a certain sample has been contaminated or changed in some way, we will attempt to explain its failure to dissolve by hunting for some interfering factor; we will not argue that it is just not soluble. The important fact illustrated here is that it is only because we conceive of solubility as a specific property, character, or feature of a substance—only because we have some idea of what solubility *is*, apart from the dissolving behavior that a soluble thing will normally exhibit—that we can make sense of the very idea of negative conditions which, because they are conceived as indefinite rather than infinite, we could never completely describe.

Returning, now, to the case of pain, we might ask whether something similar could be said by way of justifying Malcolm's undeniably sound contention that the list of negative circumstances here is indefinite. Malcolm himself would evidently say "No." It seems to be his opinion, and it is a very widely held opinion, that there is nothing more to the meaning of a term than what is implicit in the criteria for its correct application. Indeed, he would presumably insist that it is actually senseless to puzzle about a thing's essential nature, or about what it is that we mean by a word, *if* we are clear about the appropriate criteria. As he remarked in connection with the word "dreaming":

> . . . we must admit [*i.e.*, on pain of self-contradiction] that there is a criterion for the use of "He dreamt" and also that it does not tell us what a dream *is*, does not give us the "essence" of dreaming (whatever that might mean), but gives us the conditions that determine whether the statement "He dreamt" is true or false.[9]

And again, after arguing that one's waking impression of having dreamed is the criterion of having dreamed, he insists:

> I am not maintaining that a dream *is* the waking impression that one dreamt. . . . Indeed I am not trying to say what dreaming *is:* I do not understand what it would mean to do that.[10]

5. THE BEHAVIORIST'S ASSUMPTIONS RECONSIDERED

Although Malcolm may wish to deny that he is a behaviorist, his remarks on dreaming recall the behaviorist's argument given at the beginning of this chapter. If dreaming really were an inner process logically distinguishable from its outward behavioral criteria, we could then legitimately ask how we know that it is reliably correlated with those criteria. Granting the behaviorist's assumption that lawful relations between distinguishable kinds of occurrences can be established only by a form of instantial generalization based on publicly observable instances, we should have to answer by saying that this correlation cannot strictly be known. And if we were to accept the verificationist principle that it makes no sense to speak of correlations that cannot, even in principle, be known, we should then be forced to agree with Malcolm that talk about an inner process of dreaming would not even make sense.

Notice that if we accepted these crucial assumptions, we should also be committed to reject the account I have given of solubility. According to my analysis, when we rely on dissolving as a normic indicator of solubility, we implicitly assume that dissolving indicates the presence in a substance of a specific feature, one that could be present even in the absence of dissolving if conditions are not normal. Yet our only means of ascertaining the presence of this specific feature is by reference to the dissolving that occurs under normal conditions; we simply have no other criteria by which its presence can be determined. Since the specific feature in question is distinguishable from an actual process of dissolving, our confidence that the latter provides a reliable indicator of the former must be capable of some kind of empirical justification. But the possibility of this justification is completely ruled out by the crucial assumptions in point.

It might be urged at this stage that these assumptions are easily refutable by the observation that we can make sense of theoretical science only if they are rejected. We cannot, after all, *observe* such things as electrons, and there is no way of establishing lawful relations between them and what we do observe by instantial generalization. An answer of this sort is not wholly decisive, however, for it can be argued—paradoxically, I admit—that theoretical science ought to be interpreted as a mere instrument of prediction.* In order to rule out these assumptions and, with them, all the isms that arise from them, a far more penetrating argument must obviously be found.

A useful means of locating such an argument is to consider the drawbacks of a line of thought offering the possibility that one might have one's cake and eat it too. This approach requires us to weaken the verificationist's criterion of meaning so that sense can be made in speaking of items for whose existence only very indirect evidence is possible. Assuming that this weakening of the criterion is reasonable, we may then defend a principle of universal causation by a process of instantial induction. The events we observe generally have both causes and effects; therefore, probably all events have both causes and effects. Given this principle, we may proceed to argue that since certain observable events do not have observable causes or effects, their causes or effects must be unobservable. Talk about the latter will make perfectly good sense because we can provide indirect inductive evidence showing that such causes or effects probably occur. Since this procedure would allow us not only to speak of unobservable physical events but also to regard mental events as the unobservable causes of observable behavior, we could consistently reject both instrumentalism and behaviorism without abandoning the inductive principles characteristic of traditional empiricism.

While the later stages of this approach may seem highly promising, its initial stages are obviously fallacious. If we are to establish a universal causal principle by instantial generalization, then our subsequent failure to find a cause or effect for an observed event will require us to *abandon* this principle rather than use it to infer that some events have unobservable causes or effects. To deny that

* See Ch. I, p. 14 f.

we are required to do this is to make nonsense of induction as a reasonable form of inference. Plainly, if our success in finding a cause for a given event is to count in favor of the principle of universal causation, then our failure to find such a cause should count against it. Since there obviously are events for which no observable cause can be found (such as certain spontaneous movements of human beings), any attempt to establish a principle of universal causation by instantial induction is bound to be a failure. In fact, the conclusion that this approach yields is that the statement "Every event has a cause" ought to be regarded as simply false.

The well-known reluctance of most philosophers to accept the outright falsity of "Every event has a cause" can be expected to prompt the objection that the causal principle does not have to be justified by instantial induction. Indeed, it might be said that the grounds for accepting this principle are similar to the grounds for accepting the inductive principle itself. This latter principle plainly requires some kind of justification; and if its justification is to be given by the fashionable argument that inductive generalization is an indispensable tool for reasoning about the world and that its acceptability is presupposed by our very concept of a reasonable material inference, it would appear that a similar justification could be given for the causal principle itself.

Although I would argue that the term "cause" is far less clear than those who insist upon the causal principle like to admit,[11] I believe that the above objection is entirely sound at least to the extent of insisting that the inductive principle is not intrinsically more credible than many other principles we commonly rely on in our reasoning about the world. As the first step of my all-out attack on the claim enshrined in what I have called assumption (4) of the behaviorist's argument, I want to show that if an obvious implication of the causal principle is accepted on its own merits, then this claim must be rejected as untenable. As stated at the beginning of this chapter, assumption (4) imposes a very strict necessary condition on any attempt to provide an empirical warrant for a lawful connection; it insists that to justify such a connection, we must in some way observe a constant correlation between events of the appropriate kind. To deny this assumption is obviously not to deny the weaker claim that if we do observe such a correlation, we may infer (*ceteris paribus*) that the lawful relation holds. This weaker claim is something I willingly grant; it is the stronger thesis that leads to behaviorism, and it is this thesis that I wish to deny.

The relevant implication of the causal principle—hereafter called "The Causal Assumption" for short—might be expressed in rough-and-ready terms as follows:

> Things normally behave as they do because of their nature and the character of their surroundings, and they will not exhibit new or unexpected behavior unless they have actually undergone some fairly specific change.

Assuming that this assumption is tenable, it immediately allows us to speak of unobservable occurrences in a manner that assumption (4) clearly forbids. If a thing begins to exhibit a marked change of behavior, we may now infer that it has undergone some kind of change, whether we are able actually to identify this change or not. If, further, the behavior the thing exhibits is of a recognizable kind, and if similar things also occasionally exhibit this kind of behavior, we can infer by the principle of analogy ("From like effects one can infer like causes") that there is a common cause responsible for this kind of behavior. Not knowing what this cause is, we cannot of course describe it intrinsically. But we can nevertheless award the cause a name and conceive it as *the cause* of the behavior in point. There is, naturally, a risk to this procedure, but it does not follow that the procedure is thereby illegitimate.* Our commitment can be defended not only by reference to the specificity of the kind of behavior produced but also by reference to our current theories about the sort of thing that could be expected to produce this behavior. In general, the justification of our practice in such a case will be determined by the extent to which the various considerations bearing on the possible occasions of that type of behavior point to a unitary cause.

If the Causal Assumption just mentioned is sound, it is thus clear that assumption (4) is unacceptable. Of course, the reverse is true as well. The question therefore arises as to which of these assumptions is worthy of our support. Part of the answer to this is fortunately implicit in the argument of previous chapters. Ever since Chapter II, I have persistently attacked what I have called the "foundations" picture of meaning and truth, and assumption

* Ch. I, p. 22.

(4) is just a fragment of this picture. As stated in the behaviorist's argument, this assumption involves the idea that there is a particular level of knowledge with respect to which all empirical questions must ultimately be settled. This level is determined by public observability, and it is because an inner mental state is not susceptible of public scrutiny that its relation to any outer criteria was said to be incapable of empirical support.

To reject the foundations picture completely is thus to reject assumption (4). My basic reason for abandoning this picture was built on the fact that even observation claims are not theoretically immune to suspicion. If a man claims to see a needle in a haystack, or a bear in the bush, we do not immediately accept his claim as true. The acceptability of a man's spontaneous claim always depends on our knowledge of the kind of object observed and on our assumptions concerning the man's reliability as an observer. (Are the objects in point easy to see? Are they liable to be mistaken for other things? Does the man have good eyes? Is he honest, sane, sober, and unlikely to be carried away by a vivid imagination?) It is, in fact, only relative to *general empirical assumptions* regarding both the perceiver and the perceived that *any* observation claim is considered acceptable, and not all these assumptions can be directly verified by observation. To establish this last point, it is not necessary to argue that at least one of these assumptions will concern the general regularity of nature. It is entirely sufficient to note that in accepting any observation claim whatever, we must always presuppose that someone—either a given observer or someone looking over his shoulder—is at least for the moment a reliable observer. This assumption obviously could not be tested by direct observation because any such test would presuppose what it sets out to prove.

Given, then, that the acceptability of an observation claim is conditional on the acceptability of a number of general empirical assumptions concerning both the observer and the observed, it is plainly impossible to maintain that an empirical statement is *ipso facto* suspect if it is neither an observation claim nor a statement that is derivable from such claims by a form of reasoning based on inductive generalization.* On the contrary, *every* observation claim

* The same argument plainly holds good for introspective claims. On this see Ch. II, pp. 33-36.

and therefore every inductive generalization based on such a claim presuppose empirical statements that the claim or the generalization could not possibly establish. Since there are certain empirical statements whose acceptability is presupposed by every observation claim whatever, it follows that not all empirical statements owe their justification to a noncircular process of inductive generalization, if they are general, or to direct observation itself, if they are singular. Some of these statements must rather have a *prima facie* credibility that is justified in some other way. This means that assumption (4) collapses as totally unwarranted, and the behaviorist's argument, since it is based on this assumption, collapses as well.

6. SOME BASIC FEATURES
OF EMPIRICAL REASONING

My claim above, that there are general empirical assumptions whose acceptability is presupposed by *every* tenable observation claim, immediately prompts the question of just how these presupposed claims could possibly be justified. The general answer to this question, at least stated roughly, can only be this: the presupposed claims are justified by the success we have in operating on them. To give any other answer is implicitly to abandon the essential demand of empiricism.

The answer just given was stated very roughly because an important qualification must immediately be made. Obviously, any assumption sufficiently plausible to be accepted by sane men can always be protected in such a way that it becomes immune to refutation. This may be done by introducing new assumptions that accommodate any initially recalcitrant facts to the assumptions previously held. To cite a simple example suggested to me by Paul Feyerabend: If a man assumes that all sons really hate their fathers, he can accommodate the plain fact that some sons show striking affection towards their fathers by assuming that such behavior is merely the expression of a deep-seated hostility that a son is unconsciously bending over backwards to hide. Clearly, in order to provide a reasonable justification of our basic assumptions, we must avoid this kind of obscurantism. We must be prepared to retain as much simplicity as possible in our conceptual scheme, and not complicate it merely to protect an assumption that is dear to our hearts. To see the absolute necessity of this is to appreciate the germ of truth in the verificationist theory of meaning. When we isolate our basic assumptions from any possibility of refutation, however indirect, we thereby drain them of any assertive content.[12]

If some of the refutable assumptions presupposed by the acceptance of an observation claim are rendered justifiable largely by the success we have in operating on them, it turns out that our reasoning about observations is essentially the same, in abstract formal structure, as our reasoning about scientific hypotheses. As the epithet "the hypothetico-deductive method" indicates, the standard way of justifying a scientific hypothesis is to show that the predictions, or deductions, they allow us to make are regularly successful. If these deductions fail, or if the hypothesis turns out to be inconsistent with other hypotheses regarded as more firmly established, then the hypothesis is generally modified or rejected.*

It is easy to see that the same pattern of reasoning is involved in our treatment of observation claims. Suppose a man reports that an object before him is red and triangular. If, contrary to our normal presumption concerning adult language users, we have no good reason to think he is a reliable observer, then his claim is acceptable only to the extent that its implications are in line with other claims that we trust. On the other hand, if he is regarded as a reliable observer, then his claim would be rejected only if it were incompatible with claims we have greater reason to trust, for instance the claims of a whole group of reliable observers who were known to be in a good position to observe the object. Of course these other claims could come under attack as well (see p. 42). After all, if the claim of a man known to be reliable were wildly out of line with those of his fellows, some kind of explanation would obviously be in order. And further investigation could conceivably lead us to accept his claim in preference to the claims of others. This might happen if it became known that the others had been eating peculiar mushrooms noted for their bizarre effects on a man's vision.

It is important to observe that the need for explaining conflicts

---

* As I shall show in subsequent pages, the scientific method of forming and testing hypotheses is rather more complicated than these off-hand remarks suggest. See Ch. VII, pp. 168–176, and Ch. IX, pp. 244 f.

between claims having a strong *prima facie* acceptability is a crucial factor in leading us to develop scientific theories and to revise many of the concepts and assumptions on which we have been operating. The conflict between the claims, "That substance is plainly soluble" and "A sample of it did not dissolve," might naturally lead to a new theory concerning an unknown type of water-impurity. And the conflict between the common-sense assumption that substances get lighter when heated and the observed fact that metals such as mercury react in precisely the opposite way actually did lead to a radically revised conception of fire. Recall that for the ancient Greeks and even for the medieval Schoolmen fire was conceived as one of the four basic kinds of sublunary material; it was not regarded as a *state* of a concrete thing until long after the scientific revolution of the seventeenth century.*

The traditional tendency to underestimate the remarkable complexity of the concept of observation goes hand-in-hand with the tendency to underestimate the complexity of the concept of an avowal or introspective report. To expose this tendency as seriously myopic is to make plain just how the basic structure of empirical reasoning can be essentially the same regardless of subject matter. Although this mode of reasoning is largely dialectical in allowing us to rely temporarily on assumptions we cannot fully justify at the moment, it is nevertheless maximally critical because it permits us to challenge any one of our assumptions, though not, of course, all of them at any one time.† This mode of reasoning is also relentlessly empirical because even though it does not allow us to base all our knowledge on an allegedly indubitable foundation of raw experience, it constantly leads us to subject nature to searching interrogation and to wring answers from her that she is not always willing to give. Because it is both maximally critical and thoroughly empirical, it is accordingly a justifiably rational mode of reasoning. Not only does it allow us to slide between the traditional extremes of dogmatism and skepticism, but it tends to bring about a certain dissatisfaction with what we have, and leads us on to new intellectual vistas, where exotic worlds of giant waves and tiny particles dominate the view.

* For further remarks on this example, see p. 169, footnote.
† See p. 58.

7. AN EXTERNAL APPROACH TO
THE CONCEPT OF PAIN

Having ruled out assumption (4) and, with it, the behaviorist's basic argument, I am in a position to say something positive about such inner states as pain. In the last chapter I argued that pain may be said to have external criteria, and that these criteria are essential to the concept of pain. I made no attempt, however, to say what sort of state pain is—as distinguished, that is, from its criterion characteristics—and this is what I shall attempt to do now. In order to make sure that no assumptions lacking a clear intersubjective sense are unwittingly smuggled into my discussion, I shall begin by considering how we might conceive pain if, like a colony of possible Martians, we had never felt it ourselves but were in possession of the Causal Assumption and were at home with the pattern of scientific reasoning described above. In proceeding this way, I also hope to make vivid the logical structure of our reasoning about such states as pain.

Assuming that we are playing the Martian role and brooding about the meaning of "pain," one of the first things we might notice is that there is an easily identifiable kind of stimulus, often involving the outright destruction of living tissue, and an easily identifiable kind of response, both characteristically associated with those circumstances in which the word "pain" is applied with maximum confidence. Since this kind of stimulus and this kind of response constantly occur in connection with a wide variety of human beings—the response sometimes not preceded by the stimulus, and vice versa—it would be reasonable to think that the stimulus produces some fairly specific effect, which in turn results in the familiar kind of behavior. It might therefore occur to us that if there actually is such a specific effect, a language-using creature could perhaps be trained to utter certain sounds when that effect is believed to qualify his condition. This expectation is of course borne out in fact, since utterances of "I am in pain," "It hurts," and the like are such sounds. We may also note, however, that when human beings are well trained linguistically they are normally capable of giving highly reliable information about their immediate surroundings. It might occur to us, accordingly, that if certain specific effects are indeed evoked in human beings by the action on them of pain-inflictors, as intelligent language users they should also be able to find ways of *describing* these effects. This last hypothesis is also borne out in fact, since human beings do tend to use a wide variety of words in this descriptive capacity and agree among themselves on their appropriateness. (The words used would include "stinging," "blinding," "pulsating," "stabbing," and "nagging.") All of this gives us good, though admittedly indirect, evidence for the idea that pains are at least "inner" states or episodes typically produced by a certain kind of stimulus and typically resulting in a characteristic kind of behavior, some of the latter being intelligent verbal behavior.

To conceive of pain as even a Martian could conceive it is thus to go a long way beyond the confines of philosophical behaviorism. It is also, oddly enough, to go sufficiently far so that something even Malcolm's account left high in the air is easily explained, namely, the distinguishing features of "negative circumstances," where the usual criteria for pain do not guarantee application of the word. Since the importance of understanding these circumstances has already been stressed, I shall proceed to outline their distinguishing features.

According to the Martian account, "pain" quite clearly refers to an inner state or occurrence, a very specific one that is normally brought about by the application of a certain range and type of stimuli, and which produces in turn a characteristic kind of behavior. (Strictly, as a moment's reflection shows, what is brought about is actually a *disposition* to exhibit this kind of behavior.) Typical or paradigm pain-producers are cuts, burns, knocks, and slaps; and typical or paradigm pain-behavior is crying, groaning, swearing, blanching, and perspiring.

Although a striking feature of the behavior criterial for pain is that it is normally brought about spontaneously, it is nevertheless possible to exhibit such behavior deliberately and artfully, when no spontaneous inclination to exhibit it is present. For this reason, it is not difficult to list a host of conditions that are negative so far as behavioral criteria are concerned: when one seeks to deceive, to keep a stiff upper lip; when one pretends as in a play; when one has been hypnotized; and so on. These conditions are negative because they imply that the spontaneous, thoughtless tendency to pain-behave is absent. Because there are, similarly, things that can be done to eliminate what we take to be the characteristic effects of being cut or burned—anesthetics can be given, for example—we can list a whole range of circumstances where the presence of the usual pain-inflictors does not guarantee, or even count very highly in favor of, the presence of pain.

The strategy of identifying "negative circumstances" is thus perfectly straightforward once it is admitted that pain is conceived as an inner state only characteristically related to a certain kind of behavior and circumstance.* Anything that can bring about the behavior characteristic of this inner state when the agent is believed on good grounds not to be in this state, and anything generally efficacious in inhibiting natural pain behavior and thus presumably capable of preventing the agent from being in such a state, can reasonably count as negative or abnormal. Hence, to identify things of this kind we have only to consider what things might function as such producers or inhibitors. Of course, as pointed out in connection with solubility, there is no way of knowing in advance what all these producers and inhibitors might be. Malcolm was therefore quite right when he said that the totality of these negative circumstances is indefinite, rather than just very long and difficult to complete.

Everything I have said so far about pain is very cautious, for the intrinsic nature of pain, taken as an inner state, is still open to dispute. Obviously, pain is thought to have intrinsic qualities as well as some sort of location in a person's body, and these features are capable of raising as much philosophical difficulty as pain's "inner" status. In order to round out my discussion of pain—indeed, to take it beyond the Martian stage just attained—I shall try to clarify the status of these perennially puzzling intrinsic features.

8. THE QUALITY AND LOCATION OF PAIN

Pain is generally said to be a feeling or sensation, one that all but masochists mind having. It is also said to be locatable here or there

---

* Note that the preceding remarks apply only to what might be called strong or intense pains. Mild pains must be conceived by analogy with these, and verbal behavior will provide the most important key to their *differentia*.

in or on a person's body. One may have a pain in the arm, leg, or abdomen, or even, as is typical of sinus headaches, in a very determinate region of the forehead. This talk suggests that pains are best conceived as objects, which, like nerves or cells, may be here or there; but as many writers have noticed, every statement that prompts this interpretation appears to be equivalent to another statement that does not. Thus, "I have a pain *in my arm*" asserts no more than, and may be rephrased as, "My arm pains me" or "My arm hurts." And these latter locutions, far from suggesting that pain is a peculiar object that may be here or there, imply that it is rather a feature, in some sense, of a part of one's body. Instead, therefore, of locating pain *in* one's arm or leg, it seems closer to the facts to say that a certain region of one's arm or leg pains one.

There is unfortunately one serious drawback with this attempt to objectify pains: the peculiar phenomenal qualities we commonly ascribe to pains apparently cannot be represented in the form of translation just considered. A pain may be said to be blinding, pulsating, nagging, burning, stinging, or stabbing, and it is hard to see how anything having these peculiar properties could be itself a property of part of one's body. Thus, while we can easily translate away a reference to the location of pain by construing "The pain is here" as having the force of "It hurts or pains here," we evidently cannot do something similar with a reference to the intrinsic quality of the pain. The locution, "It pains me throbbingly here," which would be the natural translation for "I have a throbbing pain here," is presumably not respectable English.

There is, fortunately, a possible way out of this difficulty. Notice that in describing pains as stinging, burning, stabbing, nagging, pulsating, and blinding, one is using language metaphorically. Bugs and nettles may sting, hot coals may burn, wives may nag, blood may pulsate, and gouging may blind—in an entirely straightforward, literal way. But the same is not true with pains. They do not literally burn, stab, sting, or pulsate; they do not actually nag, and they cannot blind. When we use these words we are trying to say something *indirectly* about the quality of our pain, and we do this in at least three ways. First, we sometimes try to throw light on our pains by relating them to certain typical causes of pain. Thus, a stinging pain is the sort of feeling that one typically gets from nettles and bees; a burning pain is the sort that typically results from burns; and so on. Second, we use words such as "nagging" or "pulsating" to bring out the quality of our pains by analogy with the behavior of such things as wives and currents. There is, after all, a notable similarity between the nagging of a wife and the quality of certain pains: the pain, like the wife, may irritate mildly but relentlessly; it remains with you, a constant source of frustration. There is also a marked analogy between the rhythm of certain currents and the quality of certain pains, a rhythm of falling and rising intensity, a pattern of spurts and pauses. Third, we use such words as "blinding" to indicate the quality of our pains by reference to the effects they have on us: blinding pains tend to make us close our eyes in anguish, thus producing momentary darkness, and so on.

If this account is convincing as an analysis of our practice of using such terms as "stinging," "nagging," and "blinding" to describe our pains, there is then an obvious way of patching up the translation strategy. To characterize a pain as stinging, burning, stabbing, nagging, or blinding is just to characterize the quality of the hurt, which may be felt as here or there. The reason that we cannot advance a plausible translation of "I have a stinging pain in my foot" into the "My foot pained me stingingly" idiom is not that the former captures something that *could not* be captured by the latter, but only that since there is no such word as "stingingly" in common use, there is no such word to be used figuratively. The ontological point is not, however, affected by this linguistic accident, for we could obviously introduce such words as "stingingly" into our current idiom so as to guarantee the above-mentioned translation.* But once we understand the force of such words as "stinging" in "I have a stinging pain in my foot," once we understand that they are used to describe the quality of the hurt, we have all the grounds we need for saying that pains are not conceived as peculiar objects but as "qualities": the difficulty of finding a straightforward translation is thus of no significance whatever.

Before tackling the puzzle about the location and qualities of pain, I said that pain is best understood as a state or condition of a person, the criteria for which are "outer" and behavioral. The

* For further discussion of this problem, see Ch. VI, p. 147, footnote, and pp. 149–152.

question arises as to whether this is really correct, modest as it seems to be. In the light of what I have just said about the so-called location of pain, might it not be better to say that pain is a condition of a *part* of a person's body, rather than a condition of the person himself? I think not, mainly for the general reason that it is the person who is stimulated and the person who responds.* To insist that it is, say, the leg that is stimulated and the leg that responds is not just to overlook the complex variety of pain-behavior, much of which is entirely verbal, but it is also to treat the leg as a quasi-person itself, as a thing that feels and acts—and this, of course, is comically crude. Still, if pain (and thus feeling pain) is a condition or state of a person, it remains puzzling how "X's foot hurts in a way that can be described as 'stinging' " can be a less misleading way of expressing the force of "X has a stinging pain in his foot." After all, the latter says something directly about X, while the former seems to speak not about X but about his foot.

The way out of this difficulty can be traced, I believe, as follows. To say that a man feels pain, or is in pain, is plainly to say something *about him*. Since to be in pain is not *eo ipso* to exhibit specific behavior, when we say that he is in pain we are at least saying that he is in some particular condition (or state). Now, what do we add to this claim when, in response to the question "Where does he feel pain?", we answer, "He feels pain in his left foot"? One thing is clear: we certainly do not implicitly retract our previous claim that he is in the feeling-pain condition (or state). We rather make our claim more specific. He is not just in the feeling-pain state; he is in the feeling-pain-in-his-left-foot state. But if this is what our additional remark comes to—a more determinate specification of his state—then there is obviously no problem about how feeling-pain can be a state (or condition) of a person and yet be described in such a way that one might naturally take it to be a condition of a *part* of a person's body.

Although this last argument is apparently unproblematic, it does prompt a query about the exact force of the expression "a feeling-pain-in-the-left-foot state." How, exactly, are we to understand such a contrived locution? The answer to this is obvious: the locution in point is simply a perspicuous description of what we

---

* See Ch. IX, p. 250, footnote.

ordinarily call a "pain in the leg"—perspicuous because it does not tempt us to think of the pain as a peculiar inner object, or even as something adjectival qualifying just a part of a person's body. The locution is specially formed, in other words, to emphasize that a pain in the left foot is a condition of a person *as a unitary agent*, a condition which, because it disposes one to favor, attend to, worry about, and so on, a certain region of one's left leg, is described in relation to that leg. Thus, while no "feels" are rawer, more immediate, and more undeniably insistent than pains, they are not strictly locatable either as objects or as episodes—at least it is not philosophically perspicuous to regard them as locatable in this way. This is a consequence, not only of the arguments just given, but of the familiar facts about phantom limbs, where, though a person may have no legs at all, he may nevertheless claim to feel pain in either one of them. In such cases we do not, of course, accept the descriptions offered at face value: lacking legs, a man cannot literally, as we ordinarily say, feel pain in one of them. But this is just a consequence of the character of the criteria that govern the expression "feeling pain in the leg." As an experience, as an inner state characteristically associated with specific dispositions, the man's feeling-pain-in-the-leg state need not differ at all from that of anyone else; and for this reason we might say that his state is such that if he actually did have legs, it would correctly be described as "a feeling of pain in the leg." To put this in another way: the perspicuous locution "a feeling-pain-in-the-left-leg state" differs from the ordinary locution "a feeling of pain in the left leg" in that while the former applies, or can apply, both to normal and to legless men, the latter applies only to men with left legs—and is, therefore, unperspicuous philosophically, since it leads to gratuitous puzzles about the nature and location of pain.

If the argument here is sound, pain is thus not too far from what common sense has always taken it to be, namely, a covert state whose presence accounts for a familiar kind of observable behavior. This covert character of pain is entirely compatible with both the facts of language-learning and the privileged access that each man has to the pains he feels—something that the entire argument of Chapter IV attempted to establish. In order to perfect this account of pain it is, I believe, only necessary to discuss a number of

borderline cases, where there is some uncertainty about whether
"pain" is strictly applicable or not,[13] and then probe the general
question of the relation of sensory experiences to brain states. But
because the latter question is far more complex than is usually
thought, I shall save it for Chapter IX, where the problem of mind
and body is specifically discussed.

VI
Sense Impressions

If the form of reasoning distinctive of theoretical science is merely a special case of the kind of dialectical reasoning needed for all empirical knowledge, then we have no reasonable alternative but to accept physical theory as providing a factual account of the actual character of the world. This outcome makes it impossible to brush aside the classical problems concerning perception, sense data, and sensible qualities, which immediately arise from the apparent conflict between common sense and a literal interpretation of basic physical theory.

I. SENSE IMPRESSIONS AND THEORETICAL SCIENCE

It has, of course, been a familiar theme of recent philosophy that it takes far more than a scientific view of the world to prompt the classical problems of perception. In fact, it is often thought that if our everyday language does not commit us to accept such bizarre entities as sense contents or impressions, some of these classical problems cannot arise. The error of this approach is, however, patent, since even if the language of everyday life were thoroughly behavioristic (which it is not), reflection on the physics and psychology of perception would immediately incline us to postulate some sort of subjective sensory experiences.* A "naive" conception of sensible qualities such as color seems very obviously to be out of line with the contentions of physical science; and if we are not to take the desperate step of purging sensuous *qualia* from our entire world, it is natural to follow John Locke and in effect relocate them in the "minds" of perceivers. To yield to this temptation is admittedly to open the door to a host of classical difficulties, but we can always draw at least some comfort from the apparently well-established fact that sensuous purples seem to emerge only as the result of stray radiation and thus presumably qualify the state of a perceiver rather than the character of some remote cause.

The comfort to be drawn from this approach may be wholly illusory, some will say, unless it is possible to block forever the historic line of thought that results in solipsism. Since the arguments of the last few chapters inevitably lead to some form of scientific realism and, in turn, prompt one to speak of sense impressions with renewed confidence, the problems raised by the solipsist's argument may appear to assume formidable dimensions. It will be wise, therefore, to have another look at this threatening old argument; if the problems clustered about it cannot be dispelled once and for all, our temptation to speak freely of subjective sensory experiences is perhaps disasterously misguided from the start.

A careful look at the solipsist's argument (see pp. 61–62) is very heartening, since if the preceding discussion is sound, that argument is shot through with error. For one thing, although nothing has yet been said about the exact character of a sensory experience (or a "subjective appearance"), it is clear that if such things are to be postulated at all, they must be understood as having some sort of "outer" criteria. This is indeed a condition of their being encompassed in an intersubjective language.† Yet if sensory experiences must be understood in this way, it follows at once that solipsism, or indeed even skepticism about the existence of a common external world, cannot possibly result from admitting their existence. To conceive them as having outer criteria is to conceive them

---

* See pp. 8–10.
† The reasons why a scientifically inspired language must be intersubjective were explored in Ch. II (see esp. pp. 61–62) and Ch. III (see esp. pp. 173 f.).

in relation to an outer, public reality; and if the criteria for their existence is ever satisfied, there is then no room for general doubts about either the existence of a world of bodies or that of the sentient creatures whose experiences they are.

The possibility of interpreting sensory experiences in this indirect way requires, of course, that one abandon the "foundations" picture of knowledge on which the solipsist's argument rests. This erroneous picture of knowledge was criticized in detail in Chapters II, III, and V, so its abandonment here is a cause for rejoicing rather than alarm. But to see clearly that it has to be abandoned is to see just how objectionable the solipsist's argument actually is.* For what it does is locate an alleged foundation of knowledge, namely subjective appearance, and then attempt to show that nothing nonsubjective can be inferred from this basis. In attempting the latter, two unacceptable principles are used, both of which have been thoroughly undermined by the argument of the last chapter:† a verification principle that traces all empirical meaning to immediate experience, and a principle that restricts inductive inference to various forms of instantial generalization.

It is important to note that, apart from employing these unacceptable principles, the solipsist's argument also provides a completely false picture of the evidential basis on which theoretical claims about the world are advanced. Consider the atomists of Chapter I whose views were challenged by the solipsist. Far from actually developing their ideas of atomic physical reality from their

---

* Solipsism must be distinguished from a stronger position that might be called "utter skepticism." The solipsist maintains that he (or perhaps any man) can at least know the character of his own psychological states, but nothing of an external world or of any other person. The basic error of this view is that it claims too much and, in doing so, is self-refuting. A man's claim actually to *know* the character of his own subjective states can be defended only by reference to a form of dialectical reasoning adequate to establish the existence of other persons and a common world. If, therefore, one can actually *know* the nature of one's own subjective state, one cannot be trapped in a logically inescapable subjectivity. (See Ch. II, pp. 31–38 and 61–62; also Ch. V, pp. 123–126.) The utter skeptic, who denies that any sort of knowledge is possible, cannot be taken seriously until he tells us what he means by knowledge. When he does this, we can expect to find either that his claim is true but unexciting (for example, "All empirical claims are subject to revision") or that it is challenging but false (for example, "Given acceptable canons of evidence, there is actually no evidence for any empirical claim").

† See pp. 123–126.

conception of sensuous appearance, they rather came to the reasoned *conclusion* that they were "immediately aware" of sensuous appearance only by reflecting on their theory of physical reality. Instead of being purely subjective, their starting point involved a public world of common-sense objects. In order to account for certain peculiarities of these objects, the atomists were led to identify them with complex systems of minute colorless particles. This theoretical development led to a conflict (at least in their judgment) concerning sensible qualities such as colors and smells, and the status of these qualities was accordingly reinterpreted. For these thinkers, there was obviously no question of starting with subjective appearance, known to be appearance, and then going on to *infer* the character of reality from this tenuous basis. These men rather started from a certain objective conception of themselves and the world, and then gradually changed this conception in accordance with the demands of further thought and experimentation.

It is crucial to realize that atomists proceeding in this way were at no stage required to drag in private concepts. The common-sense notions they started out with were patently intersubjective, and although they were led to extend the concept of an appearance to encompass such qualities as color, this latter concept does not have to be regarded as a private one. After all, the things presenting the appearances were still held to be public objects, situated in a public space and time. It is true that these public objects were reinterpreted in theoretical terms as systems of particles, but this reinterpretation could not itself destroy their intersubjective status. In fact, this status could appear doubtful only to someone who has accepted the foundations picture of knowledge and, with it, an abstractionist or associationist theory of meaning for basic empirical concepts.*

Although the atomist's approach, thus understood, seems entirely capable of escaping the skeptical problems it has faced in the past, the cost of embracing its essential spirit might be regarded as excessively high. Not only does it imply that science and common sense actually do clash, but it suggests that in accepting the scientist's view of reality we are committed to regarding the common-sense world of sunsets and flowers as in some sense an "objective

* These theories of meaning were explained and criticized in Ch. III.

appearance." Both ideas are extremely unpopular at the present time, and neither will be accepted without very strenuous argument. Besides, the atomist's approach faces some rather special obstacles. One of these is that any attempt to reinterpret sensible qualities such as color as dispositions of a physical system to evoke peculiar sensory states in perceivers seems to be circular (see p. 11). Thus, while a sophisticated form of scientific realism has no trouble eluding such traditional bugbears as skepticism and solipsism, it is far from being free of philosophical difficulties.

Since the entire tenor of my argument leads to a "realistic" interpretation of physical theory and an explicit rejection of the foundations picture of empirical knowledge, the possibility of a conflict between common sense and theoretical science remains, for me, a completely open one. In order to determine whether such a conflict actually exists, it will be necessary to have a clearer idea of the common-sense view of the world. My first step toward attaining this will be to investigate our common conception of sensory experience.

2. AN APPROACH TO SENSE IMPRESSIONS

In view of my discussion in the last chapter, I shall assume that any acceptable account of sensory experience must in some way conform to Wittgenstein's dictum that an inner process requires outward criteria. About the only recent, reasonably detailed account that meets this condition and also strikes me as intuitively plausible has been advanced, independently, by Wilfrid Sellars and by Peter Geach.[1] I shall call this "The Analogy Theory of Impressions" and begin my discussion by considering it in some detail. For the most part I shall concentrate on Sellars' version of the theory, since he developed it first and also has worked it out more extensively.

The term "sense impression," as it is used here, is intended merely as a collective label for a wide variety of sensory experiences. The items covered by it include eidetic images, afterimages, illusory and hallucinatory experiences, and the various sensory experiences one normally has in looking at, smelling, and hearing ordinary physical things, such as flags, flowers, and fire engines. In using this collective label, I do not mean to imply that there are not important differences among the items included under it. But these differences are not important for the kind of question I shall discuss.

According to Sellars, talk about sense impressions gains its basic force and usefulness in explaining aberrant perception, and it is in connection with aberrant perceptual claims that such terms as "afterimage" or "auditory sensation" might naturally have been introduced into discourse. As he views the matter, so long as a man's claims about what he sees or hears are correct or, if incorrect, can be explained by reference to his tendency to lie or jest, there would be little point in speaking of the sense experiences he has. But when, in all honesty, a man claims to see, hear, or smell something that is clearly not there, such as a floating dagger, little green men, or fuzzy spots on a grainy black field, then there is considerable point in speaking of his subjective sensory experiences. It is indeed with reference to them that we characteristically *explain* the facts (a) that he utters the particular words that he does utter, and (b) that his utterance is not just a species of raving but an intelligent, sometimes even thoughtful report, reflecting the man's rationality. Thus, some explanation as to why Macbeth spoke of a dagger rather than a donkey must be available to common sense; and while "an heat oppress'd brain" might account for an inclination to rave, it could not explain why he used those specific words, nor could it explain (and this is perhaps the most important point) why his use of those words was *intelligent, coherent, and in its way even defensible.** Such an explanation can be given, however, by reference to the peculiar hallucinatory experience he must have had; and an experience of this sort is, for Sellars, just a special kind of sense impression.

If having certain sense impressions is indeed able to account for the occurrence and rationality of a man's aberrant perceptual claims, just what characteristics must these impressions be understood to have? Sellars answers this question by providing a dual characterization. First, an impression of a red triangle (to take a representative, simple case) may be regarded, extrinsically, as "that state of a perceiver normally brought about by the influence of

* Some philosophers, in an evident effort to avoid speaking of sensory experiences, have tried to explain the intelligence of aberrant perceptual claims by reference to a man's thought, "It was *as if* I were actually seeing a dagger." These attempts ultimately fail because they cannot account for the rationality of these peculiar "as if" thoughts.

red, triangular objects on the eye."[2] Second, regarded intrinsically, such an impression is conceived as something analogous, in
certain limited respects, to objects that are red and triangular on
their facing side. These two modes of characterization are plainly
designed to do justice to an impression's twofold explanatory force,
which was mentioned above. If an impression of a red triangle is
that state *normally* brought about by the influence of red triangles
on the eye, then the fact that a person has such an impression would
explain why he should use words appropriate to the presence of
red triangles, even when no such things can be found in his immediate vicinity. And if an impression is conceived as analogous
to the facing surface of a triangular, red object, then the fact that
it has the features the analogy demands—for instance, a feature
analogous to the color of a physical object—can explain why a
man's words can be taken to be intelligent and rationally produced.

Before attempting to sift Sellars' account with any care, I might
point out that as just stated it fits in nicely with what I said about
pains in the last chapter. For one thing, it gives sense impressions
just the same intersubjective yet parasitical status that pains re-
ceived on my analysis. They are not private objects, nor even basic
sensory particulars, but rather states or attributes of a person that
are specified in relation to observable states of affairs. Again, like
the concept of a nagging pain, the concept of an impression is
in part an analogical one, given content by analogy with something
both public and familiar. Finally, since they are conceived as inner
states capable, like pains, of issuing in characteristic verbal responses, a man's privileged access to them can be easily understood
according to principles already discussed. As in having a pain, one
may have an impression and yet fail to make any response that
would enable others to identify it, being entirely clear oneself what
its presence tempts one to say, and even why one should have this
temptation.

3. A BASIC PROBLEM WITH THE ANALOGY THEORY

Although this view of sense impressions undoubtedly does fit in
well with what I have said about pains, and thus ought to tempt
me very strongly, it unfortunately seems to involve a serious dif-

ficulty. Let me lead up to a statement of this difficulty by a little more exposition. For Sellars, and even for Geach, an impression is something adjectival, a state of having-something or being-impressed in a certain way.* An impression cannot therefore be understood as a peculiar object; indeed, the act-object distinction, so familiar in traditional discussions of sense impressions, is emphatically repudiated as a real distinction.† To speak of *an* impression is thus to speak in an unperspicuous, even misleading fashion. It would be much better to speak of having-an-impression, all in one breath; for this latter locution would always remind us that the state in point is strictly incapable of being broken down into a relation between a man and a peculiar psychic object. To say that a man *has* an impression of X is thus to say that he is in a having-an-impression-of-X sensory state; and since "having-an-impression-of-X" is to be understood as a syntactically simple predicate, we would not be tempted to make the existential inference from "Tom has an impression of X" to "There is an impression, Y, which is related to Tom in some way." The most we could infer is "Tom is in some sensory state or other."

The problem that Sellars' account prompts is this. If a relational analysis of "Tom has an impression of X" is to be rejected as factually misleading, then we must regard the analogy that Sellars mentions as holding between the having-an-impression-of-X sensory state and, say, a facing surface. But what kind of *analogy* could this possibly be? Sellars calls it a "formal, trans-category" one,[3] but this terminology does not make the force of his position immediately obvious. If an impression of a red triangle is to be understood as analogous to the facing surface of a red triangle, it would appear that the state of having-this-impression would have properties analogous to shape and color. But how could this be? How could a nonextended sensory state possibly be analogous to a facing sur-

---

* Geach uses the locution of "seeing" to make the same point: ". . . may we not at any rate say [that is, in the case of double vision] that there is something, my seeing, that splits into two when I push my eyeball. . . ? It does seem to me reasonable to say this sort of thing" (*Mental Acts*, p. 128). Notice that Geach speaks of *his seeing* splitting, rather than something *that* he sees splitting.

† Sellars maintains that the distinction is rather a nominal one, like that between smiling and a smile. This distinction is discussed below; see esp. pp. 145–148.

face that is colored and extended, that is red and triangular? The answer to this question is simply not clear.

Note that if an analogy between visual images and colored surfaces were to be drawn in the most natural way, two highly debatable ideas would presumably lie behind it. The first is that colors are to be interpreted "naively" as the sort of occurrent sensuous quality that has always proved scientifically disturbing. The other is that visual images may be accepted as peculiar inner objects, items with an odd sensuous surface. These items would of course be *like* outer surfaces in a very obvious way; they could even be said to be mental pictures of the latter. If the analogy were drawn in this way, it would of course be easy to account for the phenomena Sellars' theory was designed specially to explain, namely, the reasonableness of aberrant perceptual claims. A man making such an aberrant claim could then be said to be responding to a mental picture of the object or objects that his words would normally describe. Since the picture might sometimes be difficult to distinguish from the real thing, the reasonableness of his words would be patent.

Accepting a simple-minded analogy of this sort would admittedly be out of the question for most philosophers today, because the two ideas on which it is based are extremely unpopular.[4] For the sake of maximum clarity, however, it is worth asking just what is supposed to be wrong with these two ideas. Exactly why are we, or might we be, so eager to reject them? To give a little punch to this question, notice that if our task here as philosophers were what it is sometimes said to be—namely, to give a reasonably unbiased analysis of what a plain man might ordinarily say—it would not be unreasonable to conclude that such ideas might very well be reflected in ordinary discourse.

Consider the case of color. To think of colors as Lockean powers,* or as dispositions to reflect radiation of certain wave lengths, is surely to go a long way beyond the world-view of unaided common sense. Not only does a scientifically influenced view of color strike the innocent beginner at physics and philosophy as wildly paradoxical, but in practice it even wrenches a sophisticate's sensibilities to conceive colors in anything but a "naive" way. In fact there is something dehumanizing about rejecting the naive

---

* Locke regarded colors as powers of an extended object to produce color-sensations in a sentient being. See p. 11.

picture in everyday life. If two lovers, eyes inches apart as in the Vigeland sculpture, were to think of each other's eyes as simply molecular structures reflecting different mμ's of electromagnetic radiation, and do this without a change of interest or posture, their mutual attraction would seem as strange and inhuman as the mating behavior of Grey Walter's electronic "tortoises." Their view of each other, in the earthy circumstances in which they sit, would simply be too far out of line with our ordinary view of two human beings in love to be believable or understandable. The scientific view of golden hair and blue-green eyes is not the view we live with in our everyday, practical affairs.

Just as it is natural to think of a young woman's hair and eyes in a "naive" rather than a coldly scientific way, so it is natural to think of mental images as if they were objects, with almost a life of their own. It is a commonplace that after looking at a very bright light, a person will have highly vivid images, which gradually fade with the passage of time. It is entirely natural to say that many such images can be produced in this way and that their number can easily be determined by a simple process of counting. In comparison with this common mode of description Geach's remark that his "seeing . . . splits into two" in double vision is highly anomalous, suggesting that activities can be split apart like dried peas. There may be philosophical merit in this way of speaking, but it cannot be denied that it *seems* far out of line with the way we ordinarily speak and presumably think.

A moment ago I raised the question of why, as philosophers, we should want to reject a so-called naive conception of sensible qualities and an inner object analysis of sense impressions. I think it is clear why we might want to reject the former: it is evidently out of line with what physical science shows us our world is really like. But what about the latter? Exactly what is wrong with the idea that images are inner objects? For some thinkers the difficulty is again based on scientific considerations. We know, at least in general outline, what the human brain and nervous system are like, and we know, or think we know, that there is no place in them for peculiar sensuous objects.[5] For others, there are important philosophical arguments, which presumably do not rest on empirical premises. Since scientific considerations cannot militate against the adequacy of a proffered analysis of a common-sense notion, it is clear that only philosophical arguments are relevant if we are concerned to unearth a just analysis (whatever that may be) of colors and impressions as they are ordinarily conceived.

In recent years the most familiar philosophical objections to an inner object interpretation of sensory experiences have been associated with behaviorism—the basic idea being that there could be no intersubjective means of *verifying* whether such objects actually exist. For reasons given in the last chapter, objections of this sort can no longer be taken seriously. There is nothing in principle objectionable in speaking of unobservable things and events. Since "outer" normic criteria can be provided for inner objects just as easily as for inner states or episodes, what is needed here are special reasons for interpreting mental images as belonging to one category rather than another. Several reasons of this sort were brought out in the last chapter when pains were discussed, and similar reasons seem to lie behind the claims of Sellars and Geach. I shall try to develop these reasons now, leaving the analysis of color to Chapter VII.

4. OBJECTIONS TO IMPRESSIONS
AS INNER OBJECTS

Although Sellars is anxious to reject the inner object interpretation of sense impressions, he would not want to deny that we ordinarily describe our images as if they were as thing-like as men or trees. In fact he would presumably agree that for ordinary purposes this mode of description is "entirely in order as it is." What he would want to insist upon is rather that, like the smiles a man may properly be said to "wear," the images we describe as "fuzzy" or "red" have the conceptual status of nominal objects, and accordingly require an adverbial analysis. Thus, the distinction we properly draw between a mental image and the "act" or state of imaging it is, in his view, just a nominal one, like the distinction between smiling and a smile, serving and a serve, or shaking hands and a handshake.[6] And just as "Hilda wore a wan smile" is best understood as asserting no more than the nonrelational fact that Hilda smiled wanly, so, he would contend, "Jones has a sense impression of X" is best understood as asserting no more than the nonrelational fact that Jones "is impressed" in a certain fashion or mode.[7] The fact that we do not ordinarily describe impressions or images in this perspicuous way is thus irrelevant, so far as Sellars' basic contention is concerned. He would cheerfully admit this fact—and then go on to argue that the familiar mode of describing impressions is just as unperspicuous, philosophically, as the familiar mode of describing smiles.

To appreciate the arguments that might be advanced in defense of Sellars' contention, it may be useful to consider why, and in what sense, the familiar mode of describing smiles may be held to be unperspicuous. However unlikely it may be, it is at least possible to imagine a man thoroughly befuddled by the relational form of "Mary wore a seductive smile." If the man had studied enough traditional philosophy to be concerned with the distinction between things and relations, he might conceivably ask such questions as these: Just how is that seductive smile related to Mary? Does it cover her lips as her slippers cover her feet? Might it exist, interesting as it is, after she is gone? Might it materialize one summer night like the smile of the Cheshire cat? Or is Mary's "ownership" of her smile "logically nontransferable," as philosophers say? If it is the latter, exactly why is it nontransferable? Why couldn't Sarah, who is just as seductive, wear it too?

Questions of this sort, though decidedly bizarre, are really no more bizarre than many questions philosophers constantly pose in connection with such items as "statements" or sense impressions. In the present case, however, it is easy to show just why they are misconceived, and showing this amounts to showing why the relational form of smile attribution is not conceptually perspicuous. If "Mary wore a seductive smile" is equivalent to the less misleading "Mary smiled seductively," not one of these bizarre questions could reasonably arise. In answering the question of how her smile is related to her, one would only have to say: "Her smile is not actually 'related' to her at all, for it is not an independent object. To speak of her smile is merely to speak in a convenient, nominalized way of what she *did* and how, or in what manner, she did it. What she did was smile, and she did it in a seductive manner. The reason that Sarah cannot wear Mary's smile is that Sarah, being a different person from Mary, cannot perform Mary's act of smiling. They may both smile, and smile just as seductively, but the act of the one person is not the act of the other."

Assuming that all of this is true of smiles, is it at all reasonable to say that something similar is true of mental images? A first step toward answering this can be made by noting that the sense in which a man *has* a mental image is presumably the same as that in which a man *has* a feeling or headache. Yet, according to the analysis of pain given in the last chapter, "Jones has a pain" is not strictly a relational statement. To say that a man has a pain, far from implying that he is actually related to a peculiar object which may itself throb or sting, is only to say that he feels-pain, that some part of his body pains him or hurts.* This being so, the similarity of the "has" in "Tom has a headache" and "Tom has an image" would strongly suggest that the latter is not strictly a relational statement either, that it, too, is a conceptually misleading locution, equivalent to something like "Tom images in a certain mode."†

Once this suggestion is made, it is easy to see that the same basic considerations favoring an adverbial analysis of pain also apply to sensory experiences generally. Take the statement "Tom has an afterimage." If this were a genuinely relational statement, we could then legitimately ask: Just where is this image that Tom has? Is it in his head, his eye? Or is it, as some philosophers have suggested, no *where* at all, belonging to some nonspatial realm of consciousness? And what about the relation of *having*? Is this relation perhaps a causal one? If it is, it can hardly hold between a *person* and an image; it must presumably hold between the image and certain events in his body. But what events could these be? If they are supposed to be physiological events, describable in the language of the laboratory, we should then be committed to the impossible idea that the ordinary, nontechnical notion of having a mental image is not analyzable in ordinary terms.‡ Again, if the relation of having

---

* See Ch. V, pp. 132 f.

† In traditional terminology it would be said that imaging has *modes* rather than relations to objects. As Collingwood put it: ". . . for Descartes the grammar of the sentence 'I see a blue colour' is not like the grammar of 'I kick a bad dog' but like the grammar of 'I feel a transient melancholy' or 'I go for a fast walk'. The colour, the melancholy, the walk, are not objects of an action, they are *modes* of an action; their names have an *adverbial* function in the sentences in which they occur. . . . On the Cartesian view . . . a blue colour is a feeling of which I am conscious exactly as a slight exhilaration is a feeling of which I am conscious; in neither case is there any object of feeling. . .," *The New Leviathan* (Oxford: Clarendon Press, 1942), pp. 30–31.

‡ This is discussed at length in Ch. IX; see esp. pp. 249–256.

did hold between the image and certain physical events in the brain, in what sense could the image be properly attributable to the person *as a unitary subject?* Would we not have to say that what has the image is not the person at all but rather these events in his brain? Since this would be patently unsatisfactory, should we rather say that the relation of having is a purely mental one, perhaps a relation of direct apprehension? But what is this relation, and how is it attached to the *person* who is said to have the image and to speak or move as the result of having it? How, indeed, is this relation to be understood as ruling out the possibility of multiple "ownership" of the image, of Tom having Harry's image as well?

As in the case of pain, all of the above questions arise from the relational analysis of having an image or sensory experience; and if we can accept the adverbial analysis distinctive of the Cartesian tradition, each one of them drops away as every bit as confused and misconceived as the analogous questions raised above concerning smiles. In my opinion anyone familiar with the history of futile attempts to fit together a relational interpretation of "Tom has a mental image" with the conception of persons as unitary subjects of mental and physical attributes should find the alternative adverbial interpretation infinitely preferable.[8]

5. ON THE METHOD OF PHILOSOPHICAL ANALYSIS

Earlier I suggested that if the proper approach to philosophical analysis is essentially descriptive and uncritical—a matter, at least occasionally, of considering what one might ordinarily say about some phenomenon—it would be tempting to think that the idea of mental images as inner pictures is firmly enshrined in ordinary discourse. In rejecting this conception of images as adequate even at the level of common sense, I am obviously employing a different method of analysis. For the sake of maximum clarity in what I shall subsequently argue, it will be useful to make a few explicit remarks about the kind of method this is.

An important point to make at once is that even so-called ordinary language analysts have rarely proceeded in a purely descriptive manner, which seems to be the ideal of descriptive linguistics. The analyses of philosophers are rather always partly critical, a

matter of "making sense" in some way of the locutions being analyzed. As is clear from preceding chapters, the critical principles
involved in much recent philosophical analysis are untenable, implying a verificationist criterion of meaning and an excessively
narrow conception of legitimate inductive reasoning. Although I
reject these critical principles, I too am concerned to "make sense"
of ordinary discourse. My analytical approach is in fact far from
novel, lying squarely in the tradition of R. G. Collingwood.[9] Like
Collingwood, my general strategy is to unearth, to the extent that I
can, the basic presuppositions of consistent thought about the phenomena chosen for investigation.

In accordance with this conception of analysis, my concern in
the present chapter has been to isolate the basic presuppositions
underlying common-sense discourse about mental images, perceptual experiences, and the like. Since these presuppositions inevitably extend to such abstract, categorial notions as those of
things and relations, the adverbial interpretation of impressions that
I favor at the common-sense level is based on more deep-seated
considerations than merely what a plain man might be inclined
to say about his sensory experiences. In fact, since plain men are
notoriously vague and inarticulate about what they mean by such
terms as "physical thing" or "sensory experience," my interpretation of the meaning of these terms involves a significant idealization
of common-sense discourse, one designed to render it both consistent and philosophically unproblematic. I contend that my approach here is not appreciably different, in general outline, from
the actual approach of most analytic philosophers.

6. ANOTHER LOOK AT THE
ANALOGY THEORY OF IMPRESSIONS

Since I am now committed to reject an inner object interpretation of sense impressions, I am also committed to reject any version
of the analogy theory that requires this interpretation. Sellars' version does not possess this drawback, and for this reason I want to
return to it and attempt to free it from its original air of paradox.
This air of paradox arose from the theory's peculiar trans-category
aspect, from its assumption that there could be a significant analogy

between items apparently so disparate as red triangles and non-extended sensory states. My immediate task will be to show that this assumption is actually not as questionable as it might appear.

To formulate my task in these terms is to assume that a so-called naive conception of colors and other sensible qualities actually is enshrined in ordinary discourse and actually is essential to the common-sense view of the world. I shall advance a detailed argument in favor of this assumption in the next chapter; for the time being, I shall simply assume that the assumption is justifiable. It is only by doing this that I can immediately come to terms with the analogy theory as Sellars develops it.

It will be useful to approach Sellars' theory by recalling some of the basic similarities between sense impressions and feelings such as pain. Although we commonly describe pains as stinging or burning, this mode of description does not actually commit us to regard them as peculiar inner objects. We might say that such locutions as "Tom felt a stinging pain" are actually metaphorical and assert no more than that Tom was in a stinging-pain state—even though, in describing his state this way, we are forced to complicate our language in a slightly unusual fashion. The justification for doing this is that while describing pains as if they were stinging or burning objects is practically very convenient, such descriptions lead to gratuitous puzzles when taken literally. Similarly, although we describe images as if they too were objects, green in color and square in shape, it does not follow that a penetrating analysis of such descriptions need leave us with images as puzzling inner objects.

Given this degree of similarity between sense impressions and pains, it is not difficult to see how we might extend it. When pains were discussed, it was shown that they are generally described in three distinct ways: with reference to their typical causes (burning, stinging), with reference to their typical effects (blinding, enervating), and by analogy (nagging, pulsating). The first two modes of description are obviously applicable to sense impressions. An impression of a red triangle is the sort of sensory state that is typically brought about by viewing red triangles under good light. This is a description by reference to a typical cause. But an impression of a red triangle is also the sort of sensory state that inclines an English speaker to say "I see something red and triangular." Remarks of this kind are naturally made when the speaker is in front of something that is actually red and triangular, but they might be made in good faith even when such objects are not there—in which case it is the impression alone that evokes the remark. Both of these modes of description are obviously compatible with an impression's being understood as a sensory state, as a state of sensing. Different *modes* of sensing are thus picked out partly by reference to certain of their typical causes and effects.

So far as the analogical form of description is concerned, an important point must be kept firmly in mind, namely, that analogies are not out-and-out similarities; they hold only in certain respects. Now, there is clearly one respect in which certain states of imaging are analogous to physical objects: the descriptions commonly given of them are *formally* analogous. Whether one conceives of an image as an inner picture or as the merely nominal object of a sensory state, one would naturally describe it in the very same words that one would use to describe certain public objects. The *formal* analogy between the image, or state of imaging, and certain physical objects would arise from the roughly invariant syntactical features of the words that are used in describing both the image and the appropriate physical objects.

If we take "*s*" as a prefix to indicate the secondary use of words in phenomenological description, we shall find, then, that words so prefixed are used in a manner that is formally analogous to the use of those words when the prefix is lacking. Specifically, we shall find that "s-red" is related to "s-shape" and "s-extension" as "red" is related to "shape" and "extension"; and "s-red" will also be related to "s-green" and "s-orange" as "red" is related to "green" and "orange." The analogy is merely formal because it is based on the syntactical interrelations among certain classes of words used for two types of purposes, namely, describing public objects and describing the merely nominal objects of sensory experience. The description of an image as s-red is thus like the description of a pain as throbbing, a feeling of melancholy as transient, or a tickle as unbearable. The fact that the image, the pain, the feeling of melancholy, and the tickle are treated *as if* they were genuine objects is not itself of any great philosophical significance; it is merely a convenient form of description, which could in principle be replaced by a less misleading form, though at the cost of introducing some rather complicated terminology. Thus, just as the ordinary

"Tom felt a twinge" could be rephrased as "Tom suffered in the twinge mode," so "Bill had an s-red afterimage" could be rephrased as "Bill sensed in an s-red mode" or "Bill sensed s-redly."

Sellars has actually insisted that the analogy he sees between impressions and physical objects is merely formal.[10] This being so, the fact that his analogy is trans-category turns out to be unproblematic. For regardless of the category of the item that is described indirectly by such words as "red" and "triangular," it may still be true that these descriptions are interrelated in a manner that is formally analogous to that in which "red" and "triangular" are interrelated when used in their primary sense. A virtual isomorphism between the interrelations of different classes of words is entirely compatible with their use in reference to different items. In the present case it is only claimed that there is an *analogy*—a similarity in *certain* respects—between the interpretations of certain words in their primary and secondary uses. And this claim is certainly reasonable enough; indeed, it seems a very modest one to make regarding such puzzling things as mental images.

Although the Analogy Theory of Impressions, thus interpreted, does seem fairly modest, it conveys a good deal of information. What it tells us, specifically, is that certain sensory states—the sort that are brought about in certain typical situations and that result in certain characteristic forms of behavior—have a family of phenomenal attributes that are indirectly picked out by verbal constructions of a nominalized sort. The constituent adjectives of these constructions, though used in a secondary sense, retain most of the formal interrelations they possess when, in their primary sense, they apply to perceptible features of public objects. To know what the attributes of a sensory state are—to understand what one means in speaking of them—is to know how they are interrelated among themselves and how they are related to attributes of other kinds. These complex relations are spelled out by what Sellars calls (see pp. 140–141) the intrinsic and extrinsic modes of characterizing impressions. The former provide an indirect means of giving the interrelations among the family of phenomenal attributes, and the latter relate members of this family to attributes of other kinds, such as ordinary physical redness. To understand these relations and interrelations is to understand everything that is understandable respecting the common-sense notion of an impression. In this respect the notion of an impression is exactly similar to the concept of pain, at least as it was analyzed in the last chapter.

7. CAN SENSE IMPRESSIONS HAVE
UNNOTICED FEATURES?

A useful way of rounding out this treatment of sense impressions is to consider the light it throws on the familiar question whether a sensory experience can have features that it does not seem to have. Using the terminology developed in the last section, this question can be formulated more precisely by asking: "Can a man have an s-red mental image without realizing that it is s-red?" To pose the question in this way is to see that the answer is an obvious "Yes." A man might have absolutely no conception of phenomenal redness, and so be utterly unable to entertain the idea of anything's having that quality.

Although the answer just given is an immediate consequence of the old idea that there is nothing intellectual or cognitive about a *sensory* experience and that "Percepts without concepts are blind," it ought to be acceptable on the grounds of common experience. A man can surely have an afterimage, or even a split image of the sort produced by finger-poking experiments, and yet fail, at that time, to ascertain all of its features. Was the afterimage really s-yellow in the center and s-green towards the edges? Did the double image produced in the experiment really seem to result from a splitting, or did it rather occur as soon as the eye was pressed? These questions are quite legitimately asked; and what is more, they can be properly answered. The man can have another afterimage produced by just the same visual stimulus, and he can spend an entire afternoon poking his eye and heeding the results. To the extent that the subsequent images are produced under just the same conditions as the first ones, to that extent there is a *prima facie* presumption that the images are of just the same kind—a presumption that is backed by the causal hypothesis embedded in the concept of an image by the extrinsic mode of characterization. In the absence of concrete evidence indicating that the conditions have appreciably changed, philosophical doubts about the similarity of the earlier and later images are just as empty here as anywhere else.

Once the infallibility of introspection is cast aside and every tatter of direct verificationism is abandoned, there is no longer any ground for puzzlement about unnoticed features of impressions. In fact, if the conception of an impression developed in this chapter is at all sound, there cannot possibly be a problem of this sort. If an impression is conceived as something whose existence can explain the intelligent, rational character of certain reports, the very demands of a good explanation must render it possible for an impression to have features that are not reflected in such reports. That is, if the fact that a man's impressions have certain special features is to explain the *reasonableness* of certain things he wants to say about his experience, then the presence of these features cannot logically depend on the attitude he takes toward his experience or the opinions he has about it.

VII
Common-Sense Colors and Theoretical Science

The object of this chapter is to investigate the basic presuppositions underlying common-sense discourse about colors. I shall be treating color as a specific example of what philosophers call a "sensible quality," and my aim in examining it will be to ascertain the extent to which such qualities, ordinarily understood, are compatible with the view of physical reality that seems to be implied by theoretical science.

1. THE COMPLEXITY OF COLOR

As every painter knows, a thing's true color does not normally vary with its surroundings. In order actually to change its color you must paint it, dye it, or perhaps boil it in water. For most things, it will not be sufficient merely to change the quality of the lighting under which it is viewed. Accordingly, if a man were to think that his tie has actually changed color because, though blue on his entering the dimly lighted dining hall, it looks black when he is sitting at the table, one could normally infer that he does not fully understand what is meant by the word "color" or by the word "blue." It is simply too elementary a fact about color that a blue thing need not look blue at all times, in all conditions of illumination. This brings out an extremely important theoretical point about color: colors such as blue are not just sensible qualities immediately discernible at any time merely by sight. They are rather persisting features of public objects normally discernible only in fairly standard conditions and when viewed by normal observers.

The relation between apparent color, real color,* standard observers, and standard conditions of perception is thus an extremely intimate one, presumably based on some kind of definition. The precise term whose definition establishes this relation has, however, been a chronic source of dispute in philosophy. For traditional empiricists, it was generally thought that the term in question is "real, or physical, color." They were inclined to think that *apparent color* is the logically simpler notion of the family, and that this notion provides a basis by which to define the other three, which are considerably more complex. Since they were also inclined to think that apparent color could in turn be defined by reference to sense data, their view naturally led to the varieties of phenomenalism that repeatedly occur in the history of their movement.

2. IS THE CONCEPT OF COLOR A DERIVATIVE ONE?

In recent years there have been frequent attempts to salvage the spirit of the traditional empiricist position without falling into the morass of phenomenalism. Although these attempts are highly problematic, the arguments they are based on have at least a very striking initial plausibility. The most popular argument relies on the notion of an ostensive definition, and another is based on the indisputable fact that such remarks as "X looks red" are normally

* When I speak of real color, I mean the color that a given thing would normally be said *actually* to have, not the color it has "naturally" (for example, the natural color of a bleached-blonde's hair), or when viewed in its normal habitat (for example, under water). I shall try to make this sense of "real color" clear in what follows, but in doing so I should not be understood as denying that there are plenty of borderline cases where it would be difficult to apply the term, or that "real" does not have a variety of uses that my discussion does not take into account. For a discussion of some of the ways in which "real color" is commonly used, see J. L. Austin's *Sense and Sensibilia*, G. Warnock, ed. (Oxford: Clarendon Press, 1962), pp. 65–77.

far more cautious than "X is red." According to the first argument, children learn to discriminate the qualities of color appearances long before they are able to grasp such rarefied notions as *standard observer* and *standard conditions of illumination.* This being so, the concept of actual color they later attain must be a derivative one because it presupposes these rarefied notions. According to the second argument, the facts stated by "X is red" and "X looks red" must differ in complexity because the former statement is less cautious than the latter. Since the facts stated here are logically related, the presumption is that the latter is a component of the former —that something's being red is its looking red plus something else. Because a complex is obviously best analyzed in terms of its elements, rather than its elements in terms of the complex, being red must be analyzable in terms of looking red, rather than the other way around.

In spite of the initial plausibility of these popular arguments, both are ultimately unsuccessful. In fact any argument, carried out in common-sense terms, that purports to reduce actual color to appearances is bound to be unsuccessful as well.* To say this is not to reject a basic principle involved in the appearance analysis, namely, that if an object actually is red, it will look red to standard observers in standard conditions. In rejecting such an analysis one need not even deny that the principle just mentioned unpacks part of the meaning of "X is red." All that has to be denied is that the notion of actual color is a derived one, which is logically more complex than the related notions of apparent color, standard perceiver, and standard conditions of illumination.

3. IMPLICATIONS OF THE CAUTIOUS FORCE OF "X LOOKS RED"

In order to see exactly why appearance analyses of actual color are bound to fail, it is useful to begin by considering the argument based on the cautious character of "X looks red." The first point

---

* If one departs radically from common-sense terms, one might be able to make a case for something like this reduction. But the reduction will not then provide an analysis of a common-sense notion, which is what concerns me here. I shall return to this question at the end of the chapter.

to note is that the caution involved here may result from importantly different considerations. If, for example, the conditions under which an object is seen are in any way questionable, then its apparent color may be a very uncertain guide to the color it actually has—and so a use of "It looks red" may indicate one's caution regarding these questionable conditions. But a use of "It looks red" may also indicate a degree of uncertainty about the determinate color that an object *appears* to have. One may be wholly confident that a thing looks red, but be in some doubt as to whether it looks crimson, vermilion, scarlet, or indeed any other particular determinate shade. This point is sometimes expressed by saying that while anything that is red must *be* some determinate shade of red, a thing may look red without *looking* any determinate shade of red.[1] Philosophers who have explicated "looking red" by reference to red sense data have naturally been puzzled by this fact, but if it is related to the cautious character of "looks" talk, it loses its air of paradox. For to characterize a thing's look is typically to indicate the way it strikes you; and a thing may strike you as being red without striking you as being any particular shade of red—in which case its determinable look would be due to a generic mode of conceptualization.

These initial remarks bring out a very important point: in ordinary uses of the "looks" locution, we are describing a thing's appearance in a way that is essentially comparative. To say that X looks red is usually to say that it looks as if it is red, as if it actually has that color. Thus, although you are not entirely certain that you are seeing the thing under normal conditions or that your eyes are not on this occasion slightly deceiving you, you might nevertheless be entirely certain that the thing you see does at least look to you, now, as if it were red, as if it actually had the sensuous quality that red objects have when viewed under standard conditions. Again, although you might not be confident about the thing's exact shade, you might be extremely certain that it at least looks red, that it has the generic look of a red thing viewed under good light.

This comparative use of "looks red" has an important application to the argument from complexity mentioned above. Although looking red, in a comparative sense, is an obvious component in the fact of something's being red, the notion of such an appearance plainly cannot be used in analyzing the notion of a thing's being red.

On the contrary, since looking red, in this sense, is a matter of look-
ig the way red things actually do look, indeed is analyzable in this
way, we are forced to admit a case where a constituent of a fact is
to be analyzed in terms of the complex of which it is typically a
part. To put the point in this way may seem heavy-handed, but actually it serves to highlight one of the dangers involved in regarding
facts as complex objects that, like frogs, can be dissected into parts.

4. IS THERE A PURELY OSTENSIVE CONCEPT
OF APPARENT COLOR?

In view of the preceding argument it should be clear that if any
looks or appearance locution is to have a chance of providing an
analysis of actual color, it must obviously be understood in some
noncomparative sense. The idea that there is such a sense of appear
words is what is stressed by the ostension argument mentioned
earlier. According to this argument, a child could be taught the use
of such words without any reference to actual color: he could
learn to respond reliably to objects which are in fact red or blue
with the words "red" and "blue," but his subsequent behavior under abnormal conditions could show that his color concepts really
apply only to appearances. Thus, when under yellow light he will
call red objects "orange," blue objects "black" (or whatever), and
so on. Since he has no conception of atypical conditions, and no idea
of any contrast between "is" and "looks," he plainly cannot have
the concept of actual color. But because his responses accurately
describe the quality of apparent colors, it is reasonable to think that
he has the concept of such appearances, even though he does not
understand, as we do, the relation between such appearances and
the true colors that things actually have.

While this argument may seem fairly convincing at first glance,
it actually fails to show that the child has any proper concept at
all, let alone the concept of a particular kind of color appearance.
As argued in Chapter IV, consistency of response cannot itself
prove anything more than consistency of parroting. And to argue
that such consistency must at least show what H. H. Price has
called a "recognitional capacity," involving a mere "experience
of the same again,"[2] is to overlook the crucial fact that the child's

responses may be interpreted in the light of an indefinite number of rival hypotheses, and that this number can be diminished only when one is prepared to answer the questions: "The same *what* again? How is this recurrent thing, feature, event, state or episode to be understood?" That questions of this sort are simply bypassed by the ostension theorist is a painful old story, illustrating the stubborn tendency of empiricists to leap from the fact that they, with their particular sophistication, would think of the child as responding verbally to an appearance (or to a sense datum or to a physical object) to the unwarranted conclusion that the child's verbal response must show a grasp of some favorite concept that applies to the thing that is thus regarded as eliciting his response.

Although the child's verbal behavior is consistent with the hypothesis that he is responding to his own subjective sense data, or sense impressions, this hypothesis can be ignored here because it leads directly to phenomenalism, which was ruled out in Chapter III. For the sake of clarifying some of the basic philosophical puzzles about colors, it will prove instructive, however, to consider the consequences of granting the child a primitive concept of one or the other of two kinds of color appearance. For convenience, these may be called "subjective apparent color" (or *SAC*) and "objective apparent color" (or *OAC*). In view of previous discussion these kinds of apparent color may be regarded as noncomparative. As its name implies, *SAC* is the color that a thing appears to a given person to have at a particular moment, though it may not appear this way generally. *OAC* will then be the color a thing appears to have to any normal observer in the circumstances in question. An example of *SAC* would be the grayish appearance that a red object presumably has to color-blind Jones; and an example of *OAC* would be the orange appearance that is apparent to any normal perceiver who views a white object under a strong orange light.

5. COULD SAC OR OAC BE PRIMITIVE COLOR CONCEPTS?

The possibility that the child's primitive color concept is that of *SAC* actually requires little discussion, since it is far too subjectivistic for the task at hand. For one thing, *SAC* is admittedly a subjectively apparent quality of a public thing, such as a tree or book. This means that anyone who has the concept of *SAC* must have the concept of a thing presenting a subjective appearance and the concept of a subject to whom the appearance is presented. To have these further concepts is not only to have some notion of a common time and space in which these subjects and objects find their objective location, but it is also to have some conception of the objective qualities that these entities have. The latter is obviously needed because the idea of an objective thing must have some empirical content; it cannot be the idea of a bare X, or substratum. One is committed, after all, to make sense of a *definite* thing, different from others, that presents this subjective appearance to one subject and that subjective appearance to another. Given this necessity of distinguishing a thing from its subjective appearance, it follows that even if we were to agree that the child's concept of a public thing could be given empirical content without reference to color—and this means without reference to visual shape, visual size, visual position, and the like—we would nevertheless have to insist that some of the other qualities of a public thing must be logically incapable of analysis in appearance terms. Yet the basic qualities describable in common-sense terms are sensible qualities; and every consideration that can be advanced in favor of reducing objective color to *SAC* can also be advanced, *mutatis mutandis*, in favor of reducing any other common-sense quality (such as hardness) to its subjective appearances as well. Since, from a common-sense point of view, not all sensible qualities can be reduced to subjective appearances, and since there is nothing special about the case of color, there is no basis for thinking that color is so reducible.

A final difficulty with this approach stands out as soon as one recalls the complexity of actual color. I have already established that the concept of actual color presupposes the concepts of standard conditions of visual perception and standard color observers. In order to effect an analysis of actual color in terms of *SAC* one would therefore have to have a great deal of information concerning which conditions are standard for color perception, how standard color observers are identified, whether one is a standard observer oneself, and so on. But as shown in Chapter III, when phenomenalism was discussed,* all this information cannot be generated from a privately subjective starting point. There is simply no tenable logical route that will allow a man to move merely from the way things happen to appear to him, with his own peculiarities and in his own special circumstances, to the way they will appear generally.

The other possibility, that the child's concept is that of *OAC*, avoids this last difficulty faced by *SAC* because there is nothing about it that is not intersubjective. Even so, it could not possibly succeed. For one thing, it does not avoid the difficulty concerning the arbitrariness of giving color an appearance analysis while refusing to demand a similar analysis of other sense qualities. If phenomenalism is to be avoided, some sense qualities will have to be given an alternative analysis. As mentioned above, *OAC* is identifiable only with respect to certain conditions of perception, and it is also something that is necessarily apparent to suitably situated observers. These observers and these conditions of perception are not, however, just objectively apparent; they are objectively real. And since phenomenalism is to be rejected, they must be characterized somehow in nonappearance terms. I shall argue in a moment that it is impossible to characterize them satisfactorily without reference to physical color itself. But even if they could be characterized satisfactorily in terms of tactile or auditory properties, at least some of these properties could not be given an appearance analysis. Yet if *they* do not require such an analysis, why should it be demanded of color? I can think of no satisfactory answer to this question.

Turning to the special drawbacks of the *OAC* analysis, we might consider how a standard observer could possibly be identified. Notice that the normality of such an observer will necessarily concern his ability to discriminate at least apparent colors. Ordinarily, one would expect to test this normality by determining whether a person can correctly identify or discriminate a wide range of things or shapes whose actual colors are known. This procedure is naturally

---

* See esp. pp. 76–78. Note that the age-old attempt to use the Argument from Analogy to show that things probably appear to others as they do to me is unusually hopeless in the present case. To use it I would have to base the analogy on the premise that red things present a certain kind of appearance to me. Yet this premise would not be available to me until I had succeeded in making sense of the notion of a red thing. And it is the analysis of this latter notion that is at issue here.

not available to the analyst in question. He might, however, attempt to modify it by asking an observer to identify certain apparent colors. But the question is: *which* apparent colors? It is natural to reply, "All apparent colors; the full range of OAC's that a human being could generally be expected to discriminate, or those a failure to discriminate which would require special explanation."*

The trouble with this last answer is that apparent colors are objective only with respect to certain circumstances. So in what circumstances is this whole range of colors supposed to be discriminable? Any circumstances whatever? Obviously not; what is objectively discriminable will *vary* with the circumstances. What is discriminable on a bright sunny day is not always discriminable under ultraviolet light. Shall we then say that the normality of the observer is to be determined by his ability to make maximum discriminations under standard conditions? But what conditions are these, if they are not precisely those in which standard observers can make maximum discriminations among (in this case) objectively apparent colors? And this does not just give us a vicious circularity; it implies that *every circumstance is standard*. OAC's are, by definition, objective only with respect to certain perceptual conditions; and in any such conditions what is maximally discriminable will depend on what is there and then apparent. Hence, to retreat to standard conditions in this connection is to revert to any conditions whatever, which we have already shown to fail.

The constant temptation in the above argument is obviously to break away from the "with respect to" rider attached to OAC and to speak of a whole range of apparent colors that may be discriminated in different circumstances. But to give in to this temptation is to fall back into regarding apparent color as something far more immediate and phenomenal than OAC as originally described. In fact

---

* Recall the discussion, in Ch. V, sect. 2, of normal or standard conditions, where the idea was developed that the normal is *roughly* what we are generally entitled to expect unless we have special reason to the contrary. Note also that the range of colors that a standard observer must be able to discriminate is largely determined by the range of color words in the language: he is standard to the extent that he can apply them reliably. The importance of this comes out in such claims as: "There are seven million color differences to which human beings can respond, but we use only a limited number of color concepts in discriminating objects and in describing their sensory properties," Robert Thompson, *The Psychology of Thinking* (Harmondsworth: Pelican Books, 1959), p. 64.

it is tacitly to think of *OAC* as a *derived* notion, to be elucidated presumably as follows:

> "*F* is objectively apparent in circumstances *C*" means "*F* is apparent to standard observers in circumstances *C*."

This gives us another kind of apparent color, the concept of which is simpler than that of *OAC*. Evidently this simpler sort of apparent color is not conceptually tied to particular circumstances, and can therefore constitute the full range of apparent color that can be identified without reference to any specific perceptual conditions. Yet since this kind of apparent color is presumably no different from *SAC* as described above, it turns out that the temptation in point leads one to the idea that the fundamental color concept is nothing other than *SAC*. We have already seen, however, that our concept of actual color could never possibly be developed from a basic concept of this sort.

If the preceding arguments are sound, it appears that the perennial tendency of empiricists to reduce colors to appearances is plainly misguided. To elude the difficulties that this tendency spawns, we must therefore face up to the idea that if there is a basic color concept associated with the common-sense picture of the world, it is none other than that of actual physical color. An admission of this kind raises, of course, some characteristic problems of its own, notably those previously mentioned in connection with the claims of theoretical science. But before turning to these residual problems, I want to prepare the way by explaining just how, if we regard actual color as our primary color concept, it becomes possible to give a reasonably perspicuous statement of the manner in which the notions of *OAC*, *SAC*, standard perceivers, and standard conditions of perception are interrelated.

6. THE PRIMACY OF ACTUAL COLOR

In view of my previous attacks on the foundational picture of meaning and truth I should perhaps say that to regard color as a primary concept is not necessarily to regard it as basic in the traditional sense. Nothing in the preceding argument makes it even likely that a primary concept is something totally unanalyzable from which dependent ideas are to be constructed by such simple logical operations as conjunction and disjunction. On the contrary, it is entirely possible to think of a concept as primary in the sense that it is logically nonredundant and that its use, at least in a primitive form, may have forced other, logically dependent notions on us. These dependent notions may be related to the primary notion only dynamically, as developments from it that enshrine the original version only in a modified form. How a dynamic development of this sort naturally occurs is a familiar story, implicit for instance in the discussion of normal conditions given in Chapter V.

To see how, exactly, the concept of actual color might be regarded as primary in this way, consider the following idealized history of our intellectual development. Suppose that at a certain stage of this development we had a simple battery of color words— proto-color words, perhaps—which we applied to certain sensuous features of our common environment. At this stage there need be no temptation whatever to think that these features are in any way subjective; in fact at this primitive stage we might not even have the concept of a subjective phenomenon. (When our fellows dream of buffalo, we might regard them as hunting in another world.) Admittedly, when it is very dark we could not discern the sensuous features we call colors. But then the same is true of trees, deer, and mountains. They cannot be discerned in total darkness either.

As our intellectual sophistication grows, we will naturally come to recognize a much wider variety of colors, and this recognition will be enshrined in our language by the addition of new color words. With this enrichment of our vocabulary, we shall find that our use of color words will involve more and more inconsistencies. The reason for this is that the vagaries of lighting and perspective will provide many more occasions for disagreement concerning the wider variety of color words at our disposal. (It is easier to mistake grays for whites than reds for blues.) In order to minimize the conflicts that would peril the point of speaking of colors at all, we might then begin to speak of standard perceivers and standard conditions of perception. These notions, which would at first be sufficient to minimize only the most frequent conflict, might naturally be specified in negative terms. Anyone who tended not to agree with identifications about which most observers have no reservations might be declared visually substandard; and most conditions of illumination, except for the light of common day, might be stigmatized as substandard as well. Since there will be circumstances, such as the yellowish light of the late afternoon, in which even standard observers will tend to ascribe colors to things which men intimately familiar with those things will know they do not have, the notion of *OAC* will naturally be developed. In order to explain the aberrant claims of otherwise reliable observers concerning objectively apparent colors, the concept of *SAC* might be introduced as well. It is easy to see that the concept of a visual impression is just a further development of this process, which might initially be framed to account for aberrant claims referring to nonexistent objects like pink rats.*

The story just given is admittedly idealized, and no doubt over-simplified as well. But it does at least lay bare the basic presuppositions of our ordinary thinking about colors. One of these presuppositions—one that, as Kant would say, makes our ordinary assertions about color possible—is that colors are relatively permanent features of things, which can normally be altered only as the result of some fairly substantive change in them—as might be produced by painting, dyeing, or altering with age. This presupposition makes our everyday discourse about color possible because it allows us to take certain objects as paradigms by comparison with which the colors of other objects can be determined and in relation to which the normality of perceivers and the normality of perceptual conditions can be ascertained.

The importance of having specimen examples of colors to which we can refer in cases of disputes can scarcely be emphasized too strongly. It is paradigms of this sort that give our identifications of colors an objectivity they could not otherwise have. For even if we tried to take the word of some special observer as laying down the law on the colors of things, we would have to have some way of

---

* Once the concept of a visual impression is developed, it can be used, together with the concept of a propositional attitude, to analyze *OAC* and *SAC* and thus to simplify the "ontology" of color phenomena. The possibility of providing these analyses of appearance concepts brings out the crucial sense in which *actual color* is the primitive color concept: namely, that it, unlike *OAC* and *SAC*, is nonredundant (ineliminable) in the common-sense scheme. This latter type of conceptual primitiveness is discussed carefully in Ch. IX; see esp. p. 248, footnote.

recording what his law is, so that we could apply it in his absence. To do this, we would naturally have to assume that the things he has determined as, say, red generally remain red even when he is not talking about them. But the necessity of this assumption has even deeper roots. We have to be able to identify the objects of our world, and this can be done only by reference to their distinguishing characteristics. Some of these characteristics, for instance those that distinguish our flag from the flags of our neighbors, plainly involve color. Since the identity of particular objects depends upon their identifying characteristics, if we have reason to think certain objects continue to exist when out of sight, we *ipso facto* have reason to think that they possess their identifying features when they are out of sight. Thus, if our flag is distinguished from others by its pattern of colors, then it continues to have these colors even when it is stored away from human eyes in the deepest, darkest cave.

That we can identify the colors of certain things, mark those colors by words, and generally assume that those things will continue to have those colors until acted upon by men or nature, is a fact that gives clear sense to our talk of standard observers and standard perceptual conditions. A standard observer is just a person who can generally be relied upon to distinguish a maximum variety of the determinate colors we commonly recognize. And standard conditions of perception are just those conditions in which the standard observer's ability to make these discriminations can be expected to be successfully exercised.* All of this sounds circular, of course; and indeed it is, since our conceptions of colors, standard observers, and standard perceptual conditions are logically interrelated. But the circularity here is not vicious. We do not start with a list of basic color identifications, which are immune to any sort of revision, and then build up our notions of standard perceivers and standard conditions by a straightforward reference to that list. On the contrary, it is only because a simple procedure for making color identifications generates inconsistency that we are forced to

---

* Since the growth of our knowledge, even as expressed in common-sense terms, may change our expectations regarding the conditions under which a standard observer will make accurate color identifications, it follows that the concept of standard conditions of visual perception will have an inescapable "openness" to it.

complicate our conceptual scheme by introducing these new notions.

7. CAN SCIENCE ADMIT COMMON-SENSE COLORS?

If, as the preceding argument implies, such concepts as actual physical redness are the most primitive of the common-sense scheme and directly apply to occurrent features of public objects even when those objects are far removed from sentient beings, it must accordingly follow that common sense is inextricably wedded to the "naive" conception of sensible properties that atomists have always attacked as scientifically untenable. Since I began the last chapter with a sympathetic outline of the atomist's general metaphysical claims, I must now relate those claims to the common-sense picture just unearthed, and thus ponder the question whether a "realistic" interpretation of physical theory actually does require the repudiation of common-sense colors and smells.

In order to appreciate the exact character of the question at issue here, an important conclusion of Chapter II must be kept firmly in mind. This is that a conceptual scheme cannot be attacked wholly "from without" but must rather be criticized on the basis of considerations that can somehow arise within it. Given this premise, it follows that if the common-sense framework of colored bodies is to be challenged by theoretical considerations, science and common sense must be brought into logical contact by at least a momentary merging of notions common to both. In order actually to demonstrate that there is a conflict between science and common sense, it must thus be shown that certain theoretical shortcomings in our common ways of describing things require us to complicate our world-picture by the introduction of scientific notions. This done, the next step is to show that such a theoretical enrichment of common sense will commit us to reject, or at least radically revise, the notion of a colored object that was described in the last section.

I believe that the first of these tasks has already been accomplished. Not only has the scientific method of theory construction been vindicated in the preceding discussion but in Chapter V it was explicitly shown that the logic of our ordinary reasoning about the world is such that it constantly and inevitably leads us to postulate unobservable entities and processes. Thus, in the discussion of water-solubility it was pointed out that generalizations formulated in common-sense terms constantly *break down* and require correction by theoretical principles. This happens, for instance, when substances known to be soluble fail to dissolve under what have been regarded as standard laboratory conditions. When things of this sort happen, we are led to hunt for some interfering factor— some *actual* entity or process whose presence accounts for the failure of the expected reaction. Very often, the factor discovered is not describable in common-sense terms. This is why intelligent common-sense thinking constantly tends to lead beyond itself.*

Given, then, that we are constantly forced to complicate our conceptual scheme by introducing new theoretical notions, the question arises as to whether this procedure might require us to revise or even repudiate the common-sense picture from which we began our theoretical advancement. I believe that it clearly does. Before attempting to show this, however, I must clear away a final obstacle by making a brief comment on a contemporary dogma concerning theories—one thought to imply that any attempt to point out an incompatibility between common sense and theoretical science is bound to fail. This dogma purports to be something of an *a priori* truth, one so general that it may be maintained without regard to the particular form scientific theory may take. Since my argument in favor of the incompatibility in point will involve a reference to the specific claims of a basic scientific theory, it will be useful to clear the ground by locating the error this dogma involves.

* Recall in this connection the line of thought that first led to the notion of phlogiston and then to the modern conception of oxidation. The common assumption that heating substances leads to a loss of weight because vapors, and so forth, are driven off was falsified by the discovery that metals such as mercury actually gain weight when heated. This phenomenon was first explained by the hypothesis that many metals contain phlogiston and that because phlogiston has a negative weight, metals containing it get heavier when it is released by heating. It was only when the assumption that heating drives off some of a substance's constituents was finally rejected that the theory of oxidation was developed. On this see "The Overthrow of the Phlogiston Theory," in James B. Conant, ed., *Harvard Case Histories in Experimental Science*, Vol. 1 (Cambridge, Mass.: Harvard University Press, 1957), pp. 67–115.

8. OBSERVATION LANGUAGES AND THEORETICAL SCIENCE

The dogma at issue is that the ordinary language of observation could never possibly be out of line with theoretical contentions because this language provides the needed groundwork on which all theoretical claims must ultimately rest. The idea here is the familiar empiricist one that in order for a theory to retain cognitive meaning and so survive degeneration into empty metaphysics, it must be securely tied down to an "observation language." Because a purely subjective basis for scientific knowledge is demonstrably impossible, this language must be an intersubjective "physical-thing" language.[3] Since the language of common sense is not only a language of this type, but is also the language actually used to report observations, the inference is drawn that there can be no possibility of the latter's being out of line with advances in theory.

To state this dogma clearly is to see that it is just another echo of the foundations picture of meaning and truth that has been under attack since Chapter II. Because the grounds for this general picture have already been undermined by the argument of previous chapters, it should suffice to point out that there is no reason why a theoretical language—that is, one built on theoretical primitives*—could not itself possess meaning for the very same reason that the language of common sense possesses it. As I have argued from the beginning, empirical meaning is in no way given by ostension, by an association, public or private, between word and object. The only thing salvageable in traditional ostension theories is the idea of a reliable verbal response—and such responses, like the presumed "color identifications" of the boy mentioned earlier in the chapter, are in themselves consistent with any number of different theories. Since the conceptual status of a linguistic move is not determined by the experience or physical situation that prompts it but rather by its formal hook-up with other elements of the conceptual scheme to which it belongs, there is no reason in principle why an entry move into theoretical discourse could not be made just as

---

* The notion of a primitive theoretical term will be discussed fully in Ch. IX, sect. 13. But see again p. 248, footnote.

easily as one into the discourse of common-sense colors.* It might
of course be insisted that any verbal form that gains a standard,
reliable use in language-entry transitions is *ipso facto* in some kind
of observation language, no matter how intimately caught up with
rarefied principles it may be. But an argument along these lines
would not support the contention in point, for the observation
language alluded to would not be the language of common-sense
observation, but a very different, far more sophisticated structure.

The fact that the language actually used in the laboratory for re-
porting observations is the language of everyday life adds little to
any alleged proof that science and common sense *must* be consistent. For one thing, there is surely no *a priori* reason to suppose
that the language of the laboratory is always consistent. In fact it
would scarcely be risky to suggest that most laboratory workers
probably never stop to consider how the meaning of the ordinary
language they use in describing meters and test tubes squares with
the theoretical claims they make in interpreting the results of their
experiments. Besides, from the fact that even philosophically
minded scientists—those with considered views on the relation between science and common sense—commonly use ordinary *words*
one cannot infer that these words, as they use them, continue to
possess their ordinary meaning. On the contrary, it would be
entirely natural to suppose that anyone who explicitly resolved a
conflict between his ordinary and his scientific notions (assuming
that one existed) might well continue to use many of the same
words, such as "red," in response to the same sensory experiences
as before. What would be different about his use of these words
would be their radically changed liaisons with other expressions of
his total language. Given this sort of change, one might say that
while many of the utterances he makes are still triggered by the
same sensory experiences, they would no longer have the same
meaning as before and hence would not involve the same claim.[4] An
obvious example of how this development might come about can
be seen by reference to an utterance of "That's salt," which, though
prompted in part by the familiar visual, tactile, and gustatory impressions of salt, has for the speaker the sense of "That's an aggregate of NaCl crystals."

* Queries about how "a child" could be taught the significance of these
moves are to be answered in accordance with the argument of Ch. IV.

9. MOLECULAR AGGREGATES AND COMMON-SENSE COLOR: A BASIC INCOMPATIBILITY

The points just made were intended merely to weed out initial misunderstanding and to show that a repudiation of the colored bodies of common sense might *possibly* be required by theoretical considerations. I want now to consider a few key points showing that this possibility is really a necessity. Suppose that we have taken the molecular theory of matter fully to heart and have merged it with our ordinary notions by regarding apples and billiard balls as aggregates of exotic particles. Suppose, also, that we continue to speak of these familiar objects as colored. The question then arises: can we consistently use our color words in their ordinary sense? To answer this question we need only ask another: how can a gappy collection of colorless particles possibly be colored in the occurrent, continuous fashion demanded by common sense? The answer, of course, is that it cannot: essential gappiness is incompatible with ultimate continuity.[5]

To see that the answer here is decisive, we must note that the surface of a common-sense object is categorially definable wholly by reference to its sensible properties, its visual and tactile features. One can, of course, specify a surface by reference to its function, as in speaking of the top of a certain table. But a surface can have such a function only because it is a material surface—because, in common-sense terms, it is visible and tangible. If, accordingly, we attend to the essential features of a material surface—to those features that place it in the category of material surfaces—we can see that these features must belong to every one of the surface's subregions, however small they may be. (Without these features, the regions would not count as sections of the surface.) Since color and tangibility are the essential features of a typical material surface, it thus follows that every subregion of such a surface, however minute, must have color and some species of tactile quality. But this kind of sensible continuity—for that is what it is—cannot possibly characterize the surface layer of a gappy system of particles.

Because the force of this argument seems not to be widely appreciated, it will be instructive to consider an obvious line of objection. "The cloud of particles is colored," it may be said, "only in the sense that it satisfies the criteria for being colored. Its color may, it is true, be continuous, but this can only mean that every *discriminable* region of its surface, however small, satisfies these criteria. The fact that it does satisfy these criteria is entirely consistent with its description in micro-physical terms, since to satisfy these criteria is merely to be such that standard observers in standard perceptual conditions will identify it as having some color or other."

In insisting that to be colored is merely to satisfy the criteria mentioned, the objection tacitly assumes that the following statement is adequate to define the notion of color and thus to tell us what being colored actually amounts to:

X is colored if, and only if, standard observers in standard perceptual conditions would identify X as being colored.

But the assumption here is false. The statement cited cannot *define* "color" because, as shown in section 6 of this chapter, the notions of standard observers and standard perceptual conditions *presuppose* the notion of color and can be understood only in terms of it. Thus, far from telling us what being colored really amounts to, the suggested criteria would be incomprehensible if we did not have this understanding already.

Another blunder of the objection in question is that it treats common-sense color as an essentially iffy or dispositional feature—as an object's tendency to provoke certain observers to make a particular kind of identification. But common-sense color is not iffy in this way; in fact, it is a paradigm instance of an occurrent feature. It is true, of course, that colored objects *also* possess the iffy features concerning observers—as they also possess the iffy feature of being discriminally continuous in color. But none of these iffy features can be identified with occurrent color itself.

The distinction between what is occurrent and what is iffy must in no sense be underestimated, for iffy features are analyzable in terms of the occurrent features things will actually possess *if* this or that occurs or is present. Take objective apparent color, for instance. This is an iffy feature: to say that a thing looks orange in this sense is to say that it is such that *if* standard observers were to observe it under these particular conditions, it would look orange to them. This is an essentially *conditional* fact about the object.

Without an available perceiver, no actual appearance is presented. Yet something actual, rather than merely potential, exists at the time. What actually exists is the object, which is perhaps red, and also certain objective conditions, perhaps a strong yellow light. To think that *all* of a thing's features may be wholly iffy is either to confuse the notion of an actual thing with that of a merely potential thing or—what amounts to the same thing, accurately considered— it is to follow John Locke into the trap of regarding a common-sense object as a bare particular or substratum. This trap may be initially tempting for anyone who wants to square science and common sense at any cost,[6] for to describe something merely in terms of its powers or iffy features is not to rule out a further description of its occurrent features, which could then be given in scientific terms. Even so, a trap is a trap, and a material object is *not*, for common sense, an intrinsically unknowable substratum.* It is rather a thing that, because it has certain occurrent features, may gain or appear to have others when actually placed in circumstances with certain actual characteristics. Thus, it is because an object is, say, red that it will look orange when placed under a strong yellow light.

It is worth observing that the tendency to treat common-sense objects as, essentially, substrata with various causal properties is frequently masked by two standard errors. The first consists in treating an object as the mere referent of an act of pointing. *The thing* with the causal properties is just *that*—and one points. The thing in question is thus supposedly shown to be actual, rather than merely potential, by the actual thrust of the gesture. The futility of this strategy was exposed, however, in Chapter II: a gesture of pointing cannot itself specify an object. Anything to which one can significantly point must be taken as an instance of a kind of thing, and the notion of the relevant *kind* cannot be defined by pointing (see pp. 52–55). If a definite object is successfully pointed out and then said to have certain causal properties, then, depending on the kind of thing it is, it will have a variety of occurrent properties as well: without such properties, it will not be a distinct thing capable of bringing about this or that should the occasion arise. To think that a mere act of pointing can pin down an object without

* Further remarks concerning substrata will be made in Ch. IX, sect. 2.

an implicit reference to its occurrent properties is implicitly to regard that object as an intrinsically characterless substratum.

The second standard error that masks a tacit commitment to substrata arises from the practice of describing objects in purely functional terms. In accordance with this practice, one might describe a thing pointed out as a baseball. If asked what a baseball is, one might describe the game in which it is commonly used. So long as one holds fast to functional descriptions, it will not be necessary to mention any occurrent features of the ball that might sound suspicious from a theoretical point of view. Yet some occurrent features will have to be mentioned sooner or later if the ball is not to be regarded as a substratum that somehow serves a function. If one is asked "What is the act of throwing that you say is done with the ball," one can avoid an appeal to uninterpreted gestures only by saying something like "It is an act of sending a body through the air." In giving this answer one alludes to bodies, no doubt material bodies. But no purely functional description is available for material bodies generally. To explain what, in general, bodies of this kind are, one must unearth some of the basic presuppositions underlying one's discourse. If these presuppositions are characteristic of common sense, they will concern the occurrent features of color, shape, and tangibility.* It is only because a baseball can be *seen* and *hit* by a bat that it can serve its distinctive purpose in a baseball game.

I O. THE METAMORPHOSIS OF COMMON SENSE

The foregoing discussion makes it plain that any attempt to graft a sophisticated theory of matter onto common sense by emphasizing the iffy features that a system of particles might easily have will inevitably result in a tacit rejection of the occurrent sensible properties of common-sense objects. The discussion also makes it clear

---

* Here the reader should recall my discussion of philosophical method in Ch. VI, sect. 5. In analyzing common sense I am concerned with the presuppositions of consistent, nontechnical discourse about people, trees, and sunsets. I do not mean to imply that these presuppositions are always easy to identify, or that men who think in a purely common-sense way are more likely to be found on earth than men who act in a perfectly just, perfectly disinterested way. Both kinds of men are obviously idealizations.

that to reject these occurrent properties is to reject the definitive features of the common-sense world. Fortunately, this rejection is not doomed to utter theoretical failure. Once the foundations picture of meaning and truth is thoroughly repudiated, the way is open to find new occurrent properties—theoretical ones—in relation to which an iffy, *but therefore noncommonsensical,* conception of colors, smells, and hardness can be defined. These new occurrent properties will be spelled out in physical theories of light and of reflecting surfaces, and in psycho-physical theories concerning the actual make-up of the human nervous system and the place in such a system of the phenomenal episodes ordinarily known as sensory experiences.

To appreciate just how radical a conceptual change results from admitting such new occurrent features, note that the concept of a perceiver will require even more revision than the concept of a colored wall. For not only do persons have physical bodies, which will require reinterpretation, but they have all sorts of sensory experiences and intellectual capacities—and these will require reinterpretation as well. Since I have yet to analyze some of the most distinctive features of perceivers as commonly conceived—namely, their thoughts, intentions, and the like—the details of this reinterpretation can be given only in a later chapter. Here I can only say that the result of giving up the common-sense conception of occurrent sensible qualities and accepting a sophisticated theory of matter will demand an enormous conceptual change—so great a change that even though the majority of our spontaneous utterances may remain exactly the same, the significance of what we say will be so different from before that these utterances will reflect, in the pattern of their implications, a radically revised world-picture.

VIII
Thinking

In classical philosophy a sharp distinction was commonly drawn between sensation and thought. This distinction was explicitly rejected by the Cartesian philosophers of the seventeenth century, and not everyone today would insist upon it. I have already noted the importance of the distinction,* but I have defended it mainly by repeating the Kantian claim that "percepts without concepts are blind." My aim in this chapter is to back the distinction by a detailed analysis of the concept of thought.

1. THE DISTINGUISHING FEATURES OF
CONCEPTUAL THINKING

In opposition to the traditional assumption that there is a basic concept of thinking, contemporary philosophers have been inclined to argue that there is actually a very wide variety of activities properly called "thinking" but no special feature that is either common or peculiar to all of them.[1] I shall not begin by disputing this view, although I do hope to destroy its plausibility in the course

* See pp. 97–100.

of my argument. Initially, I shall concentrate on what is at least a distinguishable form of thinking, which philosophers might term "conceptual." Such remarks as "It just occurred to me that if I am to catch the evening train, I must leave at once" may be regarded as overt verbal expressions of this kind of thinking.

An obvious feature of the mental processes involved in conceptual thinking is that they are typically unobservable. When a man says that it occurred to him, on a certain occasion, that it would soon rain, the presumption is that something did occur to him, and that what occurred to him need not have been expressed in audible terms. Since the basis for general philosophical doubts about the presence of such inner occurrences was undermined in Chapter V, there is no need to air such doubts here. We can rather safely assume that we do generally regard thinking as, at least sometimes, an unobservable activity or process, and turn our attention to the peculiar features that such processes are thought to have.

One of these peculiar features—indeed the feature that, according to Franz Brentano, is really distinctive of the mental—is that thinking is necessarily "intentional," in the sense of referring to something.[2] Thus, in the example initially given, the object of the thought was (roughly) the thinker's catching the evening train. That thinking always has an object is perhaps disputable, if everything that might be called "thinking" is considered, such as letting your mind wander, or ransacking your memory for a name you cannot recall. But there certainly is a recognizable form of thinking, the conceptual form that concerns me here, which is such that if you claim to be thinking at all, you must be able to specify what you are thinking about.

Another feature of this kind of thinking is that it is "judgmental" in character, involving the forms of thought discussed by Kant. Excepting cases of reverie and the like, to think of something is at least to entertain the idea of something's being so, being done, and so forth. I say "at least entertain the idea" because not all thinking involves belief: one may consider possibilities, rehearse intentions, and imagine fanciful situations. What is common to these cases is that the distinguishable thoughts involved are best expressed by complete sentences. If you ask a man what he is thinking (not what he is thinking *of*), a full answer will have the form, "I was thinking *that* such and such." If the man merely responded with a single word, such as "Mary," it would be entirely reasonable, though not perhaps polite, to ask: "Well, what about her? I asked 'What were you thinking?' not 'What were you thinking about?' "

According to Kant, the forms of thought are as various as the possible forms of sentences. Like sentences, thoughts may be categorical (I thought that all A's are B's), hypothetical (I thought that if p then q), disjunctive (I thought that p or q), negative, and so on. Since Kant restricted the possible forms of thought to those abstract forms recognized by the logicians of his day as standard sentential forms, he recognized far less variety than one would today. Just as there is (to take a single example) an important difference between a "material" and a subjunctive conditional, so there is an important difference between the forms of thought involving these two kinds of conditionality: "I thought that p only if q" describes a very different thought from "I thought that if p were so, q would be so as well." In general, whatever can be said can also be thought; and for every logically distinct form of sentence, there is a logically distinct form of thought.

A final feature of conceptual thinking concerns what Collingwood called its "bipolarity."[3] Anyone who engages in this kind of thinking will do it well or carelessly, logically or illogically, intelligently or stupidly. In trying to solve a problem, the thinking he does will also be successful or unsuccessful. He will normally succeed or fail in reaching the desired conclusion to a theoretical problem, and he will typically succeed or fail in making up his mind what to do in some practical situation. This bipolarity will also extend to the "contents" of the man's thoughts. What he affirms or conjectures may be true or false; what he explicitly chooses to do may or may not be realized; and what he hopes may or may not come to pass.

Taking all of these distinctive features into account, we may characterize the kind of thinking termed "conceptual" by reference to four chief marks: (i) it may be silent or "inner," (ii) it has reference or intentionality, (iii) it involves some kind of form or conceptual articulation, and (iv) it is essentially bipolar. Although these four marks are easily understandable in a general way, they are unfortunately difficult to understand in detail; in fact, most traditional accounts of conceptual thinking have failed to do justice to them all.[4] In recent years, however, a theory of thinking popular in the fourteenth century has been revived, reworked, and polished to the extent that it seems tailor-made to account for these peculiar marks. This is another analogy theory, and its recent development has again been independently initiated by Wilfrid Sellars and by Peter Geach.[5] In its new guise the theory is extremely complicated, with far-reaching, highly controversial implications. Because of this complexity, I shall begin by outlining the theory's chief contentions in a rather loose, informal way, and only later, by considering a number of penetrating objections, go on to probe its fine-grained structure. As in my treatment of the Analogy Theory of Sense Impressions, I shall concentrate on Sellars' version of the theory, since in my judgment he has worked it out in more satisfactory detail.

2. GENERAL FEATURES OF THE ANALOGY THEORY OF THINKING

The root idea of the Analogy Theory of Thinking is that intelligent speech may itself be a form of thinking, a species of "thinking out loud." This form of thinking is also held to be far less problematic, philosophically, than anything silent or unobservable. This is not just because overt speech is audible to the public ear; it is also because the form of the speech and even its reference is normally aboveboard and checkable. It may be granted that a man's audible discourse is not always a pastiche of clichés and that it is frequently not possible to determine the reference and functional form of his words merely by consulting grammars and dictionaries. Yet as we saw in Chapter IV, in order actually to *mean* something by a form of words a man must utter them in a certain frame of mind, which will involve a readiness to recognize other utterances as relevant or irrelevant to the content of what he said. Hence, if a man means something unusual by a familiar word, we can demand that he clarify his meaning in words we can understand. If he cannot do this, and if a persistent dialectical probing fails to disclose a consistent sense to his words, the presumption will be that he did not really mean anything at all, but perhaps just uttered his words in a state of confusion.*

An extremely important feature of intelligent speech is that it conforms to certain patterns, particular elements of which are often intelligible only by reference to others. If a man makes a certain remark, the point of what he is saying is often comprehensible only in relation to other things he has said or will say. These "other things" will often reflect his reasons for saying what he did, and they will be related to the latter by some principle of inference or relevance to which his speech normally conforms. As I have argued in Chapter IV especially, in mastering a language a man learns not just to identify various objects in his environment but also to conform his extended remarks to the general principles of inference, relevance, and the like, that his group accepts. If a man does not conform to these principles—if there is no connection between his remarks that can be followed by a sophisticated speaker of his language—then the presumption is that he is either linguistically incompetent or else, as would be more likely if his utterances were long and complicated, out of his mind. In either case his words would not be taken as an example of intelligent, thoughtful speech unless some special explanation were provided.

I do not propose to dwell on these principles here. I merely wish to point out at this stage that some utterances are often inexplicable except with reference to others. Some of the most striking cases of this are found in abstract studies such as logic and mathematics, but they are in fact ubiquitous in common life. If a man announces the solution to a difficult logical or mathematical problem, his announcement, let alone his confidence that he is right, is generally baffling until he indicates the line of reasoning that led him to it. When he outlines the steps he took in reaching his conclusion, we feel that his announcement is explained: we know how his solution

---

* The line between nonsense and bizarre sense is actually not as easy to survey as this might suggest. But it is at any rate only because of a kind of dialectical probing (in this case, of poems) that we can be assured that the following lines are only bizarre and not truly nonsensical: "I am aware of the damp souls of housemaids / Sprouting despondently at area gates" and "what if a much of a which of a wind / gives the truth to summer's lie. . . ?" (These lines are reprinted with the permission of Harcourt, Brace and World, Inc.; they are taken, respectively, from T. S. Eliot's "Morning at the Window," in *The Complete Poems and Plays, 1909–1950*, and from E. E. Cummings, "what if a much of a which of a wind," in *Poems, 1923–1954*.)

was worked out. The idea that it might not have been worked out at all, but rather grasped intuitively as if presented by the gods, is always highly suspect and would not, in any case, explain the man's confidence that his solution is sound. So far as common life is concerned, it is axiomatic that solutions to difficult problems are reached only by a complex process of reasoning, involving sometimes a very large number of subordinate steps.

Similar considerations apply to the explanations advanced for any distinctive human action. Such actions are not just peculiar movements explainable in stimulus-response terms; they are rather goal-directed activities, conforming to the general principles of practical reasoning. If, to take an extreme case, a man kills another in one of the farfetched ways described in detective fiction, then his action is understandable, in all its particularity, only when the line of reasoning that led him to it is laid bare. The suggestion that the man's action did not spring from a process of reasoning is just as peculiar as the idea that one can discover the solution to a difficult mathematical problem without any calculation at all. In everyday life, it would never be taken seriously.

It can scarcely be denied that most of the reasoning we do, whether in calculation or deliberation, is not audibly expressed. Yet the fundamental contention of the analogy theorist is that the principles involved in this reasoning are fully exemplified in overt discourse and that, even if we had no conception of an inner mental episode, we could fully understand these principles and use them in explaining human behavior. Thus, he would contend that if a certain part of our community did all their thinking in audible terms, the same general principles of intelligent action would be exemplified in their behavior and would enable us to explain why they say and do the things that they do. The fact that these principles could be fully exemplified in overt behavior indicates, he would add, that they may be understood as entirely public principles, of a kind that could reasonably be expected to arise in a public context.

The claim of the analogy theorist is, accordingly, that these principles of reasoning are conceptually more basic than the notion of silent thinking, that the latter is, in fact, usefully regarded as an analogical development of the concept of saying, of making utterances in accordance with these principles. The utility of interpreting the concept of silent thought in this way is that it can then be understood as a thoroughly intersubjective one, even though it applies to publicly unobservable episodes. Thus, if we assume that at some time in the distant past we had absolutely no conception of an inner mental occurrence but were entirely at home with the notion of intelligent speech, it is easy to imagine how the concept of silent thought could be forced upon us by thoroughly inter- subjective considerations. Men occasionally say or do things of such surprising complexity that it is hard to envisage their being done without calculation or deliberation. Rather than accepting it as a brute fact that such actions really are done on impulse, it would be natural to assume that the relevant thinking actually was done, though no one happened to hear it. Some men speak more softly than others, and the supposition would not be absurd that some deliberation or calculation can be done so softly that it is not audible at all. Pressing this line of thought would lead one to a conception of something like a Platonic dialogue in the soul or of a Biblical speech in the heart.

A conception of silent thought as literally a dialogue in the soul is of course highly imaginative and no more acceptable to a tough- minded philosopher than the idea that a man's soul is a subtle inner agent that duplicates, though at a deeper level, the intellectual features he himself has. Yet the conception of such an inner dia- logue is capable of development and qualification, and its imagina- tive trappings can quickly be stripped away. The first bit of strip- ping to be done would involve the natural assumption that silent thinking is like overt speech in the way that the verbal imagery we typically have in reading a poem to ourselves is like the words we utter in reading the poem out loud. This assumption must be done away with because a good share of the hard thinking a man does is often not accompanied by any imagery at all, verbal or otherwise.[6] As a consequence of this, we can only hold that while thinking may sometimes involve imagery of a certain sort, this imagery is not essential to our thinking what we do think.

The immediate result of treating imagery, or other sensuous *qualia*, as logically inessential to silent thought is that we are left with the possibility of only a very tenuous and abstract similarity between overt and silent contemplation or deliberation. Yet if there is sense in saying that we might conceivably have been driven to speak of silent thought in order to explain what is generally explainable by reference to overt activities of reasoning, a mere *formal analogy* between thinking and speaking would be entirely adequate. To conceive of silent thinking in this way would be to regard it as involving a sequence of covert episodes, elements of which have the definitive property of being related to one another in the formal manner that elements of overt discourse are interrelated. By saying that the elements of silent thought are *formally* analogous to the elements of a corresponding line of intelligent speech, I mean that while the pairs may differ materially or empirically even more radically than utterances of "It is raining" differ from utterances of "*Es regnet*," they nevertheless play analogous roles in, for instance, taking one from a given premise to a given conclusion. In this regard they would be, like arguments formulated in German or French, subject to criticism by the same formal or logical principles as apply to overt English speech.

It is important to observe that the kind of formal analogy discussed in Chapter VI was rather different from the kind involved here: there it was concerned with material characteristics while here it is concerned with what might be called functional characteristics. Thus, unlike the formal analogy between a red triangle and a certain sort of visual image, the analogy between uses of the English "It is raining" and the German "*Es regnet*" does not concern their material (their phonemic or orthographic) features but the jobs they do or the roles they play in discourse. To the extent that these empirically different uses do play analogous roles in English and German, there is a sense in which the roles they play are abstractly the same. This "abstract sameness" is what is involved when one says that the English "I," the French "*je*," and the German "*Ich*" all play the role of a first-person singular pronoun.* I shall attempt to make the notion of such roles more precise as my discussion proceeds. For the moment, I shall merely say that while the concept of a linguistic role is most easily grasped by reference to the functional similarities of linguistic activities publicly carried on in different languages, it may also be applied to those inner episodes that, issuing in intelligent remarks and actions, *do the work* of audible or visible calculation and deliberation.

* See p. 88, footnote.

Assuming that the formal analogy in point is at least intuitively clear, it may nevertheless be objected that if thoughts are to be conceived as episodes that play certain formal or functional roles, we must surely conceive them as particular role-players, as determinate episodes that involve these roles. But this objection is easily met, since, aside from their purely formal features, these episodes are distinguished from one another by coordination with the distinctive verbal forms that are said to "express" them, and the frames of mind appropriate to standard uses of these verbal forms. Thus, just as an utterance is a particular linguistic move only when it is produced in a certain frame of mind—that is, in a certain state of readiness to make additional remarks, movements, and the like of a certain sort—so an inner episode is a particular thought only to the extent that it occurs when the thinker is in a similar frame of mind. In general, the frame of mind appropriate to the thought that p is essentially the same, formally, as the frame of mind appropriate to the assertion (or whatever) that p.* If this were not so, the notion of a silent thought could not serve, as it does, to explain the peculiarities of intelligent, nonhabitual remarks and actions.

Notice that the preceding account allows both an intrinsic and an extrinsic characterization of silent thought, just as the account of impressions in the last chapter allowed both intrinsic and extrinsic modes of characterization. Intrinsically, thoughts are characterized by the formal role they exemplify; extrinsically, they are characterized by reference to their connection with specific verbal and other dispositions ("frames of mind") in ways that parallel the connection between their overt verbal expression and the frames of mind that are distinctive of them. The thought that p is, moreover, identifiable or describable by reference to the words we use for asserting, conjecturing, and the like, that p. This is done by two familiar verbal constructions: *oratio obliqua*, as in "The thought *that p*," and *oratio recta*, as in "He said in his heart some-

---

* I say "essentially the same" because the frame of mind appropriate to the assertion that p normally involves the disposition to repeat or rephrase the assertion if one is asked what one said or meant. But the frame of mind appropriate to the thought that p would be rather different in this connection: if asked what he said, a man who had silently thought that p but did not say that p would tend to reply, if English were his language, "I didn't say anything at all."

thing tantamount to '*p*'," where Geach's expression "said in his heart something tantamount to '*p*' " may be understood as equivalent to "having made a silent move that is a formal analogue of the assertion, '*p*'."

3. FUNDAMENTAL CLAIMS OF THE ANALOGY THEORY OF THINKING

When I first introduced the Analogy Theory of Thinking, I remarked that it seems tailor-made to account for the four distinctive features of conceptual thinking. It should be clear by now what the criteria for the presence of these features can be. Consider, to begin with, the unobservable character of most conceptual thinking. According to the Analogy Theory, our basis for claiming that such thinking occurs in persons generally (not just in ourselves*) is that while nonhabitual intelligent action presupposes a certain amount of reasoning, many instances of such action are not accompanied by sufficient overt speech to account for this reasoning. Since the requisite reasoning was not done overtly, it must have been done covertly, *in foro interno.*[7] Thus, the fact that Jones was able to solve the problem without overt calculation suggests that he must have done this calculation in some covert manner. The problem was too difficult to be solved without calculation, and when Jones was asked to justify his answer, he outlined the steps of a complicated proof with no hesitation whatever. The wholly public behavior of announcing a solution or of outlining a proof is therefore acceptable as a normic indicator of silent thought because our conception of such thought, like our conception of pain, involves an explanatory hypothesis—this time one concerning the possible occasions of *nonhabitual, intelligent* human behavior.

As one might expect, a report of having thought that *p* may also be regarded as a normic indicator of having thought that *p*. The basic reason for this is that a man's admission or avowal that he thought that *p*, is a bit of intelligent behavior itself. As such, it also

* Here we have to remember that the concept of silent thinking is an intersubjective one, whose general applicability is not established by reference to each man's subjective certainty that he engages in silent thought.

is to be explained by reference to various principles of intelligent action. Since the man's admission or honest avowal cannot be explained by reference to his wish to deceive or amuse, the relevant explanation will no doubt allude to his memory of what he thought. The general reliability of his memory is what justifies his confidence, and therefore our opinion, that his thought was this rather than that.

Next, consider the matter of a thought's form. Since a silent thought is conceived as an unobservable counterpart to an overt speech act, involving the same linguistic role, the form of the thought is the same as the form of the words used to express it. If, for instance, the overt verbal expression has the logical form of a conditional, then the form of the thought is also a conditional. The role of the thought in the thinking game is essentially the same as the role of the words in the asserting game. To appreciate this point, we must, of course, not confuse logical form with the sensible form—the visible or audible patterns—of linguistic tokens. The claim that a silent thought may have the form of a conditional does not in any sense imply that a man who has such a thought contains in his head a faint symbol of conditionality, such as a dagger or horseshoe.

The question of the sense in which thoughts are bipolar is closely related to the question of their form, since some of these forms are truth-functional. If a thought has the form of a so-called material conditional, it must play the same role in thought as a corresponding statement of that form plays in audible discourse. And whether something plays this role is logically independent of its specific empirical features. What is essential to such a role-player is that certain inferences may be drawn from it, whether these inferences are carried out in thought or in speech. Thus, if T is a thought of this conditional sort, then, assuming that it is true, there are other thoughts, P and Q, such that if P is known to be true, one is entitled to infer that Q is true, whether one actually does so or not. So far as the Analogy Theory of Thinking is concerned, the truth-values of $T, P,$ and Q will depend on the truth-values of their analogues in overt discourse.

It is important to note in this connection that the term "thought" is ambiguous in just the way that the term "statement" is ambiguous.* Both of these terms can refer either to an intelligent act (of thinking or of saying) or to the so-called intentional object of the act (to what is thought or to what is said). Strictly, the values true and false are not attributable to the act but to the object of the act. This does not imply, however, that these values are properly attributable only to abstract entities. On the contrary, my thoughts and my statements (in the sense in which others cannot think my thoughts or make my statements) are like the smiles discussed in Chapter VI: they are merely nominal objects, talk about which is reducible to talk about me. Roughly, "My statement or thought is true" is equivalent to "I speak or think truly" in just the way that "My smile is wan" is equivalent to "I smile wanly." Of course, there are other senses of "thought" and "statement" that are not susceptible of this kind of treatment. But the ambiguity of the terms relevant to the present discussion can be clarified without plunging into the questions of what propositions are and of how they are related to human acts of thinking and statement-making.[8]

The final distinctive feature of conceptual thought, namely its reference, is also readily understandable according to the analogy theorist's approach. Since the concept of thought is regarded as an analogical development of the concept of an assertion or statement, the reference of a thought will be conceived by analogy with the reference of an assertion or statement.† In the standard case, where the reference of an assertion is determined by general conventions, the words used will include a term or phrase that plays a certain referring role; and this role may be involved in thought as well. Thus, my thought, that *p*, may be a thought of the largest golden mountain because it involves a formal element that plays the same referring role as the expression "the largest golden mountain" plays in, say, a standard use of "The largest golden mountain exists in Peru."‡

* The term "thought" is also ambiguous in that it sometimes means "belief." The concept of belief will be analyzed on pp. 213–218.

† One must recall at this point that analogies are not identities or out-and-out similarities; they hold only in certain respects, and not in others. One respect in which a thought differs from an assertion is that thoughts cannot strictly be brought about voluntarily. The importance of this disanalogy between thoughts and assertions is indicated on p. 214, footnote.

‡ On the notion of a referring role, see Ch. III, pp. 79 ff.; also p. 204 of this chapter.

4. INTROSPECTION

One special virtue of the Analogy Theory of Thinking is that it allows us to do justice to the notion of introspection. Ever since Wittgenstein's critique of private objects became influential, philosophers have been extremely suspicious of this idea on the ground that if there were such things as inner, episodic thoughts, there could be no intersubjective means of deciding whether or not they correspond appropriately to their objects.[9] Thus, if P represents a covert thought, there could be no way (it is argued) of ascertaining whether P does or does not consistently occur in connection with, say, pains rather than feelings of joy. Indeed, it would be hard to see how the assumed reference of these inner processes could ever be understood.

While it is admittedly impossible to determine the character of silent thoughts by any direct intersubjective means, the argument against behaviorism made it plain that a direct checkup on covert occurrences cannot reasonably be demanded. Given this, if we proceed to consider the familiar fact that children must typically *learn* to keep their thoughts to themselves, to avoid blurting out everything that comes to mind, we can see the point of regarding thoughts as often barely suppressed responses that take the place, for purposes of calculation or deliberation, of overt speech. And just as overt speech is the product of a well-entrenched set of habits of right response, so, we can say, is the inner episode that replaces audible utterance the product of a set of habits—in fact the same set of habits. Because these habits of response can plainly be checked for reliability, Wittgenstein's objection to inner identifications will not apply to the thoughts springing from them. On the present view there is no conceptual gap between thinking and speaking, and our readiness to say certain things on certain occasions will provide a normic criterion for the thoughts we happen to have. Any question, accordingly, about whether a man's silent thoughts may be only wildly related to his present feelings is easily answered on this approach, since he can always express them aloud and thereby allow others to determine, if necessary, whether they do or do not correctly describe his state.

Any theory able to account satisfactorily for thought's publicly unobservable character, for its intentionality, its logical form, and bipolarity, and do justice to the age-old notion of introspection as well, plainly has a good deal in its favor. Although I think that the preceding remarks go a long way toward showing that the Analogy Theory provides a fully acceptable theory of conceptual thought, I cannot claim that it goes all the way. I must therefore pursue its analysis on a much finer-grained level. I shall attempt this by considering a number of objections, most of which are familiar in the literature. The first objection is a very simple one, but it will serve to prepare the way for the others, which have very deep roots indeed.

5. IS THE ANALOGY THEORY OF THINKING EXCESSIVELY CONTRIVED?

This objection arises from the consideration that the idea of an occurrence whose essential features are mainly formal is far too abstract and sophisticated to belong to the common-sense picture of man and the world. Surely, the common-sense notion of thinking has more substance than this. The tendency of philosophers to advance imagistic theories must obviously have some roots in common conceptions, and these conceptions are assuredly reflected in the lady's reply to the professor who announced his opposition to all such theories: "But you really do think, don't you?"

Although this objection no doubt does justice to the initial claims of the popular consciousness, it nevertheless goes astray in a crucial respect. For we do ordinarily—that is, all of us, in our nonprofessional moments—speak of silent thought, and we characterize it in *verbal* terms, by giving its gist in indirect discourse. The idea of thinking as something like overt speech is not only common to Plato, the Bible, and so-called stream-of-consciousness novels like Joyce's *Ulysses*, but it is implicit in our ordinary manner of conveying the content of our thought, which is propositional rather than pictorial. Besides, the imaginative conception of thought as a series of mental pictures is never really pressed in ordinary conversation. No one would actually insist that there are images such that if a man does not have them he cannot be thinking of Siberia or infinity, and a man's failure to detect images would never be taken as a proof that he was not thinking at all. Hence, while it is undoubtedly difficult for an ordinary person to regard thinking as occasionally wholly transparent, it is not unreasonable to say that the analogy theorist's claim is enshrined in the total corpus of our well-considered admissions regarding thought—that it may occasionally be entirely free of imagery, that its gist is best, most accurately and completely captured by sentences rather than pictures, and so on. Since the theory does have the advantage of laying bare the thoroughly intersubjective principles according to which the concept of silent thinking may have developed in a social context, it is surely not unreasonable to take it as advancing a plausible analysis of a common notion, an analysis that is perhaps surprising only because it is purified or clarified, its imaginative trappings cleanly cut away.

6. AN ALLEGED CIRCULARITY IN THE ANALOGY THEORY OF THINKING

While the last objection was somewhat superficial, this one is very serious indeed. According to it, the Analogy Theory fails because it is basically circular, presupposing ideas it purports to analyze. In attempting to elucidate the notion of silent thinking by reference to overt assertion, it tacitly assumes that the latter could be adequately characterized without reference to silent mental activities. Yet this assumption can be seen to be false as soon as one focuses attention on the frame of mind appropriate to an assertion. As is clear from the argument of Chapter IV, such a frame of mind will always involve a readiness to make further utterances if the speaker is asked, *hears and thus understands,* certain questions that might be put to him in order to illuminate the actual claim that he has made.* Also, if his assertion concerns the sensible qualities of a thing, such as its color, his frame of mind will normally involve a readiness to identify other instances of the qualities he is talking about. But to identify an object as having a certain color—to *see it as being* of this color rather than that—is not just to have a particular sense experience; it is to heed or notice something. This being so, it follows that if we are to specify everything involved in using

* See Ch. IV, sect. 1.

language to make assertions, we shall have to make some reference to silent mental activities—of taking certain noises to be questions of this or that sort, and of hearing, seeing, or feeling *that* such and such is so. Since the notion of an overt assertion necessarily involves a reference to such activities, it is clear that the analogy theorist's attempt to analyze the latter by reference to the former is inescapably circular. If we really had no conception of silent mental activities, we could not understand the explication the theory provides.

In my view this objection is entirely successful in ruling out any form of the Analogy Theory of Thinking that rests its case on an unqualified analogy between silent thought and intelligent, audible speech *as we presently conceive the latter.* I fully agree that our conception of such speech is now so rich and complicated that it enshrines the notion of silent thought already, and thus could not be used to elucidate it. But even given this admission, the spirit of the Analogy Theory of Thinking can still be saved by a fairly obvious amendment. One of the central themes of preceding chapters was that the enrichment of a conceptual system tends to modify even the basic ideas of that system. If we take this theme seriously, an obvious strategy in meeting the above objection arises at once. The basic analogy must rather be drawn between silent thought and a proto-version of overt speech, a more primitive form of speech whose elucidation does not involve reference to, or mention of, silent mental activities.

It might naturally be thought that resorting to proto-concepts here is resorting to the fictional in order to make sense of the actual, or resorting to the dubious in order to clarify the obvious. But to take this attitude is to misunderstand the basic point that the analogy theorist is eager to make. What he wants to show, fundamentally, is that the notion of silent thinking can be seen as an essentially public one, derived from other notions that apply unproblematically to publicly accessible phenomena—in a sense of "derived" in which, say, the concept of lying can be said to be derived from a simpler notion of ingenuous assertion. Yet, when one considers such derived concepts, one sees that they can rarely be boiled down to the versions we now have of the concepts they presuppose. It is clear, for instance, that circularity would necessarily result if we tried to explicate "lying" in terms of "not" and "telling the truth," for our notion of telling the truth now involves the idea of having no intention to deceive. Still, there are very good reasons for thinking that *lying* is a very sophisticated concept, which is in some sense a development from a simpler notion of ingenuous assertion. This simpler notion would have to have the status of a proto-concept, since our present notion of an honest assertion is a good deal more sophisticated.

In order to exhibit the structure of the concept of silent thinking —to show that it can be understood as a derived one, built on notions that might naturally arise in a social context—we must then be able to outline the basic form of various proto-concepts. To do this is not to suggest that, in point of historical fact, we actually did operate with these proto-concepts at an early stage of our conceptual development. It is rather to indicate that the concept of thought we now have is understandable as a development from familiar principles that can apply, in a philosophically unproblematic way, entirely to overt linguistic phenomena.

Let us suppose, then, that at a certain stage of our intellectual development our linguistic resources were such as to permit us to ascribe very complicated dispositions to our fellows but not to allow reference to any inner *mental* phenomena.[10] With reference to such a linguistic framework, we can easily define less sophisticated counterparts to our familiar notions of seeing, trying, wanting, and the like. To proto-see X, for instance, would involve training your eye on it, having some kind of sensory experience, and then uttering, or gaining a short-term disposition to utter, the words "X is. . . ." To proto-try to secure Y would involve uttering, or being disposed to utter, the words "I want Y," moving in Y's direction, groping at it, and so on. A proto-concept of asserting could then be given in a fairly natural way. To proto-assert that p would be to utter appropriate sounds in a certain frame of mind. This frame of mind would be characterized entirely in proto-terms: roughly, to follow up the one utterance with others of certain kinds, depending on what one proto-sees or proto-hears; to make movements of various sorts, depending on what one proto-senses, and so on.*

Now, proto-reasoning would be entirely overt reasoning, involving successive utterances. To the extent that one understands what

---

* See Ch. IV, pp. 91 f. and 100–101, for the basic idea of how this account would have to be filled out.

this reasoning is, one will be in a position to see how one might act or speak as a result of a proto-inference from other information. Having this concept of inference will put one in a position to explain certain forms of intelligent, nonhabitual behavior. The notion of a covert proto-thought could then be constructed: an inner episode that is formally analogous to a proto-assertion.* The episode would be analogous to the assertion in the sense that its elements would be related to one another in the formal way in which the elements of the assertion are interrelated; in the terminology used earlier, the same abstract assertive role would be involved in both of them. Also, of course, each element of the proto-thought would be related to appropriate verbal and other dispositions, these being similar to those characteristic of the corresponding proto-assertion.

Once the concept of proto-thinking is in hand, virtually non-proto-concepts of seeing, hearing, and the like could be developed, and so, stepwise, the notions of thinking and asserting as we presently understand them. This development would, I believe, meet the objection mentioned above; if the analogy is conceived as holding only between something like proto-asserting and silent thinking, then no circularity is involved whatever. But if, on the other hand, it is conceived in a less guarded way—as Geach, for instance, seems to conceive it[11]—then it runs into the objection head on.

7. AN OBJECTION BASED ON THE CONCEPT
OF INTENTIONALITY

Although the amendment just given may be taken to save the Analogy Theory of Thinking from one charge of circularity, it unfortunately prompts another such charge in its turn. This one is based on the consideration that the proto-concepts (of seeing, trying, saying) used to elucidate the notion of silent thinking are not as neutrally behavioral as they seem. Like the concept of silent thinking itself, they essentially involve the idea of intentionality. And when this idea is carefully examined (the objection goes), it

* This is, again, highly simplified, since not all silent thoughts would be assertive, even at this primitive stage.

can be shown to presuppose the concept of thought. Thus, in outlining a proto-concept of asserting, I tacitly introduced the feature
of intentionality by reference to the language used. Yet language
has intentionality (that is, reference) only because it is used to express thoughts. It is only because people *mean things* by words that
words can refer to things at all.[12]

To this objection, the immediate reaction of anyone sympathetic
with the argument of preceding chapters ought to be that it is
completely wrong-headed. If it is granted that the activity of thinking necessarily requires a conceptual scheme of some sort, the claim
implicit in the objection would seem to be that human beings in-
herently possess a prelinguistic conceptual scheme in terms of
which they can conceive the world in detail, and by reference to
which they confer meaning on words of public languages. And
surely all claims of this sort are false. We of course can define new
words once we have a language, but we cannot, in point of fact,
conceive our world in detail prior to having some language or
other. On the contrary, as the later work of Wittgenstein and even
the early work of the pragmatists has shown,[13] we develop our
conception of the world in the very process of mastering a language
that allows us to talk about it.

In spite of all this, there remains an important sense in which
words can be said to possess meaning only *because* people mean
things by them. If we look to the later work of Wittgenstein, we
can easily develop this sense without commitment to prelinguistic
concepts. Using his terminology, we can say that words have meaning because they are caught up in a system of characteristic human
activities, because they play a special role in a certain "form of
life."[14] The activity of using words in accordance with this "form
of life" is what, in fact, using them to mean something seems to
amount to. As I have shown, to use a word purposely in its conventional sense is to use it with intentions and expectations of a fairly
specific sort; it is to use it when in a certain "frame of mind."* This
frame of mind will involve a complex state of readiness to respond
in various ways (with movements, actions, other words) if this or
that should eventuate. The peculiar pattern of these responses, being essential to a purposeful and understanding use of a conven-

---

* See Ch. IV and also p. 180.

tional expression, is part of what a linguistic "form of life" consists in.

Although this favorable interpretation of the claim that words have meaning because people mean things by them would seem to be acceptable to a great many philosophers today, it unfortunately leaves us open to a modified form of the above objection, which is extremely difficult to refute. As so modified, the objection is best expressed negatively, as a challenge: "Can one, in point of fact, characterize the relevant form of life without using the intentional notions it is supposed to elucidate? It seems clear that this cannot be done. To make sense of a language-using form of life one will inevitably have to employ such intentional notions as human purpose, human need, and human interest—notions that immediately involve the phenomena of human consciousness. That notions of this sort will be essential should be no surprise; for as Brentano argued a long time ago, it is the phenomena of human consciousness that are the fundamental bearers of intentionality."

In my view this challenge is a profound and exciting mixture of insight and error. But to explore its force, it is necessary to have a more accurate grasp of the notion of intentionality. So far, this notion has been given only an intuitive significance, in terms of the reference of words and thoughts. Statements about mental phenomena have, however, certain logical peculiarities, which have been called "marks of intentionality."[15] It will be necessary to attend to these peculiarities in order to make an intelligent attack on the question at issue. What is in dispute is whether a language-using form of life can be adequately *described* without reference to inner, mental activities. If it should turn out, for example, that the logical peculiarities of mentalistic statements are *sui generis*, it would follow that the mentalistic concepts involved in these statements could not be derivative from a more primitive concept of a language-using form of life.

8. THE MARKS OF INTENTIONALITY

According to Roderick Chisholm, a distinguished contemporary defender of Brentano's thesis, sentences used to describe psychological phenomena exhibit at least one of three distinctive marks of intentionality.* The *first mark* is exhibited by a simple declarative sentence if it contains a substantive expression (a name or descriptive phrase) in such a way that neither the sentence nor its negation implies either that there is or is not something to which the substantive expression truly applies. Chisholm's example of such a sentence is "Diogenes looked for an honest man." This sentence contrasts very sharply with such nonintentional (or extensional) sentences as "Jones rode a horse," which implies, if it is true, that there is a horse that Jones rode.

The *second mark* of intentionality is exhibited by noncompound sentences that contain a propositional clause in such a way that neither the sentence nor its negation implies either that the propositional clause is true or that it is false. An example of such a sentence is "Jones asserted that demons cause schizophrenia"; neither this sentence nor its negation implies either that demons do or do not cause schizophrenia. This sentence plainly differs from such nonintentional sentences as "It is not the case that Jones died in India."

The *third mark* of intentionality is exhibited by sentences containing terms having what Frege called "indirect reference." Chisholm describes this mark of intentionality as follows:

> Suppose there are two names or descriptions which designate the same things and that E is a sentence obtained merely by separating these two names or descriptions by means of "is identical with" (or "are identical with" if the first word is plural). Suppose also that A is a sentence using one of these names or descriptions and that B is like A except that, where A uses the one, B uses the other. Let us say that A is intentional if the conjunction of A and E does not imply B.[16]

* Since writing his book *Perceiving* (see note 15 of this chapter), Chisholm has modified his views. He would still agree, I take it, that every psychological statement has one of the marks I mention, but he would deny that only psychological statements have such marks. In a recent letter to me he formulated the following sufficient condition for a more stringent sense of "intentionality," which I quote with his kind permission: "Consider the following two formulae: (1) $(Ex)(Ey) (y = a \& xRa)$, (2) $(Ex)(Ey) (y = a \& xRy)$. An expression which may occupy the place of 'R' [such as: 'believes that _____ is bald'] is intentional if there is an individual term which may occupy the place of 'a' with the result that (1) does not imply (2), and (2) does not imply (1)." I have not amended my discussion in the text to take account of this revised formulation because I believe that a discussion of his original marks is more illuminating. But see footnotes to pp. 205 and 209.

An example of a sentence of this sort would be "Tom believes that Cicero was a Roman"; from this sentence and the identity-statement "Tully is identical with Cicero" one cannot validly infer that Tom believes that Tully was a Roman.

As Chisholm points out, these marks of intentionality characterize sentences that are logically atomistic, that is, not truth-functional compounds of simpler sentences.[17] In order to get a more general criterion of intentionality, we can say that a sentence is intentional if and only if either it or one of its component sentences is intentional. Since it is possible to transform sentences with marks of intentionality into sentences which do not possess those marks by introducing technical terms (as we can transform the intentional "Jones is hunting demons" into "Jones is demonhunting," which lacks intentional marks), we shall say, following Chisholm, that a sentence is intentional even if, lacking intentional marks, it contains technical or indeed any other terms whose meaning can be given only by reference to sentences that are intentional.

In order to avoid confusion in what follows, note that in speaking of sentences as intentional, another sense of the word is being introduced. As used earlier in this chapter, it is states or episodes that are intentional. Whether mental or verbal, they are intentional because they possess a reference or so-called intentional object. It is in the very different sense of possessing the "marks" Chisholm describes that sentences are intentional. This double use of the term "intentional" should cause no difficulty in subsequent discussion, for the sense in which it is used will always be clear from the context. There could in any case be little occasion to confuse a purely formal property of sentences with the "reference to an object" of a mental or verbal episode.

9. A NOTE ON SCIENTIFIC LANGUAGE

Before proceeding with the objection raised in section 7, it will be useful unload a few more cards on the table, so that the scope of the problem at issue is more easily appreciated. According to distinctively empiricist philosophies of science,[18] the language of scientific theory is ideally extensional, with no room for expressions with Chisholm's marks. The ordinary language of scientific investigation is admittedly not extensional in this sense, for it contains modal locutions such as "it is possible that," "it is necessary that," and "If *A* were to happen, *B* would happen as well." But the empiricist philosopher typically argues that locutions of this sort ideally ought not to be there, either on the tough-minded ground that modalities are utter fictions, or on the more moderate ground that they reflect the structure of our language rather than (as their appearance in scientific language suggests) the structure of our world. According to this last alternative, modal terms are confusing "material mode" surrogates for metalinguistic expressions. The locution "It is physically necessary that *p*" is an unperspicuous representation of the metalinguistic fact that the statement that *p* is unconditionally assertable in virtue of some accepted theory; and the locution "If *A* were to happen, *B* would happen as well" (which seems to point to "real connections" in nature) is an unperspicuous representation of the metalinguistic statement that, given normal conditions, "*B* happens" is inferrable from the premise "*A* happens."[19] On either of these alternatives the empiricist's claim is basically the same, however. It is that the language of science is ideally extensional. Anything essentially nonextensional is to be regarded as at best reflecting metalinguistic ideas, which apply to the structure of our linguistic framework rather than to the world itself.

It is not my purpose to defend this conception of science here, although I shall treat it sympathetically and even base certain remarks on the assumption that its fundamental claim is sound. But because it is a widely held conception among philosophers and methodologists of science, it follows that Chisholm's views about the irreducibly nonextensional character of discourse about psychological phenomena are extremely explosive. If the language of science *is* ideally extensional, Chisholm's view has the consequence that a science of psychology—to the extent that it is a science of the mental—is strictly impossible: there would be mental phenomena about which we could not construct a proper science. The shock value of this statement for any empiricist philosopher ought to be sufficient to indicate the magnitude of the issue that the mild words of Chisholm really generate.

10. AN IMPORTANT OBJECTION REFORMULATED

With this richer conception of the intentional, we are now in a position to probe the objection of section 7 with much greater care. The point of that objection was that although we may be able to characterize the intentionality of language by reference to certain forms of life, these forms of life can in turn be adequately characterized only by reference to the thoughts, beliefs, intentions, and interests of the persons who live according to them. Consequently, any attempt to elucidate the intentionality of thought by reference to the intentionality of language is necessarily circular. Since the Analogy Theory of Thinking is built on this circularity, it follows that it must be rejected as fundamentally unsound.

In order to assess the precise force of this objection, we must be entirely clear about two points: first, we must know which form of life is relevant to the issue; second, we must know which mental phenomena are supposed to be required for describing this form of life. Respecting this first point, the amendment to the Analogy Theory given in section 6 must be kept firmly in mind. According to this amendment, our ordinary mental concepts are to be elucidated by reference to a family of proto-concepts. This being so, it will have to be the proto-concepts whose intentionality is to be understood in relation to a particular language-using form of life. Plainly, the form of life relevant here will be an extremely primitive one; it will not be the one we actually have. The objection in question, therefore, must be that even this primitive form of life could not be adequately characterized without reference to mental phenomena.

Concerning the second point, it should be noted that proto-assertion is intentional both in the sense of referring to something and in the sense of satisfying Chisholm's marks.* Given this, it would appear that if Brentano was right about intentionality, proto-assertion is either mentalistic itself or else definable by reference to something that is mentalistic in some more exacting sense. Anyone backing the objection in question must obviously endorse the last of these alternatives, for the Analogy Theory of Thinking as I have

---

* More exactly, a given proto-assertion such as "Tom is tall" may be said to refer to Tom while a sentence such as "Bill proto-asserted that Tom is tall" will satisfy one of Chisholm's marks.

developed it is built on the idea that proto-assertion may be an act of conscious thinking itself, and hence be as mental as any other act of thought. Accordingly, the basic questions at issue seem to boil down to the following: "Is not a proto-assertion intentional because, and only because, it is the manifestation of an *inner* mental process? And will not every attempt to account for this intentionality by reference to a primitive form of life be inescapably circular on the ground that an adequate description of the latter will require a reference to inner mental episodes?"

Set out in this way, the force of the objection is by no means obvious. A natural way of evaluating it—and of tracking down the ultimate source of intentionality—might be to consider just what minimal addition to a purely extensional account of the relevant form of life would be sufficient to account for the intentionality that clings to proto-assertion. If it turns out that this minimal addition will necessarily involve an explicit reference to an inner mental process, then the objection will have to be regarded as successful. But if nothing of this sort actually has to be mentioned, then the objection can reasonably be said to fail.

11. AN EXTENSIONAL COUNTERPART
TO PROTO-ASSERTION

An extensional counterpart to the activity of proto-asserting is easily envisaged in view of previous discussion, particularly the discussion of Chapter IV. From an extensional point of view, what obviously happens in proto-assertion is that an agent emits certain noises while in a frame of mind (state of readiness) to emit certain other noises and perhaps to make certain physical movements, depending on what happens, occurs, or exists in his immediate sensory vicinity. Just what these further noises or movements would be in certain circumstances could be stated, of course, only by someone who knows the language the agent is speaking and is aware of the peculiar dispositions (the proto-interests) the agent has.* But assuming that this knowledge is in hand, it would not, in principle, be impossible to construct a complex description that would represent, in entirely extensional terms, the full pattern of movements and

* Compare Ch. II, pp. 213 f.

noises that characterize the man's frame of mind and, consequently, the empirical features of his entire speech-act.[20]

Assuming that we can imagine how such an extensional description could be constructed, the next step is to ask whether anything logically essential to proto-assertion has been left out. In approaching this question it is essential to see that from a strictly scientific point of view, nothing else need be involved in proto-assertion than what an extensional description of this sort would disclose.* An organism simply emits certain noises while disposed to emit a specific pattern of further noises and, perhaps, to make certain patterns of physical movements, depending on various external features of its immediate sensory environment. One might be inclined to dispute this contention very hotly on the grounds, first, that even an aseptic scientific account must allude to the linguistic rules the speaker is following and, second, that the conditional utterances and movements distinctive of his frame of mind will depend, not on what his future surroundings might actually be, but on what he will take them to be, or on how he will interpret them. But both of these points are implicitly accommodated by the extensional description envisaged above.

Consider the agent's linguistic rules. From an extensional point of view, such rules can affect a man's behavior in two logically distinct ways. Either his behavior is merely in accordance with them, as it would be if he were incapable of formulating them, or else it results from his conception of them, which means that he is able to formulate them and indeed "has them in mind" when he acts. The first alternative is obviously accommodated by the extensional description, since the entire range of the man's rule-conforming is laid out in detail. The second alternative is also accommodated, though perhaps less obviously, because by hypothesis the man belongs to a community of proto-asserters, who do all their thinking out loud. If, then, he acts on a formulated rule, his formulation of the rule will consist in overt verbal behavior, the connection with his other behavior (his other utterances and movements) being included in the extensional description.

The matter of the man's taking or interpreting his surroundings to be such-and-such and then acting appropriately is treated sim-

---

* It is granted that patterns of neural activity might be held to be essential as well.

ilarly. For he is, by hypothesis, capable only of proto-taking—and this is nothing other than his describing, or being disposed to describe, his surroundings in such-and-such a way; which is to say, his applying, or being disposed to apply, certain words to them. And applying words to something is, from an extensional point of view, just a matter of uttering certain sounds in a particular set, in a particular state of readiness to utter certain other sounds and make other movements, depending for instance on the particular sensations one has.* Applying a word to an object is not to be understood, after all, as a matter of conceiving the object in some natural, innate conceptual system, and then relating this conception to the word one utters by *another* psychic act. If the presence of the object in one's immediate sensory vicinity is the occasion for a variety of language-entry moves that we know (on other grounds) to be appropriately related to the original move one made, then there is no longer any general question about whether one's original move did or did not involve a reference to that object—let alone a question that could be satisfactorily answered (in a public context!) by reference to a shadowy domain of psychic facts, incapable of inclusion in the above account.

But granting that from a narrowly scientific point of view the extensional account omits nothing strictly essential to proto-assertion, is there not a broader sense in which something is very obviously missing from that account? The answer, of course, is "Yes." The specific interpretation that sounds get *as linguistic elements* is simply ignored. Anyone who did not know what the sounds picked out by the extensional description *mean* to the people who use them would not be able to tell, merely from scrutinizing that description, just what assertion a particular utterance was. Admittedly, if one happened to know the language in which the utterances are to count as tokens, one could very easily decide which assertions are normally made when they are uttered. But to one who did not have this information, the extensional description would provide no decoding of the utterances at all.

---

* Here we must keep in mind a point developed in earlier chapters, namely that in order to elicit a response from a man in a certain mental set, these sensations need not be interpreted by him. The basic reason for this is that the response that in many cases is elicited by the sensation is the mental act that interprets it: for example, a throb of pain may elicit the response (given a certain set), "It hurts!"

The basic reason for this last point is simply that no matter how complex the extensional description may be, it will provide nothing more than *de facto* correlations of different sound patterns with one another, with physical movements, and with certain features of reality that *we* might regard as occasioning them. But, as I argued in Chapter II, mere correlations cannot possibly capture the meaning of a linguistic element. Not only does the meaning of a word relate to possible as well as actual things or episodes,* but its application cannot in any way be determined by the occasion, marked in terms of *our way* of viewing reality, on which it is uttered. This can be determined only by criteria internal to the conceptual scheme in point, criteria that define the relevant *kind* of thing or episode involved. Hence, to understand the application of various words we must have a conception of the *sort* of thing to which they can legitimately apply. Similarly with word-word relations. To know what certain noises mean in a certain linguistic community, we must know how they *may* be related so as to form intelligible utterances, descriptions, and so forth. And what *may* be done— what is legitimate, permissible, or sanctionable—cannot be boiled down to what *is* done.

This brings us to the heart of the matter. To know what proto-assertion is being made is to know, not just what is likely to follow upon its utterance (what noises, what movements), but what *may* be inferred from it, what *must* be the case if it is true, reasonable, or appropriate. These "mays" and "musts" are essential to the notion of an assertion because a linguistic move of this sort is possible only in relation to a system of linguistic norms or rules. It is, after all, norms or rules that specify the defining characteristics of assertions: that they have implications, denials; that they are clear, confused, consistent, self-contradictory, tautologous, and the like.

When this point is appreciated, it is easy to see why the extensional account can be, in its way, entirely complete and yet seem fearfully denuded of significant flesh. For to characterize an utterance, suitably produced, *as an assertion* is not to call attention to its empirical features—let alone describe it as springing from some arcane inner episode in connection with which such intentional objects as golden mountains "inexist." To characterize an utterance in this way is rather to subsume it under a network of essentially

* Recall the example of featherless bipeds discussed in Ch. II, p. 51 f.

normative concepts. The description of an utterance as a proto-assertion is thus similar to the description of an arm-movement as a signal, a bodily interaction with a rubber sphere as a serve, and a peculiar adjustment of an ivory piece on a checkered board as a checkmate.* All these actions—asserting, signaling, serving, check-mating—have extensionally describable counterparts, but their identity as the specific acts that they are can be understood only with respect to the particular system of principles and rules that properly specify them.

But granting that this is so—granting that the notion of a proto-assertion, or indeed of any other linguistic act, is in part a normative one—just where does intentionality enter the picture? Is it perhaps just a feature of certain normative notions? And if it is, how ex-actly is this feature to be analyzed?

The answer to this first question seems to be obvious, once one considers it. As defined by Chisholm's three marks, intentionality is patently a feature of normative statements. Consider "It is right to repay one's debts," which exhibits his first mark, and "It is morally obligatory that men refrain from murder," which exhibits his second mark. Anyone who accepts the familiar principle that prescriptive discourse cannot be reduced to, or analyzed in terms of, "naturalistic" discourse should surely balk at the idea that the intentionality of these two statements is wholly due to naturalistic facts about minds, even if these facts are themselves mysteriously intentional in some way. The same is true of Chisholm's third mark: the fact that "It is a necessary truth that 9 is greater than 6" is in-tentional does not seem to require explanation or analysis in terms of facts about human minds, either. We could not know that this statement is true if we did not have minds, nor could we formulate it. But it does not follow that its truth, or even its meaning, must be analyzed by reference to inner mental processes.†

---

* This is not to say, of course, that acts of signaling, serving, and check-mating do not have a mental component. This aspect of such acts will be dis-cussed fully.

† According to Chisholm's most recent criterion, none of the three sen-tences I have mentioned is necessarily intentional (see p. 197, footnote). This fact is not, however, damaging for the purposes of my argument in what fol-lows. On the contrary, I shall attempt to show that the logical peculiarities of sentences satisfying his latest criterion are also due to essentially normative considerations, and thus will not support his commitment to "Brentano's thesis." See the footnote to p. 209.

The fact that these three normative statements possess the marks of intentionality surely makes it tempting to trace the intentionality of proto-assertion to its essential normative features.* After all, a proto-assertion is not an inner mental process nor, as I have defined it, does it necessarily spring from such a process. But in order to evaluate this temptation it will be necessary to follow up the question raised a moment ago: "How, with respect to normative principles, is intentionality to be analyzed?" This is a very difficult question; and in order to work my way to what I believe is its answer for the special case of proto-assertion, I shall comment on another analogy, this time one holding between the normative activity of asserting and the rule-governed activity of playing chess. There are, of course, important limitations to this analogy,† but I shall base my discussion mainly on the noncontroversial assumption that both asserting and playing chess are rule-governed activities subject to evaluation by reference to appropriate norms.

12. INTENTIONALITY: ITS SOURCE AND ANALYSIS

Although we have standard material criteria of a reasonably definite kind for what is to count as the sort of piece that is to be moved in accordance with the standard rules of chess, it is not difficult to imagine other activities, associated with radically different pieces, which seem to involve the same basic rules, or at least involve rules that are formally analogous to the ones we happen to have. Thus, we might imagine (as Sellars suggests[21]) a game played in Texas, called "tess," in which automobiles of various makes are driven from county to county in accordance with rules that are the exact analogue of our rules for chess, which, let us suppose, is

* Here I adopt the position, characteristic of empiricism, that statements concerning what is necessarily true are essentially normative. Some of my reasons for taking this position will emerge in what follows.

† The chief limitation is that while the rules of chess are sufficiently neat and tidy to make the identification of a certain move (as, say, a checkmate) virtually automatic, there is so much freedom and idiosyncrasy in language-using that the identification of the move that a man is actually making can often be done only with the greatest difficulty, and not just by perusal of grammars and dictionaries. On this limitation see p. 181, footnote, and also Ch. 6 of R. G. Collingwood's *The Principles of Art* (Oxford: Clarendon Press, 1937).

unknown in Texas. In view of the close formal analogy between
the moves made in chess and tess, it would not be unreasonable to
think of chess and tess as specific varieties of the same basic game,
which might be called "bess." It would also be reasonable to think
of chess and tess players coming into contact with one another,
becoming aware of the close similarity between their games, deciding that they are both playing varieties of the same basic game, and
proceeding to engage in correspondence games, in which each side
plays with its own pieces, translating the reports of the opponent's
moves into the idiom with which they themselves are familiar. Thus
when, in such a game, a Texan moves a Volkswagen into a county
adjacent to one occupied by a Rolls Royce, the opposing side represents this move on its board by a certain configuration of pawn and
queen.

If we assume that these different bess players have not worked
out a distinct bess vocabulary into which their own special bess
moves (that is, their own tess or chess moves) are translatable, then
they would have to represent bess moves by the juxtaposition of
their own familiar pieces, relying sometimes, if they were new to
the game, on translators to tell them which of their moves are the
counterparts of certain moves of their opponents. In order, however, to distinguish bess games from chess or tess games, each side
might find it useful to employ slightly different pieces for bess.
Thus, in order to characterize a certain move as a bess move, without committing themselves to the specific form in which it was
made (that is, whether by the pieces of chess or tess), they might
flag the pieces and squares (or automobiles and counties) used to
represent it. This practice would have an obvious similarity to our
use of indirect discourse, as in "the assertion *that* it is raining," or
to the use of Sellars' dot quotes: "the assertion ·It is raining·" to
represent for English speakers a move that could be made by a
standard use of either the English "It is raining" or the French
"*Il pleut.*"[22]

Leaving the bess players for a moment, I want to consider a community of primitive speakers operating only with proto-concepts,
who have no conception of a proto-assertion made in unfamiliar
words and no means of indicating the gist of a proto-assertion in
indirect discourse or in anything functionally similar. For them, to
relate what anyone proto-asserted requires that one reproduce the

actual words used. As they see it, only members of their community proto-assert, and a given proto-assertion can be conceived only as made in specific words. According to their conventions, only one linguistic form is available for the purpose of relating what someone proto-asserted, namely, "*S* proto-asserted '*P*'." Since "*P*" may have considerable internal complexity, it is clear that "*S* proto-asserted . . ." locutions may exhibit something like all three of Chisholm's marks of intentionality, even though the speakers of the language have no conception of an inner mental process or of anything like it.

The fact that these locutions are virtually intentional—that they exhibit something like Chisholm's marks—is in no way mysterious. The reason we can infer neither " '*P*' is true" nor " '*P*' is false" from the statement "Jones proto-asserted '*P*' " or from its negation is simply that while both " '*P*' is true" and " '*P*' is false" involve an *evaluation* of "*P*," no such evaluation is either implicit in or demanded by the claim or the denial of the claim that Jones proto-asserted "*P*." Again, from the dual claim "Jones proto-asserted '*a* is *f*' and in fact *a* = *b*" we plainly cannot infer that Jones proto-asserted "*b* is *f*." The reason for this is simply that, given the primitive community in question, the identity of a proto-assertion is determined by the actual words used. Since "*a* is *f*" and "*b* is *f*" are different verbal forms, even the logical truth of "*a* = *b*" would not allow us to infer that if Jones proto-asserted the former, he proto-asserted the latter.

I said a moment ago that claims about what a man proto-asserted (in the sense just described) exhibit "something like" all three of Chisholm's marks of intentionality; I did not say that they actually did exhibit those marks. This qualification is essential because his marks were specified by reference to expressions used but not mentioned in the relevant sentences. In the examples just considered, however, the intentionality was traced to the presence of mentioned expressions, which occurred only within quotation marks. Since Chisholm's thesis evidently concerns the intentionality of sentences containing uses of terms and propositional clauses, the account of quasi-intentionality just given does not strictly affect his position at all.

The point of the chess analogy is that it suggests a way of extending the treatment just given to proto-assertions *of* "*P*" to the more general case of proto-assertion *that-p*, and thus of refuting the position Chisholm evidently wants to defend. I shall now try to effect this extension by returning to that analogy.

The proto-asserters just described correspond to chess players before they conceived the possibility of bess. For them, a checkmate could be accomplished only by particular configurations of certain familiar pieces, just as the proto-asserters could conceive of assertions as made only by the utterance of certain noises with which they are familiar. But once these proto-asserters are able to conceive the possibility of empirically different linguistic elements being used in accordance with formally analogous norms, then the necessity will arise for introducing such empirically noncommittal means of representing proto-assertions as *oratio obliqua* or Sellars' dot quotes.

It is crucial to observe that the notion these proto-asserters might gain of a linguistic move that could in principle be made in countless verbal forms may still apply only to overt linguistic activities. Although they could conceive of asserting that *p* in any number of different languages, they need not thereby have anything like the concept of silent thinking or nonproto saying. Even without these concepts, however, they would have no trouble accounting for the intentionality of proto-assertion. In order to account for the intentionality of "Jones proto-asserted *that p*," they would only have to point out that to say it is true (or false) that *p* is to evaluate the move made in asserting that *p*, and then add that such an evaluation is neither implicit in nor derivable from the claim (or the denial of the claim) that Jones made such a move. Similar remarks could be made regarding sentences exhibiting Chisholm's other marks: to the extent that they involve only proto-concepts, their intentionality is easily accounted for without any reference to an *inner* mental process.*

---

* If Chisholm's latest criterion of intentionality makes sense (see p. 197, footnote), it too would be satisfied by sentences about proto-assertions. Some of these sentences, such as "Tom proto-asserts that the king of France is bald," possess the same purely formal properties as sentences about a man's beliefs. I say "*if* it makes sense" because if I am right about belief (see pp. 213–218), Chisholm's criterion actually involves an error of quantification. As I explain it, the clause "that *p*" is quasi-metalinguistic in such contexts as "Tom believes that *p*." If I am right about this, the formula (2) of Chisholm's criterion involves an error of quantification analogous to that involved in "(Ex)(Tom said 'f (x)')."

Aside from undermining the evident position of Chisholm, these last considerations allow us to identify the key line of reasoning on which the Analogy Theory of Thinking is built. The first step is to focus attention on the rule-governed activity of proto-asserting. In considering that the function of a given proto-assertion could in principle be accomplished by a proto-assertion with very different empirical features, one makes sense of the abstract notion of a linguistic role, which could be exemplified by the use of expressions in countless proto-languages. Then, by reference to the explanatory force of statements about linguistic activities such as calculation, one elucidates and justifies application of the notion of a covert or "mental" exemplification of a linguistic role. Once this notion is in hand, the proto-concepts of the original scheme are capable of promotion to nonproto status, which converts them into the concepts we now have, with their characteristic intentionality. On this accounting the key idea of the whole Analogy Theory is thus that of a linguistic role, whose exemplification in thought is conceived by analogy with its exemplification in observable speech acts.

To explain how the intentionality of sentences dealing with proto-assertions—and therefore, after appropriate commentary, sentences dealing with assertions of the full-blooded sort—can be elucidated by reference to notions that are essentially normative is not, however, to explain the intentionality of every sort of psychological sentence.* The variety of such sentences seems virtually endless, and not all of them, at least in any obvious way, seem to concern states and processes that necessarily involve even the disposition to make covert assertions. In order, then, to appraise the preceding treatment of intentionality in its most general form, it will be essential to examine some of the cases of intentional phe-

---

* I have said enough, however, to recall an important traditional approach to the mental. As R. G. Collingwood once remarked, "A science of thought must be 'normative', or (as I prefer to call it) 'criteriological', *i.e.* concerned not only with the 'facts' of thought but with the 'criteria' or standards which thought imposes on itself," *The Principles of Art, op. cit.*, p. 171, note. In his chapter, "Psychology as the Pseudo-Science of Thought," in *An Essay on Metaphysics* (Oxford: Clarendon Press, 1940), Collingwood argued that the normative character of thought was lost sight of in the revolt against classical philosophy that began in the late seventeenth century. In his view this new approach to thought involved an egregious blunder from which modern philosophy has not yet recovered.

nomena in which the making of silent assertions is evidently not involved. The cases chosen for this purpose illustrate, respectively, all three of Chisholm's marks, and they also possess considerable intrinsic interest. They are (1) "Jones is hunting demons"; (2) "Smith is terrified that the machine he is operating will maim him"; and (3) "Harris believes that Cicero was a Roman."

13. HUNTING DEMONS AND BEING
TERRIFIED THAT . . .

If the preceding discussion is sound, the statement that Jones is hunting demons must allude to a linguistic move that is somehow involved in Jones's activity of hunting. It is not difficult to see that this is, in fact, so. If Jones is hunting demons, he must obviously have some idea of what he is after. Also, to the extent that he is actively engaged in the hunt, he must at least be operating on the assumption that there are demons. It may not be necessary for him to believe that this assumption is true, for one may evidently engage in a hunt with the idea, or fear, that it will probably turn out to be a hopeless goose chase. But he must nevertheless keep the assumption in mind—at least in the sense that, like hypotheses assumed in *reductio ad absurdum* arguments, it will constitute an essential element in the line of thought he is pursuing. And anyone hunting for demons is necessarily following out a line of thought. However he proceeds, whether with a knapsack full of holy relics or with a pistol loaded with silver bullets, he will have to relate the particular steps he takes to the general task at hand; and this will require a fairly complicated process of practical reasoning.*

If in hunting for X one is necessarily acting on the assumption, among others, that there are X's, then to specify the object of a man's hunt is implicitly to specify at least one assumption on which, in pursuing the object, he is acting. Since "Jones is hunting demons" specifies the object of Jones's hunt as that of demons, it may accordingly be taken as locating a basic assumption on which he is

---

* The form of the practical reasoning involved here is essentially this: "Assuming that there are demons, that they have such and such characteristics and are found in such and such places, the thing to do in order to hunt one down is. . . ." Further remarks on practical reasoning are made below.

allegedly acting. Once we have this assumption, however, we are in a position to evaluate it. And while such statements as "It is true that there are demons" or "It is false that there are demons" do evaluate this assumption, it is not even implicitly evaluated by "Jones is hunting demons" or its negation.* This, then, is what accounts for the intentional character of sentences of the kind in question. Although they allow us to identify a certain assumption that is, or possibly is not, at the root of a man's behavior, they do not in any way evaluate the assumption, or even provide a weak basis for evaluating it.

Turning now to "Smith is terrified that the machine he is operating will maim him," we have a statement that is very transparent in indicating, but not evaluating, a certain "propositional content," and whose intentional character is far more readily explained than the sentence just considered. The example is nevertheless worthy of special mention, because it illustrates two points of considerable importance. First, as a representative statement about a familiar kind of emotion, it allows us to see that emotions generally belong to a very different category from feelings and moods, which typically lack intentional objects. Second, the example illustrates another way in which linguistic moves may be related to intentional phenomena. Although such intentional activities as hunting, trying, and the like involve various hypotheses or assumptions in accordance with which the activities proceed, being afraid or terrified *that p*, like being angry that *p*, is a matter of being in an emotional state (of experiencing a "passion") that, roughly speaking, is brought about by the thought that *p* and is directed to the object that the thought concerns. Thus, the man who is terrified that the machine he is operating will maim him is in a terrified state with respect to the machine *because* he thinks, believes, or is haunted or obsessed by the thought that it will maim him. This general pattern in fact applies to a very wide range of cases of emotional and other states that involve propositional attitudes: being embarrassed that one is late, being pleased that one is promoted, being outraged

---

* The negation of "Jones is hunting demons," though it also locates the crucial assumption, implies nothing about whether Jones actually is, or is not, operating on it. Even if he is not hunting demons, he could still be acting on the assumption that there are such things, for he might be trying to hide from them.

that one has been cheated, or being apprehensive that there will be a war, are obvious examples.[23]

14. BELIEVING

The case of believing, while apparently capable of treatment in as immediate a way as hunting or being terrified, is actually very complicated and raises special problems. A good many of these problems are due to a widespread misapprehension as to what belief really is. The common opinion seems to be that a belief is essentially a disposition to behave, one which need not involve any tendency to engage in conceptual thought. Although Gilbert Ryle's views on belief are closer to the truth than the general opinion, they have enough in common with it to provide a useful point of departure for the critical remarks I wish to make.

According to Ryle,[24] a belief (of the kind at issue here) is essentially a determinable disposition "involving abilities, tendencies or pronenesses to do, not things of one unique kind, but things of lots of different kinds." To take his example, believing that the ice is thin is allegedy a matter of being

> ... unhesitant in telling oneself and others that it is thin, in acquiescing in other persons' statements to that effect, in objecting to statements to the contrary, and so forth. . . . It is also to be prone to skate warily, to shudder, to dwell in imagination on possible disasters and to warn other skaters. It is a propensity not only to make certain theoretical moves but also to make certain executive moves, as well as to have certain feelings.[25]

Taken strictly, this view is plainly unacceptable, because there actually are no *behavioral* propensities and dispositions that are distinctive of a belief per se. In the case just cited, the man's dispositions were obviously rooted in many things other than his belief that the ice was thin—so much so, that he may have had that belief while behaving, or being disposed to behave, in a manner almost the opposite to that described by Ryle. This would happen if the man loved the thrill of skating on thin ice, if he were suicidal or masochistic, if he were malevolent and fond of urging others on to destruction. Again, if he believed that falling into icy water was good for the health, demanded or appreciated by his gods, his belief in the ice's thinness might also lead him to skate upon it. In general, the actual dispositions the man has are a function of at least three variables, rather than one: namely, (i) his belief that the ice is thin, (ii) certain subsidiary beliefs about, for instance, the consequences of skating on thin ice—say, that one might fall through it, possibly drown, or get pneumonia—and (iii) his own interests, wants, desires, values, and the like. Since there is, in principle, no limit to the possible variations in (ii) and (iii), it is clear that an analysis of this belief (or indeed of any belief) on anything like behavioristic lines could never possibly succeed.

If a belief is not largely a disposition to exhibit overt behavior, just what is it? In my view Ryle came very close to the truth when, almost grudgingly, he admitted that a belief also characteristically involves the disposition to make "certain theoretical moves," though I would have been happier had he said "certain conceptual moves" instead. I say this because, as I see it, the word "belief" belongs to that peculiar explanatory framework, enshrined in everyday discourse and applied primarily to human actions, in which the term "reasoning" is fundamental. As I have already noted, we are working within this framework when we attempt to explain a man's actions by reference to his *reasons* for performing them. To credit a man with a belief is, from this point of view, to credit him with a reason for acting—a reason for saying and doing. Having a reason in this sense is, as Ryle saw, a disposition, but it is a disposition to affirm something to oneself and to use the proposition affirmed as a premise when reasoning, practically or theoretically, about a wide variety of interrelated subjects.*

Take, for instance, the case of Jones, who believes that a man can regain his youth by drinking from the waters of the Ucayali River in Peru. His having this belief, I contend, is essentially a disposition on his part to affirm to himself that a man can so regain his youth,

---

* It is often held that to believe that *p* is *ipso facto* to be disposed to say that *p*. But unless saying is confused with thinking "out loud," this view is false. Unlike mere thinking, saying is a deliberate act, prompted by reasons and motives. In general, one's willingness to say that *p* (to someone) hinges on three things: one's belief that *p*; one's beliefs concerning the consequences of saying that *p*; and one's wants, intentions, and interests. Thus, although I believe that Jones is a wretched golfer, I would never say so to anyone, because he might hear about it, become angry with me, and thus repudiate the friendship that I value highly.

and to rely on this thought when reasoning, in various ways, about
a wide range of subjects.* As already indicated, the kinds of reasoning in which this premise is naturally involved are both practical
and theoretical. If Jones is asked about his views on the inevitability
of growing old, his answer, whether candid or devious, will presumably involve a line of reasoning in which his idea of the Ucayali
is featured. This would be an instance of mainly theoretical reasoning in which the thought is involved. But if Jones is deliberating
about how to spend his sabbatical leave, his idea of the Ucayali may
also be involved in practical reasoning; and some of his behavior, on
the face of it not perhaps related to thoughts about regaining his
youth, may be explainable only by reference to a line of practical
reasoning in which the thought concerning the Ucayali is an
essential premise.

I take it there is no problem about how a belief may be involved
in the theoretical moves a man might make. But it may be useful to
outline a concrete case of practical reasoning, so as to emphasize
how reference to such reasoning can serve to explain the occurrence
of behavior that might, at first sight, seem entirely unrelated to a
given belief that the agent happens to have. Consider, then, the
following dialogue, which was prompted by the spectacle of Jones
coming out of a certain store with a pile of tents and shovels:

A: Why on earth did Jones buy all that equipment?
B: I've heard that he plans to take a trip to
   the wilds of South America.
A: For what reason?
B: To hunt for the Ucayali River.
A: Well, what's so exciting about the Ucayali?
B: He believes that if a man drinks from it
   he will regain his youth.
A: (Cynically) So?
B: He thinks he's getting old.
A: (Even more cynically) So?
B: Well, he doesn't *want* to be old.

* It is necessary to be vague about this variety because the subjects to
which a man may regard a certain proposition as relevant will vary with his
knowledge, intelligence, sanity, and the like. Note that I am here ignoring
the fact that beliefs may be held more or less firmly. Roughly, the strength of
a man's belief that *p* is determined by the *degree* of his readiness to rely on the
assumption that *p*—especially when reasoning about subjects of practical importance to him and to others.

What happens in this, and similar, dialogues is that an explanation of a man's behavior is worked out by reconstructing the line of thought that presumably led him to perform it.[26] In the present case, the line of thought unearthed might be sketched roughly as follows:

1. I will do what I can to regain my youth.
2. Since a man can regain his youth by drinking from the Ucayali River in Peru, this is the thing for me to do.
3. In order to drink from the Ucayali, I must, however, go into the wilds of South America and hunt for it.
4. I shall need camping equipment for hunting in the South American wilds.
5. Such equipment can be bought in the Outfitter's Store near here.
6. (Resolve) I will go to that store and buy it.

This so-called practical argument is obviously to be understood as a reconstruction of the line of thought that led Jones to the store, not as a statement of what literally or explicitly passed through his mind. Plainly, he did not have to think through every one of the above steps and then expressly resolve to go to the store. In fact he may well have made the move corresponding to (5) and then, without further thought and ado, proceeded at once to the store. Still, every step in the above sequence is involved in his deliberation at least in the sense that what he thought was *in accordance with* those steps, in the way that an enthymematic argument is in accordance with its essential missing premises.*

With these critical remarks on the analysis of "belief" in hand, we can now return to the problem of intentionality. The essential

---

* In view of this paragraph it might occur to some readers that it would be better to analyze believing that p as a disposition merely to reason "in accordance with" the premise that p. This would not be satisfactory, however. Although it is true that there is no particular bit of reasoning in which a man's belief that p *must* occur as a premise, if he actually does believe that p—instead, say, of merely presupposing or assuming that p in much of his reasoning—he must be disposed actually to make the move that p in at least some contexts of thought or deliberation. Not every premise in accordance with which a man may habitually reason can be called one of his beliefs: among other things, a belief is "closer to consciousness" than many of the propositional attitudes that otherwise resemble it, and it also has a peculiar affirmative force that some of these attitudes lack.

points to make in this connection are now entirely straightforward. In view of the preceding discussion, we can interpret the statement "Harris believes that Cicero was a Roman" as having essentially the force of "Harris is disposed to make the move ˙Cicero was a Roman˙ in various contexts of contemplation and deliberation."* But this latter statement does not imply that if Cicero is identical with Tully, then Harris is disposed to make the move ˙Tully was a Roman˙ in these contexts of contemplation and deliberation. The reason for this is simply that the truth of "Cicero is identical with Tully" does not in any way imply that ˙Cicero was a Roman˙ and ˙Tully was a Roman˙ are the *same* move, or that if Harris is disposed, under certain conditions, to make the one move he must also, whether he believes that Cicero is identical with Tully or not, be disposed to make the other move under these conditions.

Actually, the considerations just mentioned allow us to see why even stronger, necessary equivalences do not permit substitution in belief-contexts—why, for instance, we cannot infer "Jones believes that 5^3 is greater than 124" from "Jones believes that 125 is greater than 124, and it is a necessary truth that $5^3 = 125$." The reason is simply that even logically equivalent verbal forms do not play the same linguistic role. To say that "p" is logically equivalent to "q" is only to say that "p if and only if q" is logically true, or that "p" and "q" are formally deducible from one another. But to be formally interdeducible is not the same as being formally identical role-players; indeed, if it were, every logically true equivalence would be of the trivially true form "P if and only if P," and all theorems of the standard predicate logic—even those not known to be theorems—would have to be regarded as the same basic premise.† The significance of this fact for the topic of belief statements

* Sellars' dot quotes are essential here because to credit a man with a certain belief is not to credit him with the ability to reason in any particular language. (For an explanation of these quotes, see p. 207.) Note that affirming to oneself that a is f is here regarded as making the move ·a is f· in a certain context of contemplation.

† Although it is not within the scope of this book to work out a precise criterion for the formal identity of role-players, it should be intuitively obvious to the reader that empirically different role-players such as "$p \supset q$" and "Cpq" may be regarded as formally the same while logically equivalent role-players such as "$p \supset q$" and "$\sim p \vee q$" are formally different. These formal differences are clearly reflected in the rules we have for sanctioning deductions. We may use *Modus Ponens* to infer "q" from "p" and "$p \supset q$"; but even

is that while a man may be disposed to make the move ˙*a* is *f*˙ under certain conditions *C*, he need not thereby be disposed to make the *different* move ˙*b* is *f*˙, even if these moves are logically equivalent. The fact of this equivalence may, after all, be wholly unknown to him.

The argument of the last two sections was advanced to show that the intentionality of activities such as hunting and of states such as terror and belief is just as amenable to the analogy theorist's treatment as that of actual assertions, overt or to oneself. But it also sufficed to show that the enormous variety of intentional states and activities cannot receive precisely the same treatment, but must rather be handled, so far as fine points are concerned, by attention to the individual case. Thus, while the intentionality of both hunting and believing was explainable by reference to a certain conceptual move, it was also shown that such a move is not involved in these cases in precisely the same way.

15. THE PROBLEM OF THOUGHT IN ANIMALS

In order to round out this discussion of the Analogy Theory of Thinking, it is necessary to meet a final line of objection. This one consists in the claim that the Analogy Theory greatly exaggerates the extent to which thought can be regarded as linguistic. Ordinary animal lovers as well as certain experimental psychologists will surely agree that dogs, cats, and apes are capable of thought in at least a rudimentary form. Yet there is absolutely no reason to believe that the thinking these creatures do is carried on in anything like linguistic terms. Accordingly, although the Analogy Theory may seem very plausible in connection with the thought of adult

---

though "$p \supset q$" and "$\sim p \vee q$" are logically equivalent, we cannot use the same rule immediately to infer "q" from "p" and "$\sim p \vee q$"; for the latter inference we need the so-called rule of Disjunctive Syllogism and the law of Double Negation.

It may be noted that probably no two-rule players of ordinary discourse are formally identical in any strict sense. Formal identity here is rather an ideal, like synonymy. For certain purposes various role-players may be treated as formally identical even though there are known differences between them. Such treatment is justifiable because some formal differences may be irrelevant to the purposes at hand.

human beings, it can be seen to break down when directed to the case of thought in animals.

In coming to terms with this objection, the first point to note is that the mere fact that thinking is commonly ascribed to animals, whether by ordinary animal lovers or by experimental psychologists, is no guarantee that it is truly ascribed to them, or that such ascriptions are not in any way confused. To have such a guarantee one must have a fairly clear conception of what thought is supposed to be, and one must be able to show that the relevant criteria for thinking this or that are in fact satisfied by the animals in question. In my view those who ascribe thought to lower animals with little reservation typically do *not* have a clear conception of what thought is, and their basis for ascribing thought to these animals is also highly confused. This confusion deserves especially careful attention because it is involved in the views of even highly sophisticated thinkers and leads to a great deal of needless perplexity in both the philosophy of mind and theoretical psychology.

It is crucial to realize that the conception of thought that we actually employ in explanatory contexts—that is, where we want to explain a pattern of behavior by reference to the thinking the agent has presumably done—is built on the idea of *inference*.[27] Whether such thinking is practical or largely theoretical, the agent is to be understood as reasoning his way to, roughly, a decision or conclusion. A line of reasoning of this sort cannot, moreover, be understood as a mere sequence of images or thoughts spread out in time. That this is so was one of Kant's most important insights. To reason one's way from p to q is to conceive q as a reasonable inference from p, as something whose affirmation is in some way warranted or rendered reasonable by p; and to do this is to conceive the transition from p to q as being in accordance with certain principles of inference.

Apart from presupposing such principles of inference, the explanatory form of thinking in question also requires certain nonformal concepts. In thinking (as cats are often said to do) that the mouse will run to its hole as soon as it sees you, the agent is *conceptualizing* a situation in a particular way; he is distinguishing items of reality in just the way that these items are distinguished by men who use such words as "mouse," "hole," "run," "see," and "you." If, consequently, we are to credit a cat with the literal ability to entertain the thought just mentioned—and if we do this in order to account for the behavior it might exhibit—we must also credit it with a whole battery of thing, activity, and semantic concepts. Yet we have the best of reasons for believing that these concepts could not be attained without mastering a very complicated language—indeed, a language that is formally analogous to our own.

Surely no one with a clear head would actually want to credit lower animals with conceptual schemes of this sort: to do so would be to anthropomorphize them beyond all reason. Accordingly, the force of saying (as animal lovers commonly do say) that cats, dogs, or even little pet ducks know facts, have beliefs, gain expectations, and form intentions, must be explained in highly qualified "as if" terms. The behavior of these creatures is often sufficiently similar to that of a language user (who does have knowledge, beliefs, intentions, and expectations) for it to be profitable to regard them *as if* they had knowledge, beliefs, intentions, and expectations themselves. Looking at animals this way is in fact the only way, outside the laboratory, of making sense of their actions, of fitting what they do into some sort of orderly pattern. But to insist that animal thoughts, beliefs, intentions, and expectations have something more than this *as if* status is to court intellectual disaster.

Although in echoing Locke's claim that "brutes abstract not" the preceding remarks are entirely in line with the traditional conception of animal cognition, they might nevertheless seem obscurantist to a contemporary thinker. For quite apart from the tendency of lonely old ladies to treat their pets as mute, inglorious children, psychologists of noted astuteness often find it necessary to posit covert acts of animal thinking in order to account for the problem-solving behavior of experimental animals. Thus, if Köhler's apes were unable mentally to represent objects in their environment that they are not actually viewing, it would be extremely difficult to understand how they could do so many of the things they were observed to do, such as turning their backs on the buried fruit before them, running to a remote part of their cage, and bringing back the stick that enables them to unearth the fruit with ease and aplomb.[28]

In order to avoid misunderstanding, let me say at once that my previous remarks do not in any way commit me to deny that it is legitimate to postulate "intervening" processes in order to explain animal behavior. All that they commit me to deny is that it is legitimate to interpret such processes as involving the framework of thought, of concepts and inference. Thus, although something undoubtedly does go on in the head of an ape when, in the process of groping for food, it turns around and "hunts" for a stick, what I am forced to deny is that this inner episode can be interpreted, without confusion, as one of *thought* or *deliberation*.

Before pushing this point any harder, it is worth mentioning that the confusion I allege here—between thinking, properly so called, and the intervening processes in the brains of apes—shows itself in the very way the problem situation is described. The antics of the ape are not described in the neutral scientific terms that ought to be used in the laboratory, at least according to empiricist philosophers and tough-minded behavior theorists.[29] On the contrary, the behavior of these animals is characterized in frankly intentional terms. The ape alluded to above is thus described as *trying* to unearth some food, and "trying to do *A*" is entirely intentional, exhibiting Chisholm's second mark of intentionality. The claim, then, that such behavior is to be explained by reference to thinking is entirely natural, because that behavior is already viewed within the framework of thinking. Natural as such a claim is, however, it is also confused; for to the extent that a straightforward ascription of thinking to an ape is at all questionable or problematic—as those who make such ascriptions are perfectly willing to admit—to that extent the unqualified description of the animal's movements as actions, as attempts to do this or that, is questionable also.

To a scientific reader, it might still seem excessively medieval of me to deny, or even be tempted to deny, that the explanatory scheme of thinking and intentional acting is strictly appropriate for the description and explanation of simian behavior. After all, we *are* brothers to the apes; and research in neurophysiology seems to indicate that the inner workings of man and beast are essentially the same, differing in degree of complexity rather than in kind of occurrence, as my account seems so stubbornly to suppose.

This reference to the similarity of neural mechanism in man and ape is, however, misplaced in the present connection. As I have already pointed out (see pp. 204–205), the framework of conceptual thinking is not an entirely descriptive framework. That

Jones thought that p is not, in other words, a brute fact; like the fact that Jones checked Smith's queen, it involves a tacit reference to a system of *norms*. For this reason my denial that lower animals can strictly be said to think, believe, have expectations and intentions should not be taken as a form of medieval obscurantism, reflecting a metaphysical belief that only men have "souls." It is rather a reflection of the entirely familiar fact that human beings engage in a certain rule-governed activity that lower animals do not and probably cannot engage in—for reasons to be discovered in the laboratory. Another way of putting this is to say that because animals do not play a reasoning or inferring game, their actions in pawing for food are not, strictly and unequivocally, to be explained by reference to the same principles—of having reasons and making inferences—that are used in explaining the moves that are made by agents that do play such a game.

On the other hand, however, it might be held that what actually goes on in the cerebral cortex of a man when, as we ordinarily say, he occurrently thinks that p need not differ in anything but degree of complexity from what goes on in the cortex of an ape when it is "groping" for a pile of bananas. In fact, an even stronger and far more exciting claim can perhaps be made as well: what goes on in the cortex of a person under these conditions may be formally the same as—even isomorphic in structure to—what goes on in certain machines when, as one might carelessly say, they perform certain calculations.[30]

This last suggestion, which I shall not try to develop here, has two important implications for any objection to the Analogy Theory of Thinking based on the kinship of men and apes. First, the continuity of structure and functioning that presumably connects men closely to lower animals will be exhibited only by sophisticated theories successful in explaining the movements of animals and men by reference to patterns of activity in their central nervous system. There is absolutely no reason to think that this kind of continuity is in any way reflected in the descriptions of human and animal behavior that are advanced at the level of common sense. Secondly, although lower animals cannot, in a strict, unequivocal sense, be said to *think about* their environment, it can be said that certain of their inner states *represent* or *picture* aspects of their environment. The only restriction on saying this is that we do not confuse representing or picturing with the reference of thought. Unlike picturing, the latter is essentially intentional and to be explicated in semantic terms.

Let me comment on this last point in a little more detail. Since the reference of thought is to be understood in relation to the reference of language (in the devious way explained earlier), there is no question of crediting creatures lacking conceptual schemes with the ability to make such mental references. It is, however, entirely possible to credit such creatures with the capacity of representing or picturing their environment in a nonsemantic way. The sort of representation I have in mind here is discussed by cyberneticians as well as psychologists,[31] but it is perhaps grasped most easily by reference to a favorite example of the formers', a radar-controlled anti-aircraft battery. Without going into any details, it can be said that a battery of this sort has a scanning device for locating aircraft, a means of representing their position, a means of aiming the guns at this position, and a means of representing the position of the bursting shells, so that the aim of the guns can be automatically corrected if misses occur. The sort of representation involved here is plainly not a matter of electronic activity in the battery's "brain" *referring to* or *signifying* the oncoming planes and the bursting shells. On the contrary, it is entirely a matter of an isomorphism between certain patterns of electronic activity and the positions of the planes and the shells—an isomorphism that can be fully elucidated and precisely defined in the *extensional* language of cybernetic theory.

Now, there apparently is reason to think that phase-sequences of certain complex systems of cell-assemblies in the cerebral cortex of both animals and men may represent or picture their environment in a similar way.[32] If this is indeed so, then the development of neurophysiology will probably justify the tough-minded claim that the ability of man and beast to represent their environment "internally" is explainable by the same general principles. But this unitary account will nevertheless not shed light on thinking as we ordinarily understand it, nor will it show itself in an analysis of common-sense discourse. So far as the latter is concerned, there is a categorial difference between brutes and men; and to collapse this difference is implicitly to abandon the intentional framework of conceptual thought.

IX

Mind and Body

The mind-body problem has been called a world knot, where all the problems of philosophy ultimately come together. Considering the tangle of issues that constitute this ancient problem, the description is barely an exaggeration. Since I have argued that science and common sense actually clash on fundamental points, my treatment of these issues can be expected to complicate matters even more. Nevertheless, by separating the mind-body knot into two workable but still intricate strands, I can survey at least the leading issues concerning mind and body in the scope of this chapter. The first strand will involve the claims of common sense, and the other will include the more exotic contentions of theoretical science.

I. WHAT IS A MIND?

In the very strict sense of "mental" discussed in the last chapter, only such activities as thinking, intending, and hoping to achieve some envisaged goal are truly mental. Popularity, feeling, and sensing are often considered mental, too—even though they do not, in my view, possess the intentionality that philosophers such as

Brentano and Chisholm regard as the distinctive mark of the mental. I have already emphasized the importance of restricting the notion of human consciousness to encompass only intentional phenomena, but if the considerations behind my restriction are carefully kept in mind, there can be no objection to a more informal treatment here. Thus, for the purposes of this chapter, even brute feeling can be regarded as mental.

Traditionally, it has proved extremely tempting to think of a mind as a spiritual substance, an immaterial thing that actually does the thinking, willing, and so forth ordinarily said to be done by the living creatures that have minds. Without pondering the intricate and very interesting basis for this temptation, I shall only say that it is ruled out at the level of common sense by what I have already said about thinking, acting, intending, or even feeling, emoting, or sensing. I have argued that these activities or states are to be understood as adjectival to persons, taken as single logical subjects with observable characteristics. These logical subjects necessarily have such characteristics because the notions we have of their inner mental states are specially framed to account for their observable behavior—their screams, their jumps, their avowals, and their goal-directed activities.

Since mental states of the kind usually recognized are understood as inner states of bodied persons, the only consistent common-sense notion of mind that can apply to them must be something like the one suggested by Gilbert Ryle in *The Concept of Mind.*[1] According to this interpretation, a mind is something adjectival, not substantive. To speak of a man's mind is not to speak of some inner, immaterial self that he allegedly possesses. It is rather to speak in a highly abbreviated way of a large class of his special abilities and capacities—to think, to engage in intentional actions, to sense, to feel, and the like. To put this point in the terminology suggested in Chapter VI, a mind is at best a nominal, not a real, object. "Tom has a mind," like "Mary wore a smile," simply introduces a convenient noun where a verb or verbal clause is logically more perspicuous. Thus, "Tom is minded" might be regarded as less misleading than our normal idiom.

In view of this conception of mind as adjectival to a living creature, one might be inclined to think that the relation between

mind and body is nothing other than the "relation" between a certain sort of organic body and its distinctive abilities and capacities
to think, feel, act, and so forth. This inclination is, however, misdirected, although it comes closer to the truth than many familiar
alternatives. The reason it is misdirected is that we ascribe mental
and sensory states to *persons*, which are said to have both minds
and bodies. Since the material bodies in question are themselves
attributed to persons, rather than identified with them, the complicated set of abilities and capacities in which having a mind consists cannot, then, be the abilities and capacities of those bodies.[2]
They are rather the abilities and capacities of persons, which are
said to *have* bodies as well as minds.

2. WHAT ARE "PERSONS"?

In order to avoid thinking of a person as a sort of bare particular
or "thing I know not what," it is essential to see that the sense in
which a mind or body is attributed to a person is utterly vacuous,
factually. Persons are by definition both bodied and minded, and
this means that any factual statement concerning a person's physical
or mental characteristics can only attribute to him some determinate characteristic that he need not have *if* he has some other
determinate characteristic belonging to the same family. By virtue
of the very meaning of "person," such remarks as "That (human)
person has some sort of size" or "That person can think" have no
factual content at all; they are as empty as "Black dogs are black"
or "Trees have trunks." In order to make an informative statement
about a person's mental or physical features, one must rather make
a more determinate claim, such as "That person is six feet tall" or
"He can solve differential equations." The point here is the obvious
one that unless certain features were built right into the notion of
a subject of attributes, the latter would indeed have the status of a
bare particular or a classical substratum.* As it is, persons, like other
common-sense particulars, are not "bare." And attributions of

---

* In order to avoid substrata it is, of course, equally important to realize
that attribution-statements are not implicitly relational. Cf. Strawson's discussion of "non-relational ties," *Individuals, op. cit.,* pp. 167ff.

minds and bodies to persons have point chiefly in the context of conceptual analysis, where they serve to remind us that the concept of a person is the concept of a minded, bodied subject.

Although the notion of a person as a minded, bodied subject is as old as Aristotle, it cannot be denied that, so conceived, a person seems to be a very peculiar "glued-together unity," which cries out for a simplifying analysis.[3] Can such an analysis be given? According to P. F. Strawson, who has considered the matter carefully, the answer is an emphatic "No." He argues that the concept of a person must be regarded as primitive in our conceptual scheme, and thus incapable of analysis into simpler notions.[4] In one very important sense Strawson is clearly right here, for there assuredly are no simpler descriptive concepts (such as *body* and *experience*) into which the notion of a person is analyzable. There are two basic reasons for this. First, the concept of a person has an important deontic element, since persons are agents to which rights and duties are essentially ascribable. This ethical dimension is by itself sufficient to forestall any purely extensional analysis of the usual concept. Second, the apparently separable "naturalistic" elements that seem glued together in the notion of a person cannot possibly be pried apart. The fundamental reason for this is that mental states are just that—*states*, not conceptually independent things or processes. And as shown in the last four chapters, these adjectival features are also conceived in relation to the behavior that persons—taken as walking, talking, weeping, visible creatures —occasionally exhibit. Hence, for reasons amply developed in those chapters, there is no chance whatever of analyzing the notion of a person into the notions of, say, mental states and material body. The notion of a mental state presupposes the notion of a person already, and thus could not be used to analyze it.

Although analyses of this empirical sort obviously fail, there is nevertheless a radically different type of analysis that does not fail at all. This type of analysis may be traced back to Kant, who interpreted the notion of an empirical substance as a schematized version of the notion of a logical subject.[5] What is special about this type of analysis is that it distinguishes a concept's formal structure from its empirical content. In this respect such an analysis differs profoundly from the type discussed in the last paragraph, for there the aim was to distinguish the empirically significant elements that the concept ties together. Here one of the elements distinguished is understood as having no empirical content at all.

To see how this peculiar analytic strategy may be employed in connection with the concept of a person, recall that the concept of a conceptual move (thoughts and assertions being such moves) is in part a formal or normative one, like the concept of a checkmate. Now, just as it is possible to conceive of a checkmate in the abstract—that is, without reference to the shape or size of the pieces used to effect a mate in the usual game—so it is possible to conceive of a conceptual move in the abstract, without considering the specific verbal means that might be used to make such a move. (Exactly this was done when the concept of silent thinking was elucidated.) Since a conceptual move is the particular move that it is only by reference to other moves that might be made by someone using the same conceptual system (compare p. 92), it is possible to conceive of a thinker or speaker in the abstract as well. The notion of such a "pure" subject of conceptual activities might be regarded as the abstract notion of a *persona*, and it might be compared to the abstract notion of a pawn in chess—"abstract," because the pawn is here conceived merely as the player of a certain role, its physical embodiment having been abstracted away.

Even if we neglect the ethical dimension of the concept of a person, we will not thereby reduce it to a purely descriptive concept, for it will still involve the normative features that accrue to it from its relation to such notions as speaker, thinker, concept-user.* These residual notions telescope together into the abstract notion just discussed. To use Kantian terminology, the concept of a person, ethically disinfected, is a schematized version of the pure concept of a *persona*, of a subject of conceptual activities. In this way it compares to the empirical notion of a pawn, which is a schematized version of the concept of a player of a certain role in chess. Since formal notions of this sort may in principle receive different concrete embodiments (the same remark may be made in different words, chess may be played with buttons, standard pieces,

---

* There is thus considerable point to Locke's claim that the concept of a person is a "forensic" one, applicable "only to intelligent agents capable of a law." See *An Essay Concerning Human Understanding*, abr. and ed. by A. S. Pringle-Pattison (Oxford: Clarendon Press, 1924), Bk. II, Ch. 27, sect. 26, p. 199. (This reference was brought to my attention by a note in I. A. Melden's essay, "Action," *Philosophical Review*, LXV [1956], 523–541.)

or even automobiles), it appears that persons may differ radically as well, and that the concept of a person is of a higher order of abstraction than the concept of a human being.*

I shall not comment on the theoretical shortcomings of traditional theories of nonhuman persons. How immaterial spirits—gods, ghosts, angels, or devils—can count as concrete embodiments of formal notions is a question best left to thinkers with other sympathies than mine. It is interesting to note, however, that some of the other-worldly creatures of science fiction could very easily qualify as persons (that is, *persona* or rational agents), even though their physical characteristics differ widely from those of a human being. Thus, there is nothing conceptually absurd in the idea of a creature with the body of a bird or dog carrying on rational discourse, and the same is true of the more amorphous or vegetative shapes possessed by the characters in stories of life on other planets. Of course, if such characters are to be believable as possible *persona*, they must have a strong functional similarity to human beings. But this does not imply that they must bear anything like the physical image of man. Fred Hoyle's Black Cloud is an excellent example of this.[6]

But to turn away from science fiction and to focus attention on our actual world of things and persons, we can see that the only creatures capable of qualifying as persons are community-living, noise-producing Homo sapiens. Since in order to explain the full range of behavior these agents exhibit we must credit them (rather than parts of their bodies) with feelings, impressions, emotions, and the like, it follows that the persons of *our world* are sentient creatures of a very special type. That our world, as I am describing it here, is a common-sense world, and that it is possible to envisage other worlds in which persons as physically embodied are describable in a very different way, will turn out to be of the greatest importance in the later stages of my argument. For the moment, I

* The abstract notion of a *persona* is similar to the notion of a Turing machine, which is frequently mentioned in recent discussions of the mind-body problem. Although such a machine differs from a *persona* in being extensionally describable, it too is conceived in abstract, formal terms. As Hilary Putnam has remarked, a Turing machine "is an *abstract* machine which may be physically realized in an almost infinite number of ways"; see his "Minds and Machines," in S. Hook, ed., *Dimensions of Mind, op. cit.,* p. 159.

want to remain with persons ordinarily conceived and consider more pointedly the "relation" that exists between their bodies and their minds.

3. THE RELATION BETWEEN MIND AND BODY, ORDINARILY UNDERSTOOD

If, to restrict ourselves initially to the strict sense of "mental," we ask for the relation between a man's mental and physical characteristics, the answer seems both obvious and unproblematic: they are simply *different* characteristics of the same unitary subject. The reason they are actually different is that one of them is a partly formal or normative characteristic, and *no* such characteristic can be identified with one that is purely naturalistic. Thus, if the mental characteristic is that of believing something about the moon, there is no purely physical characteristic such that, unless one possesses it, one cannot possibly believe such a thing. Not only do we conceive the state of believing in a way that is logically independent of the physical processes that occur in one's head, but the very identity of a specific belief is largely determined by reference to purely normative factors such as what implies what, what negates what, and so on. By now this should be a dull old story; for if the argument of the last chapter proved anything, it was that the intentional character of mental phenomena neither consists in nor springs from their peculiar character as natural phenomena—and that as intentional phenomena they could not possibly be identified with something purely naturalistic.

But even if one grants this last contention, it may still be possible to raise another question, which is perhaps closer to the intentions of those who have worried about the mind-body problem. This is the question whether the activity that, in a particular case, gives a conceptual move its concrete empirical character is or is not the same as some physical process or other. Just as the intentional notion of proto-assertion was seen to have an extensional counterpart in the notion of making certain noises in a particular set, might not the concept of thought have a similar extensional counterpart, so that one could say that the nonformal aspects of silent thinking are purely physical as well?

In view of the well-known fact that imagery of various sorts is logically inessential to thinking, it might seem that anyone with an optimistic view of future progress in neurophysiology is bound to answer the above question with an enthusiastic "Yes." Yet if the question here is based on a common-sense picture of the world— on a picture of the world in which persons and sensible objects are basic particulars[7]—then the answer will have to be "No." The reason for this has already been foreshadowed in Chapter VII: it is simply that the scheme of common sense does not include the theoretical concepts of neurophysiology and, indeed, cannot include them without substantial revision. At the level of common sense, mental states and even sensory states are basic, categorial features of human persons; and there is no room within this conceptual network for even their partial identification with states of any other kind.[8] If our interest in scientific theory, as opposed to the possible confusions of *a priori* metaphysics, excites dissatisfaction with this dualistic picture of common sense, then we will have to pose our questions about mind and body in a fashion that is more guarded and indirect. One way of doing this is to ask if there is any reason to think that in a conceptual scheme enriched with scientific notions and built around different basic particulars (such as molecules) there will continue to be terms for phenomena that are intuitively nonphysical. If a positive answer can be given to this question, we may then consider what relations might obtain between true statements containing these terms and statements containing the more familiar terms of theoretical physics.

4. THE DEMANDS OF THEORY

The fundamental reason why the acceptance of a micro-theory of matter—and here I restrict myself to the implications of admitting any modern version of the molecular theory—demands a radical revision of the basic logical subjects of the common-sense world is that the latter are categorially specifiable in terms of occurrent sensible qualities, which are incompatible with reality microphysically conceived. Thus, as argued in Chapter VII, there is no place in the molecular structure commonly called air for the sensuous fragrance of lilacs and roses, and no place on gappy surfaces for spatially dense reds and purples. All these sensuous features have to be located somewhere else. This means that the very unity of the common-sense objects whose identity is determined by sensible qualities is inevitably shattered by our theoretical advance. We are thus left with the job of retracing the unity of molar objects in terms appropriate to the complex systems that these "objects" really are.

This conceptual revolution does not, of course, require us to junk such terms as "red" and "green." What has to change—and change profoundly—is the allover shape of our conceptual scheme: the sense we can attach to such categorial notions as physical thing, sensible quality or change, and the full pattern of inferences that we can sanction. The fact that these conceptual convulsions clearly show themselves only in a fairly rarefied level of discussion does not in any way imply that it is false to say, as Sellars does,[9] that from the point of view of physical theory there are no such things as the colored objects of common sense. This claim is strictly true, and failure to appreciate it can only issue in philosophical error. Although we can admittedly go on using a large share of the language of everyday life, it does not follow that we can consistently be speaking of the same things. To the molecular biologist, the golden strands of the maiden's hair are glory bereft, for they are simply polypeptide helixes reflecting radiation.

5. THE UNITY OF THE PERCEIVER

A good way to begin the exploration of the deep-seated changes required in our conceptual scheme by the acceptance of a new domain of basic micro-things is to concentrate on the concept of a perceiver, for it is with respect to him that the sensible qualities of the common-sense world are to be reconstructed—for example, as powers of a physical system to affect him in a certain way. The main difficulty to be faced here is that of finding a way of reconciling the essential unity of a perceiver with the plurality of the (largely) physical system that, on scientific principles, he is supposed to be. Fortunately, the way out of this difficulty has been foreshadowed in earlier discussion. I have already shown that the concept of a person has a purely formal dimension and that it is possible to make sense of a subject of conceptual activities in the abstract, without considering its mode of embodiment. This being so, it is open to us to argue that certain gappy molecular systems have sufficient *functional* unity to serve as admissible physical realizations of this formal unity. Just as one could admit squads of well-trained fleas as individual pawns in a game of chess where pawns are regarded as primitive unities, so one can admit squads of particles (which are not, as squads, primitive unities in a factual sense) as physical embodiments of persons (which are primitive unities in a formal sense).

Let me expand on this point, which is very important and not just a piece of woolly metaphysics. The root consideration here is that systems of particles, to the extent that they have a functional unity sufficient for being singled out as unities, have the status of the compound substances of classical philosophy. The unity they have is thus conceptually derived; it is to be analyzed and understood by reference to the laws governing the simple substances, the individual particles, that compose them.[10] The unity of a person, on the other hand, is not a derivative one. The fact that S is a subject of conceptual activities is not analyzable into facts about simpler subjects, whether molecules or more elementary thinkers, that in some way compose S. For this reason, it has always proved tempting for philosophers to argue that while a man's body may be a compound substance, he himself, as a subject of conceptual activities, must be a mind, which is a simple, immaterial substance.* If I am right, however, the error of this last temptation consists less in the appeal to an unobservable, immaterial substance than in a serious confusion between an essentially formal unity and a purely

---

* Compare the classic statement of Descartes in his Sixth Meditation: ". . . when I consider . . . myself inasmuch as I am only a thinking thing, I cannot distinguish in myself any parts, but apprehend myself to be clearly one and entire. . . . But it is quite otherwise with corporeal or extended objects, for there is not one of these imaginable by me which my mind cannot easily divide into parts, and which consequently I do not recognize as being divisible; this would be sufficient to teach me that the mind or soul of man is entirely different from the body, if I had not learned it from other sources," *Philosophical Works of Descartes*, Vol. 1, E. S. Haldane and G. T. R. Ross, trans. (London: Cambridge University Press, 1934), 196.

factual one. Like the primitive unity of a pawn in chess, the primitive unity of a subject of conceptual activities is a formal one that
can be described in abstract terms. And a unity of this sort is entirely compatible with the derivative unity of some compound
substance that may constitute its physical embodiment.

6. THINKERS AND PHYSICAL EMBODIMENTS

Even if the primitive unity of a person as a subject of conceptual
activities is consistent with an embodiment in a complex substance,
can we agree that a purely physical embodiment is really appropriate? The question I am posing here naturally arises for anyone with
doubts about mind-body identity. These doubts are by no means
silly, for conceptual activities are not in any obvious sense always
physical activities, involving only physical movements on the descriptive side. If traditional theorists were right, thinking would in
fact always involve an activity strictly indescribable in physicalistic
terms. My previous argument commits me, of course, to reject
this radical claim about thinking, but if one considers that persons
are ordinarily understood to have all sorts of sensory experiences
that seem paradigmatically nonphysical, the idea that it would ever
be reasonable to regard human beings as, empirically, nothing but
composite physical systems becomes extremely doubtful.

In order, however, to explore the precise extent to which the
abstract notion of a *persona* might be realized in a purely physical
system, we can begin by ignoring the question of sensory experiences and concentrating on conceptual activities proper. The point
in proceeding this way is that there is nothing essentially conceptual about sensory experiences, and that such experiences are
no more essential to thought than sensuous imagery. As argued in
the last chapter, silent thought is conceived in an empirically transparent, purely formal way; and this leaves open at least the logical
possibility that a person, considered solely as an intelligent agent,
might be a purely physical system on the descriptive side.

Is there any reason to think that this latter possibility might gain
concrete support by progress in neurophysiology? Except for one
fundamental reservation, I am strongly inclined to say "Yes." The

basis for this inclination consists not only in what strikes me as exciting developments in the allied sciences of cybernetics and
molecular biology, but also in the fact that a good share of our
thinking is already known to be accompanied by characteristic
patterns of cortical activity.[11] Since we ordinarily conceive silent
thinking in a largely formal way, it is entirely reasonable to suppose
that it may occasionally be identifiable, in its empirical aspect, with
various patterns of neural activity. I say "may occasionally be
identifiable" because of my fundamental reservation mentioned
above. This is that although silent thinking *need not* involve verbal
or other imagery, it often *does* involve such imagery, particularly
verbal imagery. I regard the presence of imagery—assuming, for
the moment, that it is incapable of physicalistic reduction—as an
obstacle to a wholesale identification of the empirical aspects of
thinking with cortical activity because we conceive of thinking in
such a linguistic way that verbal imagery must sometimes be accepted as part of it. To maintain that verbal imagery is *always*
nothing more than an accidental accompaniment to our thinking is
implicitly to reject the concept of thought we actually have and
run it together with the idea of an inner process that pictures reality
in the sense discussed in the last chapter.

7. MAN'S PURELY EXTENSIONAL COUNTERPART

From a narrowly scientific point of view, one might of course be
strongly tempted to cast aside the ordinary concept of thinking
and replace it by a theory of brain activity having no place for
normative elements. This temptation might be supported by the
following considerations. First, it is a cardinal principle of contemporary empiricism that the peculiar task of the sciences is to
present a purely factual picture of man and nature. Since the ordinary notion of thinking, being based on the idea of inference,[12]
is not a purely factual notion, it strictly has no place in a *science*
of human behavior. Second, even though mental imagery may
occasionally occur when, as we ordinarily say, a man is thinking,
this mere imagery can hardly be essential to the basic process that
provides a fine-grained explanation of his subsequent actions. If the
imagery is irreducibly nonphysical, it is at best an accompanying

"epiphenomenon" to this process. Finally, the traditional idea that inferential thinking is always at the root of a language user's non-habitual actions is scientifically unacceptable because (a) it exaggerates the extent to which human behavior is actually based on reasoning and (b) it obscures the general principles that explain the complex behavior patterns of the entire range of higher animals. I have amplified this second point in the preceding chapter (see pp. 221 ff.), and in connection with the first criticism it is perhaps sufficient to say that in using the notion of inference to explain such familiar facts as the utility of "incubation" for problem-solving, we are inexorably led down the metaphysical path to unconscious inference and Freudian dynamics. To take this path is not just to lose out on the chance of explaining such phenomena by theories that are beginning to emerge with the help of the neurophysiologist;[13] it is to abandon all hope of uniting psychology with the physically more basic science of molecular biology.

In my view all of the above considerations are extremely reasonable, and they are evidently in the minds of hard-headed psychologists who abjure "animism" in psychological theorizing and endeavor to explain human and animal behavior by reference to neural mechanisms. Of course, the ultimate reasonableness of this empirical picture of man can show itself only in the future development of theoretical psychology. That it is already accepted by many cyberneticians and neurophysiologists is nevertheless a familiar fact, one that is fearful to some and happy news to others. All that I can say about it as a philosopher is that it seems to involve no conceptual difficulties whatever—so long, that is, as it is not advanced as a reconstructed picture of a *person*. If it is to attain its proper purpose, it must be clearly understood as describing a person's *extensional counterpart*, or those aspects of a person that can be fully captured in neutral scientific terms. Since such distinctively human activities as acting with a purpose and choosing a course of action cannot be captured in these terms, they will not appear in the scientific picture. This does not mean, again, that the picture leaves something out that strictly belongs there. In order to see exactly why nothing strictly factual need be omitted, it will pay us to look more closely at the concepts of purposive activity and free, responsible action.

8. PURPOSIVE ACTIVITY

The crucial fact about the concept of purposive activity is that it is an intentional one. Thus, "Tom's purpose in doing A was to achieve B" exhibits Chisholm's second mark, since neither it nor its negation implies either that Tom does or does not achieve B. In view of the argument set forth in Chapter VIII, the mere fact that the concept of purpose is intentional assures us that it can no more be elucidated in materialistic or cybernetic terms than can the reference of thought. This means that vitalists and others who recoil with horror or dismay from the frequent claims of the cyberneticians and behavior scientists that purpose is really nothing but feedback mechanisms in action are not entirely misguided. They go wrong, in fact, only in insisting that the cybernetician's account is factually incomplete, that it omits reference to the spiritual process in which the true essence of purpose consists.

The error these defenders of spirit make at this point is by now familiar: it is the confusion of a concept's normative dimension with a supposed reference to an exotic domain of ethereal occurrences. Like the intentionality of hunting (see pp. 211–212), the intentionality of purpose itself is to be elucidated by reference to the normative concepts of a linguistic move and of practical deliberation. Roughly, to explain an agent's intelligent, nonhabitual action by reference to his purpose is to outline, if only very schematically, the line of practical reasoning that lies behind the man's action and thus accounts for it (see pp. 214 ff.). And we have already seen that all of the naturalistic or brute facts involved in such reasoning are capable of capture by an extensionally described counterpart to the asserting activity.* Hence if the cybernetician puts his claim in a more guarded way, namely that in his terms he can account for everything that in point of brute fact occurs when a man is acting for a purpose, then his claim may be entirely correct. He definitely goes wrong only if he advances his account as an explanation of what purpose is, of how we are actually to understand it.

* For reasons already given, this extensional counterpart might occasionally involve reference to verbal imagery. This fact is, however, irrelevant to the issue in point, as will become clear in later sections of this chapter.

9. FREE, RESPONSIBLE ACTIONS

A well-known objection to any essentially physicalistic account of human beings is that their ability to perform free, responsible actions points to a spiritual power or agency within them that, not subject to ordinary causal laws, permits their behavior to be unpredictable in a way that inorganic nature is not. Although it is not possible here to enter fully into the complex battle that still rages over the freedom-determinism issue,[14] it is crucial to see that objections of this sort, whatever else is wrong with them, rest fundamentally on the type of confusion just mentioned in connection with purposive activity. That is, they contain an important sliver of conceptual truth which, thoroughly misunderstood, is used as a wholly inadequate prop for a misconceived claim about the ultimate furniture of our world.

In order to locate the sliver of truth these objections contain, we must again note that the concept of a deliberate action is an intentional one, like the concept of thought it presupposes. As already indicated, intentional activities are not to be explained, *qua* intentional, by antecedent or concurrent causes; they are rather to be explained by the wants, intentions, and lines of thought that prompted the agent to perform them. This is simply a basic principle of the framework of intentional action. Now, deterministic laws concerning the behavior of natural bodies do not include the intentional terms of action description, for what is purely natural is extensionally describable (see p. 199). Thus, such laws can only tell us what may or may not happen, not what can or cannot be *done*.* This, then, is the sliver of truth on which the objection rests —that what can or cannot be *done* is not implied by deterministic laws. But far from indicating that free human actions spring from a nonphysical power or agent that may interfere with natural regularities, this sliver of truth really only tells us that the sense of the word "can" appropriate to the morally significant statement "He can *do* otherwise" is not the "can" of physical modality.

---

* Of course, such laws, when conjoined with statements describing the movements one must make in performing certain actions, can lead us to the conclusion that the appropriate actions cannot be done. But we can conclude this only because we are assured that the appropriate criteria for the action's being done cannot be satisfied. For further discussion, see the papers mentioned in note 14 to this chapter.

If, however, the "can" in the statement criterial for a man's free-dom, "He can do other than what he does do (or is doing)," is not the "can" of physical modality, just what is it? The answer to this, as I have argued elsewhere,[15] is that it is the "can" of ability-in-certain-circumstances. What one wants to know if the freedom of a man's act is at all in question is whether he was actually able, in the circumstances of its performance, to do something else instead. And what a man is able to do in certain circumstances is not de-termined merely by what he does not do in those circumstances. A failure to perform a certain action in circumstances C implies—that is, without collateral information about the kind of action it is—that a man lacks the corresponding ability only if he has also willed or chosen to perform that action. Our use of "can" in this sense is in fact built on the idea that *a man need not do what he can do* and that in order to find out what he can do we must in effect find out what he will do if, in the circumstances in question, he wills or chooses to do certain things. And this assumption, far from con-tradicting determinism, is in one very important sense fully in line with it; for it is presumably only because a measure of determinism does hold in nature that men are *regularly* capable of doing things they have done before.

10. THE PROBLEM OF SENSORY QUALIA

Having seen that with the possible exception of sensory experi-ence, there are no brute facts about human beings that cannot be accommodated in a purely physicalist picture, we are now in a position to take a closer look at this possible exception. Is there, or is there not, something irreducible about sensory experience, so that a scientific picture of human beings will have to include what might be called "sensuous *qualia*" as well as physical processes? One point, at any rate, is entirely clear: our commonsensical notions of feelings, sense impressions, and the like will not be included here. The reason for this is that they are conceived in relation to human bodies and behavior as ordinarily understood, and the very con-ception of such bodies will have been thrown aside by theoretical developments. Hence, if the new picture does contain a place for

the sensuous, the latter will have to differ substantially from anything describable in common-sense terms.

In recent years a number of philosophers have advanced arguments the import of which, when brought into line with the distinctions I have been drawing, is that no special terms for sensuous
qualia are needed for an adequate scientific picture of sentient
organisms.[16] They have even gone so far as to argue that the introduction of such terms would be out of line with a reasonable
methodology, and would pose far more problems than they could
hope to solve. Thus, as J. J. C. Smart has recently said:

> ... if such terms were admitted into the scientific picture, there would
> have to be special irreducible laws which relate the complex neuro-
> physiological processes to the corresponding sense data [or sensuous
> *qualia*]. These laws would have to be isolated offshoots from the main
> network of scientific explanation: as H. Feigl has put it, these laws
> would be 'nomological danglers'. ... Wherever we look in science we
> do not find anything analogous to the sort of ultimate law which
> would have to be postulated by the Subjectivist. It would have to be
> an ultimate law which would relate something simple, a sense datum
> with an unanalyzable *quale*, to a very complicated and nonhomo-
> geneous process involving millions of neurons (and hence countless
> millions of millions of ultimate particles) and depending on numer-
> ous feed-back mechanisms of complicated sorts. This does not seem
> quite believable. ...[17]

II. THE PHYSICALIST'S ATTACK ON QUALIA

Although the above remarks by Smart may seem to support a
doctrine of physicalism, they really only highlight an agonizing
problem that has always haunted reflective atomists, prompting
Anaxagoras as far back as 450 B.C. to attribute *qualia* to his micro-
scopic basic elements. Contemporary materialists tend to avoid
this ancient problem by arguing, in effect, that it does not exist.
Their approach here rests mainly on two distinct lines of thought.
First, it is sometimes argued (for instance by Smart) that ordinary
sensation concepts are really "topic neutral," and do not therefore
commit us to anything like irreducible sensory *qualia*. To say that
one has a yellowish afterimage is to say no more than that some-

thing is going on in one that is like what goes on when one is looking at something yellow. Since what goes on in the latter case is not intrinsically specified, there can be no serious objection to the idea that the so-called afterimage is really a brain process. Second, it is frequently argued that while we may, in ordinary life, take such words as "mental image" to refer to something nonphysical, developments in neurophysiology make it reasonable to think that these alleged items would have to be in one-to-one correspondence with neural states anyway, so that it would not be necessary to allude to them in explaining any aspects of human behavior. In view of the methodological soundness of Ockham's Razor, which tells us not to multiply entities beyond necessity in constructing our theories, we ought therefore to accept a materialistic theory of sentient organisms and either eliminate all mentalistic words from our scientific vocabulary or else reinterpret them as referring to neural processes.[18]

It is hardly necessary to say that arguments of this sort could gain currency only at a time when introspection is no longer taken seriously. But introspection does not have to be defended in order to rebut these arguments. Consider the argument based on the alleged topic neutral character of sensation concepts. The first point to note is that if I am at all correct about theories, this argument is in an important sense irrelevant to the issue. It rests on a proffered analysis of common-sense concepts, and I have argued that these concepts would have to be twisted entirely out of shape when transposed into the scientific picture, where micro-objects are basic particulars. Hence, even if Smart were right about our ordinary concepts (which he is not), we might still be tortured about sensuous *qualia* in the scientific picture. This possibility cannot be taken lightly, because once we have abandoned the common-sense conception of color, the temptation would be extremely great to follow the example of Locke and regard sensuous expanses as features, in some sense, of the perceiving subject.

Smart's analysis of the ordinary notion of sensory experience is, however, erroneous, for we are entirely capable of characterizing an image or an impression in an intrinsic way: this is done by the device of formal analogy. It is useful to observe, moreover, that even if it were possible to effect a simple merging of ordinary and theoretical concepts without distortion of any kind—so that we could proceed to ask whether specimens of the former and specimens of the latter have the same *de facto* reference in the way that "yellow" and "the color of ripe lemons" have it—the intrinsic mode of characterizing mental images would provide a solid barrier to the identification of the phenomenal and the physical. The reason for this is that phenomenal color, being an analogue of ordinary objective color, has the ultimate "continuity" of the latter;[19] and no predicate of neuron clusters or even molecular aggregates specifies a property involving the *same sort* of continuity—as Smart himself admits.

The second line of argument in favor of physicalism—the one resting on a presumed dispensability of phenomenal terms at a utopian stage of scientific investigation—involves one of the same basic difficulties that infects the first argument, and it must accordingly be reinterpreted if it is to have any chance of success. The difficulty in point is, again, the erroneous assumption that science and common sense may be brought together without clash, so that correlations can be established between items falling under these distinct types of concept. In order to remove this difficulty it is necessary to restate the dispensability thesis in some such way as this: the growth of our scientific knowledge of nature and sentient organisms can be expected to result in a comprehensive conceptual scheme containing no special, irreducible concepts applying to items or features of items that are not wholly physical. Put more concretely, the doctrine here is that phenomenal terms of the common-sense level, such as "yellowish afterimage" or "stinging pain," will become either redundant or entirely pruned away as our theories develop, and no new terms of a comparable phenomenal import will have to be added in their place. The picture of sentient organisms that will eventually emerge will then be wholly physicalistic (on the factual side).*

The first thing to notice about this doctrine is its essential vagueness, at least as stated here. In envisaging a stage of our conceptual development where phenomenal terms are either absent or otiose, it tacitly assumes that we are reasonably clear about what a phe-

---

* It is essential to appreciate that the development envisaged here may be purely ideal—in the sense that it may actually be worked out only in imagination by someone who takes on the metaphysical task (discussed in Ch. VI, sect. 6) of analyzing the presuppositions of scientific thought at some utopian stage of our intellectual development.

nomenal term is supposed to be. Yet in one sense, a sense crucial to the doctrine, it cannot be supposed that we are clear about this at all. The basic reason for this unclarity is that the examples we can give of phenomenal terms belong to the language of everyday life, and this language is admittedly to be radically metamorphosed in the final picture. The failure of the final picture to include the examples in point can thus be accepted by physicalist and non-physicalist alike: the issue that separates them will still remain high in the air.

It might naturally be argued that we have at any rate an intuitive idea of the phenomenal, an idea that anyone can be expected to have who has reflected on the experience of having an afterimage or of seeing a rose. But this intuitive idea, to the extent that it is at all significant, just seems to stand in the way of the physicalist's claims. For it would certainly appear that any conceptual scheme with a reasonable claim to comprehensiveness must make *some kind of place* for the phenomena ordinarily classified as colors, impressions, and the like—even though these phenomena can no longer be understood as features or states of unitary subjects. It seems entirely clear, accordingly, that in the vague, intuitive sense of "phenomenal," no reasonable development of our conceptual scheme could possibly dispense with phenomenal terms.

12. SCIENCE AND COMMON SENSE:
THE METHODOLOGICAL CONNECTION

Although the remarks just made have mainly an intuitive significance, they call attention to an aspect of the relation between science and common sense that deserves special comment. Thus far, I have been largely concerned to oppose the widespread assumption that theoretical terms owe their empirical significance to their relations with the observation terms of everyday life. Having repeatedly insisted that the latter are in fact incompatible with the claims of physical theory, I might seem to have committed myself to regard common-sense concepts as strictly irrelevant to the mind-body problem. But this is so only in a sense. In repudiating a logical connection between the terms of common sense and theoretical science, I am not in any way repudiating a very strong methodological connection between them; and this methodological connection is of crucial importance to any adequate statement of the mind-body problem.

Speaking somewhat roughly, the crucial methodological connection between theoretical and common-sense concepts is that the former are to be conceived as developments from the latter, involving improved counterparts that can do everything the latter can legitimately do, as well as much else besides.[20] To the extent that these improved counterparts involve a repudiation of a common-sense idea, as happens in the case of sensible qualities, the repudiation must be viewed as *demanded* by our enriched conceptual scheme. Thus, while common sense must constantly give way to the pressure of theoretical progress, every departure from it must be backed by powerful considerations, and all the claims that we can justifiably make at the common-sense level must have their counterparts in the new picture—unless, that is, solid reasons can be given for regarding those claims as in some way fundamentally erroneous.

From the standpoint of scientific methodology, to envisage the structure of a future scientific world-picture is in part to envisage the picture we now have as changed or metamorphosed by the introduction of new theoretical principles. (It is only if we think of it in this way that we can take the new picture to be a picture of *our* world.) If we restrict the scope of these new principles to those implicitly discussed since Chapter VII—the molecular theory of matter and, say, a physiological theory of the functioning of cells in the nervous systems of animals—we can then pose the question already discussed in a much more determinate way: might the picture that results from admitting *these* new principles be an entirely physicalist one, lacking even metamorphosed tatters of common-sense colors and impressions? In my view, the answer must be an emphatic "No!" Although the introduction of these new principles will require a radical change in our conception of a material body, of sensible qualities, persons, and their sensory experiences, it will not require the actual repudiation of anything phenomenal. All of the reasons we ever had for speaking of the phenomenal will, in fact, remain with us. It will still be necessary to account for the reasonableness of aberrant perceptual claims, and the necessity of revamping our conception of a sensible quality will increase, rather than diminish, our inclination to explain such claims by reference to phenomenal occurrences. To put the point bluntly, there is nothing in *these* new principles that demands the purgation of the glory—the pinks and purples, the aromas and $c\sharp$s —from our entire world. The most they require is that we relocate this sensuous splendor, and the common-sense conception of a sensory experience provides the obvious hint on how this relocation is to be accomplished.*

13. A NEW GUISE FOR
THE PHYSICALIST'S APPROACH

Since the molecular theory and the anticipated success of neurophysiological speculations cannot possibly destroy the artist's world of glowing sunsets and fresh spring bloom but merely, in a sense, relocate its sensuous richness, it might seem that *any* version of physicalism is bound to be a dismal failure. It happens, however, that there is another approach the physicalist can take. The idea is this: although the sensuous phenomena that delight the artist undoubtedly do exist and will continue to be reflected in our conceptual scheme, though in a metamorphosed guise, they are nevertheless purely physical—as physical as a photon. This claim is not to be understood as a mere matter of verbal acrobatics, involving an arbitrary redefinition of the term "physical." What it affirms is that sensuous phenomena are describable without loss in terms that legitimately belong to an ideal language of physics. Properly understood, this claim is by no means trivial; in fact, in one of the two ways it may be understood, it seems to be false. Still, even without elaboration, this new version of the physicalist's claim ought to bring an immediate sense of relief. It implies that whatever exactly it is that he wants to assert, the physicalist need not at least be blind or mad, nor understood as trying to foist upon our unwilling ears

---

* It may in fact be said, if my conjecture about the development of our ordinary color concepts is sound (see Ch. VII, sect. 6), that the first step towards this relocation was actually taken within the common-sense scheme itself, when we progressed beyond proto-color to the more sophisticated concept that is internally related to *SAC, OAC,* and even to the concept of a sense impression.

the grotesque and eerie idea that the objects of our esthetic interests have always been *nothing but* colorless atoms and a disheartening void.

The claim that sensuous phenomena are really physical phenomena may be understood, then, in two different ways, one of which is more risky than the other. According to the less risky interpretation, sensuous phenomena may reasonably be called "physical" because even as commonsensically conceived they lack most of the characteristics that led traditional thinkers to classify them as mental, and because in the future scientific picture they are bound to have a place in what will be, on the whole, a physical theory of sentient organisms. As was shown in Chapters V and VI, sensory states are not modes of an immaterial spirit, nor do they possess the intentionality that is distinctive of a mental process. An image *of* a red triangle has, in other words, only a pseudo-intentionality, and the sense in which a man *has* such a thing is not to be assimilated to intelligent awareness. Again, since sensory states do, in a sense, exist in space—that is, in association with animals or men—the traditional idea that they are mental because they are nonspatial can reasonably be abandoned as well.* After all, there is no good reason to suppose that a reinterpretation of sensory states based on scientific considerations will make them less spatial than this.

It is clear that this first interpretation of the physicalist's claim does not really affect the basic issues concerning the relation between the physical and the phenomenal. On the contrary, sensuous phenomena are merely said to be physical in the sense that, as scientifically understood, they will be a species of natural process, capable of representation by terms bound up in the nomological network of a scientific theory concerned with the peculiarities of sentient creatures. Since the intuitive difference between such phenomena and those typically discussed by the physicist is not in any way denied by this appellation, and since it is not claimed that they exist anywhere else than in association with the organic sys-

* For a discussion of the points made here, see Herbert Feigl, "The 'Mental' and the 'Physical'," *op. cit.* It should be clear that phenomenal "spatial" relations, such as *s-next-to*, are simply phenomenal features of a complex sensory state. Also, it should be clear that sensory states or occurrences will have the same sort of spatial location as any purely physical *state* or *occurrence*.

tems popularly called animals, the decision to call them "physical" can be disturbing only to Cartesians, vitalists, and the like. Because, however, there obviously are other senses of "physical" that are not innocuous in this way, it will be useful to tag the term with a subscript and say, following Meehl and Sellars,[21] that an event or entity is *physical₁*, or *physical in the broad sense*, if its corresponding concept belongs to a network of scientific concepts adequate for the description, explanation, and so forth of objects and processes in space and time.

If the second interpretation of the physicalist's claim is to be more exciting than the one just discussed, a much stricter sense of "physical" must obviously be involved. In particular, a phenomenal item cannot be held to be physical if the scientist's concept of it is theoretically primitive,* applicable only to certain organic systems of a high degree of complexity, and merely hooked on to a set of physical concepts so that the group as a whole can form the heart of a conceptual scheme adequate in principle for all natural phenomena. To regard something as physical merely because it meets these conditions would simply amount to avoiding the basic problem the physicalist wants to resolve. What must be maintained, if the physicalist's thesis is to be a serious challenge to many traditional forms of mental-physical dualism, is that the phenomenal terms of the conjectured utopian conceptual scheme will not be theoretically primitive but rather definable by reference to a set of other terms which, like "photon" or "electron," are ade-

---

* That is, primitive in the sense in which common-sense *color* was shown to be primitive in Ch. VII. A primitive concept in this sense is, of course, internally related to other concepts, for wholly "simple" concepts are fictions. What is distinctive of a primitive concept is that, like *common-sense color*, it cannot be given an explicit definition. Also, it is essential to note that while "red" and similar primitive predicates of the common-sense scheme are observation terms, this is strictly an accidental fact about them. To say that a predicate is primitive in the sense in point is only to say that it is nonredundant or essential to its conceptual scheme, and to say that it is empirically significant is only to say that it plays a significant role as a descriptive term (rather than, say, a logical connective) in a conceptual scheme that is applied to reality. It often happens, as in physics, that the primitive predicates of the scheme are furthest away from language-entry positions, or that there is maximum distance between them and the terms used in observation reports. But it should not be inferred from this that they are only "partly interpreted." This whole essay is an argument against such an inference.

quate for the basic theoretical description of *inorganic* phenomena.[22] In order to give a name to this tougher sense of "physical," I
shall again follow Meehl and Sellars and say that the referent of a
term meeting this last condition is *physical₂* or *physical in the
narrow sense.*

Intuitively, the idea that phenomenal states or occurrences are
physical in the narrow sense strikes me as patently absurd. But in
order to evaluate it fairly, it is necessary to be far more exact about
the character of phenomenal terms in a conceptual scheme where
micro-entities are basic particulars. As before, I shall restrict myself
to discussing a conceptual scheme built around a molecular theory
of matter without saying exactly what this theory is (except that it
is a *particle* theory) or how it conceives the ultimate constituents
of molecules.

14. A FIRST APPROACH TO SENSA:
STATES OF NEURON CLUSTERS

The best way of working out the structure of the phenomenal
terms in point is to attend to the line of reasoning we would naturally pursue in accommodating the changes demanded by the
incorporation into the common-sense picture of the theoretical
principles just mentioned. The initial steps of this line of reasoning
have already been given. The sensible qualities of common sense
lose their primitive, occurrent status and become dispositions of
molecular aggregates to evoke certain phenomenal effects in perceivers. These "phenomenal effects" might initially be regarded
as the familiar impressions of common sense, but because perceivers
are, empirically, compound substances rather than basic particulars
(see pp. 233–234), the concept of an impression must be revamped
as well. Part of this revamping would seem entirely obvious. Since
we are now operating on the physicalist's assumption that whenever, according to common sense, a man has a sense impression,
certain clusters of cells in his central nervous system are activated
in a particular way, it would be entirely natural to regard impressions as states of those cell clusters. A man would now be understood as *having* an impression only in a derivative sense; his having

it—as we can continue to say—will now be interpreted as a matter of his cerebral cortex being in a certain state.* From the finer-grained view of molecular biology it can, of course, be said that certain molecular systems constitutive of the appropriate cell groups are in this particular state.

In order, however, to account for everything that the common-sense concept of an impression was able to account for—and indeed to accommodate the fact that common-sense men view the world in a common-sense way—we must obviously build phenomenal features into a our new conception of an impression. The natural way to do this is to conceive these new impressions, which to avoid possible confusion we can call "sensa," by analogy with their common-sense counterparts. That is, like a common-sense impression, a sensum has a variety of phenomenal features, $f_1, \ldots, f_n$, related to one another in a manner analogous to that in which the features of its common-sense counterpart are related. I say it is "natural" to conceive them this way because we want them to explain what was explainable by reference to a common-sense impression, and an analogy with, for example, newly interpreted physical surfaces would not allow this—one reason being that the latter are no longer ultimately continuous in a way that a phenomenal expanse presumably is. (I shall return to this point in section 17.)

Notice that while the notion of a sensum may be built upon the notion of a sense impression, the phenomenal features of the sensum are conceptually primitive in the new scheme in just the way that occurrent colors were primitive in the old.† This does not mean, again, that the concept of a phenomenal feature must be formed by ostension, for my whole argument demands the repudiation of this alleged mode of concept formation. All that it does mean is that

* Cf. the discussion, in sect. 2 above, of a person conceived as an embodied subject of conceptual activity. Having an impression is not a conceptual activity, but because we refer to impressions in order to explain such activities (for example, aberrant perceptual claims) it is natural to keep them tied to a unitary subject.

† That conceptual primitiveness is compatible with methodological derivativeness was a theme of my earlier discussion of color in Ch. VI, sect. 7. At that time I argued that while *color* is primitive in the common-sense picture, it may yet have developed from a cruder concept of proto-color, which had no logical relations with appearance-concepts.

the concept of such a feature is not capable of being boiled down to other concepts of the scheme, that it is not logically redundant in that scheme. And saying this involves no backhand commitment to the "simple" concepts of traditional empiricism. Although the concept of a sensum cannot be boiled down to other concepts, it still has essential relations to them; in the terminology of Chapter V, it has normic criteria. Thus, a sensum of this sort is not only a state (derivatively) of a perceiver typically brought about in certain physically describable situations, but it has phenomenal features of such a kind that sophisticated language users who "experience" it are inclined to make certain characteristic claims about either themselves or their surroundings: for instance, "I have a red after-image," "There is a red object before me," and "Something before me looks red." Because of this complicated fabric of conceptual connections, the concept of such a sensum is entirely intersubjective and applicable on a wholly public basis. Indeed, so far as the purposes of ordinary life are concerned, it would hardly differ from its common-sense counterpart. As I have indicated, the difference in meaning between the new term and the old need only show itself at a fairly rarefied level of analysis.

15. ANOTHER BREAK WITH PHYSICALISM

The conception of a sensum just outlined has two immediate consequences that bear directly on the physicalist's radical claim. The first is simply that his claim must be erroneous. The reason for this is that the concept of a sensum, since it involves the primitive notion of a phenomenal feature, cannot be wholly reduced to physical concepts in the narrow sense of the term. The second consequence is that sensa have the status of "emergents"; they are strictly emergent states of systems of neurons.[23] They have this status because, involving conceptually primitive phenomenal features, the fact that a neuron system is in a sensum-state is not entailed by basic physical$_2$ laws about the behavior of individual neurons (or their constituent molecules), together with a description of the special relations they bear to one another in this system. Thus, there is nothing about the neurophysiologist's specification of what a neuron is which, together with the statement that neurons may be connected together in complex systems, implies that various states of such systems may have phenomenal features.* Our knowledge that they occasionally do have such features is rather based on a presumed discovery of a lawful relation that happens to hold between specific systems of neurons interrelated in a certain way, on the one hand, and a peculiar, irreducible, phenomenally characterized state of such systems on the other. The same basic point holds true, *mutatis mutandis*, if one speaks of systems of molecules rather than systems of neurons. In either case we are left with emergent phenomenal states.

16. A SECOND APPROACH TO SENSA: HOBBESIAN EPIPHENOMENA

A philosopher with strong physicalist leanings can be expected to be extremely uncomfortable with the description of sensa just given, and he will naturally wish to hunt about for some alternative. It happens that such an alternative can be found; but while it is, in its way, entirely reasonable, its consequences may prove even more upsetting to a physicalist than the original description. Generally speaking, this alternative approach differs from the one already discussed in that it models sensa not on sense impressions but directly on common-sense bodies. When consistently developed, this approach yields a species of epiphenomenalism, according to which sensa are not group-states but particulars in their own right,

* This argument recalls a famous passage in Leibniz: "Supposing that there were a machine whose structure produced thought, sensation, and perception, we could conceive of it as increased in size with the same proportions until one was able to enter into its interior, as he would into a mill. Now, on going into it he would find only pieces working upon one another, but never would he find anything to explain perception"; see *The Monadology*, para. 17; trans. George Montgomery in *The Rationalists* (New York: Doubleday, Dolphin Books, 1960), p. 457. If we read "brain" for "machine" and "neuron" for "piece," we have essentially the argument in the text. Note, however, that Leibniz' argument is not the naive one that if mental states occurred in the brain, we ought to be able to see them if we opened a man's skull. The point of his argument does not rest on a simple-minded conception of perception. (In order to *see* mental states, they would no doubt have to be capable of reflecting radiation.)

which fleetingly exist, from time to time, in association with brain states. As before, this approach would not require us to stop speaking of a *man's* having a sensory experience. It would merely require that this "having" be elucidated by reference to an epiphenomenon (or a "phantasm," as Hobbes would have it) that exists in association with certain patterns of activity in regions of a man's brain. I shall not discuss this peculiar approach here,[24] but merely say that it can be worked out in an entirely consistent, reasonable way, and that it has at least two possible, or arguable, advantages over the approach mentioned earlier.

The first possible advantage of this Hobbesian approach is that it allows one to dispense with the highly puzzling notion of an emergent state in favor of another sort of basic particular which, though lawfully related to particulars of very different types (such as molecules), is in itself no more problematic than any other sort of basic item. Second, this approach also allows a more straightforward treatment of phenomenal qualities. On the group-state approach these qualities will be perspicuously described in some adverbial form, since they characterize a brain state as a sense impression characterizes a person's state; yet a straightforward adjectival description is perspicuous for epiphenomena. The choice of this type of description for epiphenomena can be defended not only on the practical ground that adverbial descriptions are clumsy and unnatural, but also on the theoretical ground that certain "objects" of our experience, which we can no longer regard as actual features of physical objects, seem very obviously to satisfy the postulates of a pure geometry themselves, and hence need not be described in the indirect manner that is distinctive of the first approach. The conception of a sensum as a group-state is, after all, a twofold analogical development from the concept of a common-sense object, which directly exemplifies geometrical features. And although we can no longer hold that *such objects* actually exist, we are not compelled to admit that no sensuous objects exist which *directly* exemplify such features.* On the contrary, it is entirely natural to say that there are such objects and that they are epiphenomena.[25]

---

* This also provides a direct and immediate means of getting "content" into a world-picture sketched largely by bare equations. Cf. the last part of sect. 18 below.

17. A BASIC FEATURE OF PHENOMENAL QUALITIES

My reason for introducing another possible conception of sensa without discussing it fully was to draw attention to a very basic consideration that blocks the physicalist's attempt to accord the phenomenal a physically derivative status. This basic consideration concerns the fact that the structured logical space of sensuous qualities characteristic of common-sense bodies is in no way broken into or shattered by the acceptance of a micro-theory of matter. By saying that this logical space is not broken into or shattered, I mean that the peculiar formal relations in which these qualities stand to one another are not in any way disrupted by the new principles. The latter merely tell us that certain sorts of things, such as molecular aggregates, cannot have such qualities, not that nothing can have these qualities at all. Since these formal interrelations are fully exemplified by features of our experience, the adoption of new basic principles about the constitution of matter can only require us to regard these interrelated features as qualifying different items. Because these formal relationships appear in two guises in the common-sense picture from which we start our theoretical forays—namely, as features of physical objects or as derivatively conceived, adverbial features of the inner states I have called "impressions"—their relocation in a scientific picture of micro-things could naturally appear in two guises as well: either as features of fleeting particulars or as adverbial features of states of micro-groups. Since a relocation of this kind is not a reduction to what is narrowly physical, in either of these latter guises the features in point will continue to resist a classification as physical$_2$.

In connection with this last point, it is worth pondering a fundamental feature of visual impressions that not only blocks the efforts of the physicalist but adds a certain plausibility to the Cartesian approach. I allude to what might be called the phenomenally dense character of visual impressions. I have already explained how the continuity of common-sense color is incompatible with the gappiness of a molecular surface, but it is important to see that the same fundamental difficulty arises when we consider the relation of a phenomenal expanse to sets of neurons or aggregates of molecules.[26]

Whether we are speaking of a common-sense visual surface or the s-colored character of an afterimage, we are speaking of something that is ultimately continuous in at least a quasi-spatial manner: every region, however small, that counts as a subregion of the surface or the image, is itself colored or s-colored.* Groups of particles, whether neurons or molecules, are not, however, continuous in this way; and this means that the state of an array of such things, to the extent that it is not an emergent one of the sort already described, cannot itself constitute a phenomenal expanse. The states of the members of a gappy array simply cannot add up to an ultimate "spatial" continuity of the sort in question.

One might, of course, be tempted to rebut the above consequence by relying on such analogies from common life as the continuity of printed color that is constituted by a field of tiny color dots closely packed together. But analogies of this sort are entirely useless to the physicalist, since they lead at best to Cartesianism. For by hypothesis the redness of the dotty surface is *not* continuous; it is really (according to common sense) a continuity of red-and-paper color, which merely looks continuously red when viewed from some distance away. Since this analogy involves a distinction between appearance and reality, it can be nothing but a troublemaker for the physicalist, for it points to a distinction between a gappy molecular reality and a continuous sensuous appearance—and this immediately yields the Cartesian idea that phenomenal expanses are confused awarenesses of physical structures.† Consequently, if we do not want to tread a Cartesian path, it is best to ignore all analogies with common-sense perceptual situations and try to meet the difficulty in some other way.

It might seem that the obvious approach to take here is to argue that phenomenal expanses are not constituted by the states of particles in a side-by-side array, but by a synchronized activity of the

* I say "in at least a quasi-spatial manner" because if one interprets the afterimage as a group-state rather than as an epiphenomenon, one cannot say that it *directly* exemplifies geometrical features.

† A similar difficulty arises with suggestions based on electronic models, according to which one part of the brain may be said to "scan" another. If the theory of the brain is a particle theory, then the expanse that somehow results from the scanning is still at odds with the gappy character of the scanner.

whole array.* Unfortunately, this approach fares no better than the one just considered. The relevant activity of the whole array can be nothing other than the group-state already discussed, the phenomenal features of which are emergent, or else a state that in some way "gives rise to" an expanse, which leads us back to epiphenomenalism. Since in a particle theory phenomenal expanses must be associated with complex states of particle systems that either are or, granting emergence, are not definable in terms of the states of individual particles, it appears that if we have no special reason for accepting Cartesianism—and it is hard to see how theoretical science could provide such a reason—we are inevitably left with the alternatives previously described.

18. A FINAL APPROACH TO THE PHENOMENAL-PHYSICAL RELATION

The argument of the last four sections may be taken to have the general consequence that in any conceptual scheme in which micro-particles are basic particulars, there will be an awkward disparity between sensuous phenomena and physical$_2$ aggregates—a gap that, whether in the name of emergent group-features or fleeting epiphenomena, must inevitably be bridged by laws having the disquieting character of "nomological danglers." The question naturally arises, then, whether the basic particulars of physical theory need be thing-like and whether, if they need not, the disparity just mentioned is perhaps ultimately escapable.

To anyone familiar with the ins and outs of twentieth-century philosophy, the posing of these questions will immediately recall the persistent attempts of Bertrand Russell and others to deny the first and, by blocking out a "pure process" picture of the world, to affirm the second.[27] The significance of attempts along these lines has, of course, been lost to subsequent philosophers whose intellec-

---

* In his *Analysis of Matter, op. cit.,* p. 281, Russell attempted to reconcile phenomenal continuity with a physical process involving discrete physical elements by considering the analogy of the cinema, where rapid, stacatto movements of distinct shapes are seen as one shape in slow, continuous movement. It is clear, however, that an analogy of this kind can only support Cartesianism, since it involves the distinction, fatal for the physicalist, between appearance (to the senses) and reality.

tual horizons are limited by common-sense concerns. But it has left
its stamp on the work of Wilfrid Sellars, who has recently insisted
that, properly understood, there are no insurmountable *a priori*
difficulties with a "pure-process" approach.[28] He has even gone on
to suggest—in a dark but pregnant passage—that if particles could
come to be regarded, by physicists, as "singularities in a space-time
continuum," then we should no longer be left with an inescapable
problem about nomological danglers. On the contrary, the alternative would then be open of saying that

> . . . although for many purposes the central nervous system can be
> construed without loss as a complex system of physical particles,
> *when it comes to an adequate understanding of the relation of sensory
> consciousness* to neurophysiological process, we must penetrate to the
> non-particulate foundation of the particulate image, and recognize
> that in this non-particulate image the qualities of sense are a dimension
> of natural process which, when 'cut up' into particles in terms of those
> features which are the least common denominators of physical proc-
> ess—present in inorganic as well as organic systems alike—become
> the complex system of particles which, in the current scientific image,
> *is* the central nervous system.[29]

Although the general drift of Sellars' complex remark ought to
be reasonably clear in view of the preceding discussion, a few key
points must be kept in mind if its full significance is to be appreciated. First, while Sellars is careful to say that the theoretical development he mentions is merely a possibility, which could be realized, if at all, only by a virtually utopian science of sentient
organisms, it is important to realize that it is not, even as a suggestion, utterly visionary or mad. What is distinctive of the development he envisions is the substitution of "events" for things (or
particles) as basic particulars of the scientific frame. And this substitution is by no means intrinsically improbable. It is by now a
commonplace that billiard-ball interpretations of subatomic particles are no longer taken seriously, and popular accounts of the
dematerialization of matter and of the relativistic world of events
in space-time already foreshadow the continuum that Sellars describes. Thus, while the basic entities of contemporary physics still
seem to be thing-like in at least their formal structure, the possibility
that Sellars describes is not so visionary and unrealistic that it is not
worth very serious consideration, especially by those whose chief

attraction with "materialism" is that it allows them to dispense with nomological danglers.

Second, it is essential to appreciate that the "events" that are basic in the suggested picture are of a radically different logical status from the events of a particle theory or of everyday discourse.* The latter events, unlike the former, are largely derivative objects: like Nero's fiddling or Rome's burning, they are typically conceived as activities of, or happenings to, objects of other types, which are continuants.[30] Precisely the opposite is true of pure-process "events": they are basic, and in relation to them the things or so-called continuants of the scheme have a derivative status, being analyzed as systems of these "events." As Bertrand Russell once put it, speaking of electrons in a world of process:

> . . . there is a certain relation R which sometimes holds between events, and when it holds between x and y, x and y are said to be events in the biography of the same electron. If x belongs to the field of R, "the electron to which x belongs" will mean the relation R with its field limited to the terms belonging to the R-family of x; and the R-family of x consists of x together with the terms which have the relation R to x and the terms to which x has the relation R. "This electron" will mean "the electron to which this belongs." In order to mention some particular electron, we must be able to mention some event connected with it, e.g., the scintillation when it hits a certain screen. Thus, instead of saying "the event z happened to the electron E" we shall say . . . "z belongs to the R-family of x."[31]

The significance of this last paragraph for contemporary battles in ontology is at least threefold. First, the arguments of Strawson[32] and others that events are mainly derivative objects incapable of serving as basic particulars do not strictly cut against the suggestions of Sellars and Russell. The reason for this has, in fact, already been given: it is that the "events" in question here are not events in the ordinary sense, but rather "events" in an extraordinary sense, whose features are to be spelled out in a futuristic science of natural process in space-time. Second, the frequent claim of contemporary philosophers that in order to make "identifying references" to the items of our world, we must have common points of reference to which we can *repeatedly* appeal,[33] need in no way be

---

* I shall distinguish these exotic "events" from the usual variety by flanking them with scare quotes.

denied by a defender of pure process. The persisting objects of reference admittedly needed for intersubjective discourse may be interpreted as sets of events just as easily as persisting substances. After all, the persisting objects of common sense are not entirely immutable; they constantly undergo changes of state. And this sort of unity and diversity is adequately captured by an "event" interpretation. As Russell put the point in 1927, "when we throw over 'substance' we preserve the causal chain, substituting the unity of the causal process for material [i.e. substantial] identity."[34] Finally, since an event ontology may, in this way, include persisting things as derivative objects—that is, as objects definable in terms of "event" sequences—a pure-process picture is not really as bizarre as it might appear. On the contrary, it may, on most counts, differ from the "thing" picture only in the way that different axiomatizations of the same geometry will differ.[35] The reason for this is that the step-by-step procedure by which events are, as it were, constructed from facts about changing things is just the reverse of the procedure by which changing things are, as it were, constructed from facts about "events." Consequently, apart from questions about which terms are to be understood as conceptually primitive, the basic pattern of inferences concerning "events" and things will be exactly the same in the pure-process and the substantial-thing pictures, and the differences between these pictures, at least when one is talking about molar objects, need only show themselves at a fairly rarefied level of analysis.

In view of this sort of symmetry between thing and "event" ontologies, one might wonder how the adoption of the latter sort could possibly help with the problem of nomological danglers. The answer to this is that the structure of space-time might be such that not all "events" would fall neatly into the Russellian *R*-families that constitute the persisting things of particle theories. The particulate counterpart to these *R*-families is, after all, a gappy structure, not a plenum; so if we wish to avoid the nomological danglers that are inevitable with such structures, we shall have to pin our hopes on the possibility that not every event will fall into a distinguishable *R*-family. This possibility would allow us to say that particle theories, since they can in effect capture only those "events" of the continuum that fall into such families, give us only an approximately accurate picture of the world, one reflecting only major structural features, and that this lack of ultimate faithfulness is what led us to suppose, at a less sophisticated stage of our theoretical development, that our world involves an irreducible dualism of gappy aggregates and continuous *qualia*. This dualism would, that is to say, be dispelled as an illusion, arising from the intrinsic inability of a particulate image to represent a continuous reality of punctiform "events."

But supposing that reality is a continuum of the kind described, just how do sensuous *qualia* fit into the picture? Are we to think of physical "events" as Minkowskian slices of phenomenal fields? In order to appreciate the proper answers to these questions, it is useful to reflect on what Russell called the "abstractness" of physics. It is a very familiar fact that basic theoretical entities are mainly specified by reference to their structure, to those of their features that are describable in the language of mathematics. For most theoretical objects or events, our knowledge is entirely limited to the character of this structure, and we cannot, as William Kneale put it, "even conjecture what the content is that embodies the structure."[36] What we in fact suppose, in science, is that a set of things embodies a certain mathematical structure, and that what lacks a certain structure cannot exist in a certain region. Kneale continues:

> That transcendent [i.e. theoretical] hypotheses are concerned *only* with structure has often been overlooked in the past, because scientists and philosophers have mistakenly allowed themselves to slip some imaginative elements, such as perceptible hardness, into their concepts of the objects mentioned in the hypotheses. Berkeley pointed out quite correctly that the hypothetical entities of the physicists were unimaginable, but he concluded wrongly that because they were unimaginable they were inconceivable.[37]

A mathematical structure cannot, of course, exist in nature without content, for it is only in virtue of having certain intrinsic features that a thing or process can exemplify such a structure. Yet so far as our theories are concerned, this nonformal empirical content is not explicitly brought into the picture at all.*

---

* This brings out another reason why sensa cannot be wholly reduced to physical$_2$ events and processes: the latter are conceived so abstractly as to be bereft of this sort of content, while the content of the former is actually *presented* in our experience.

Now, there is certainly no reason to think that the "content" of scientifically conceived inorganic processes is sensuous, of the sort involved in the experiences of sentient creatures. On the contrary, we have the best of reasons to suppose that sensuous *qualia* exist only in connection with organic structures of a high degree of complexity. (These reasons are, of course, largely commonsensical, but there is nothing in theory that cuts against them.) Hence if any natural process has sensuous *qualia* as, in some sense, an intrinsic feature, such a process is no doubt to be found in the four-dimensional counterpart of an active nervous system. A process of this kind will of course be enormously complex, involving *R*-families of "events" corresponding to countless millions of micro-particles. The exact nature of such a process is, however, something to be ascertained by a utopian theory of sentient organisms. So far as philosophy is concerned, one can only say that there are no logical difficulties with the idea of such a process, and that if it finds a place in the science of the future, we shall no longer have a problem with nomological danglers. The last word on the sensuous-physical relation is thus a scientific one; philosophy can tell us where to look for it, but not what it will be.

X

Conclusion

Philosophy, as Plato saw, is essentially a dialectical study, and after more than twenty centuries of philosophical debate it is no exaggeration to say that any serious philosophical claim can be adequately appreciated only in relation to its traditional alternatives. The views of mind and nature defended here go hand-in-hand with a particular conception of empirical knowledge, one developed as an explicit contrast to the "foundations" picture distinctive of traditional empiricism. From the standpoint of this latter picture of knowledge, which is widely accepted even today, the claims I have made concerning mind and nature are highly dubious. For this reason, a brief critical review of the main consequences of this traditional conception of knowledge will provide a useful foil by which to illuminate the central argument of preceding chapters.

As the label implies, the root idea of the foundations picture is that there is a particular type of knowledge that provides the ultimate foundation on which the rest of our empirical knowledge is built. This basic type of knowledge, since it supports the whole of what we know, is not only regarded as maximally certain but it is commonly held to be immune to any sort of rational revision. We may indeed revise our ideas of what we can infer from this basis, but the basis itself can never change. To the extent that we have isolated this basis successfully, we are securely placed on epistemic bedrock.

Most of the quarrels between philosophers accepting this picture of empirical knowledge, and most of the fundamental problems they explicitly recognized, arose from two main questions: "How is the basic level of knowledge determined?" and "What forms of inference may legitimately be employed in developing the epistemic consequences of this basic knowledge?" As I have indicated, empiricists usually answered the first question by saying that basic knowledge is essentially indubitable and concerns observational data directly evident to an observer. The standard answer to the second question is that we are entitled to develop the epistemic consequences of our basic knowledge either by deduction or by a form of instantial induction. Deduction, although it preserves the certainty of our basic premises, does not really increase the range of what we already know; it rather articulates this knowledge, making it more explicit. Induction does allow us to reach beyond the level of what is immediately known, though at the cost of introducing uncertainty. What, more specifically, it allows us to do is *generalize* from what is already known. If, for example, it is evident that items of certain kinds have invariably been correlated in a certain way, then we may normally infer that such items are probably always so correlated.

For hundreds of years, empiricists regarded the foundation of empirical knowledge as essentially psychological. Whether they were scientific atomists, phenomenalists, or even, like Berkeley, subjective idealists, they all tended to agree that what is known immediately, intuitively, and with maximum certainty, is for each observer his own psychological states. Not only was a *theory* of mind largely unnecessary—to know what mind is, you have only to take a close inner look—but no purely scientific considerations could ever shake a man's conception of what he directly experienced. The subject that was intrinsically problematic for these thinkers was the nature of the alleged external world. Tending to restrict themselves to instantial induction as the basic form of nondeductive reasoning, those who were consistent naturally ended up with skepticism, solipsism, or some form of phenomenalism. This outcome was virtually inevitable, because if you can never directly experience a connection between the data of sense and an alleged external cause, you can never infer such a connection by generalization from what you do directly experience.

The horrors of solipsism and the futilities of phenomenalism made Wittgenstein's "private language" argument a straw worth grasping at, and his later work contributed heavily in prompting philosophers to seek a new foundation of knowledge in what is publicly observable. Those accepting this alternative naturally argued that observational knowledge of an intersubjective sort may be wholly certain and unchallengeable. Since many of them also accepted the traditional assumption that the only justifiable form of inductive reasoning is at bottom instantial induction, they naturally fell into the same difficulty respecting the connection between what is publicly observable and what is not that earlier empiricists had respecting the connection between what is subjectively apparent and what is not. This difficulty inevitably led them to defend behavioristic interpretations of so-called subjective experience and operationalist or instrumentalist interpretations of theoretical science. Their basic assumption regarding the foundation of knowledge also required them to insist upon the unchallengeable status ordinary concepts such as *physical object, sensible quality, and person.*

In preceding chapters detailed arguments were directed against all of these consequences of the foundations picture. It was also maintained that any view based on this picture can be expected to possess crucial limitations of two related sorts. One is that the legitimacy of certain kinds of knowledge—whether it concerns the external world, the mental states of others, or such theoretical entities as photons—will inevitably be ruled out or at least attenuated by some reductive form of interpretation. Views of this sort are thus excessively restrictive regarding the possible objects of knowledge: they inevitably limit rather than increase our intellectual horizons. The other limitation is that views based on the foundations picture are far too conservative in holding fast to favorite concepts. Whether the foundation of knowledge is said to involve immediate experience, observable behavior, or common-sense bodies, the basic concepts applicable to the foundation are always regarded as logically immune to rational revision. This attitude is essentially obscurantist, because it prevents theoretical advances from ever changing our conception of what we are observing, sensing, or doing when we think. In opposition to all of this, my argument has been that the entire range of our empirical knowledge cannot possibly be developed from a given set of basic concepts, no matter what they may be. As we increase our knowledge we rather generate new concepts, and in generating them we are constantly forced to revise the ones we started out with.

The root argument underlying my attack on all forms of the foundations picture can be set down very simply. The acceptability of any supposed basic claim presupposes a set of background assumptions with reference to which the claim is to be understood and evaluated. If, for convenience, all putative basic claims may be called "observation claims," a little reflection will show that the associated background assumptions will concern three things: the nature of the observer, the character of the objects observed, and the particular means of observation. Philosophers have admittedly not been explicitly aware of all of these assumptions, but they are nevertheless lurking in the background of their arguments. No philosopher has ever held that an arbitrary claim ought to be accepted merely because it is advanced with confidence. Basic claims are supposed to be certain just because they are a special sort of claim—because they concern a special kind of object, and because they are arrived at in a special way by a certain kind of agent. Thus, for most traditional empiricists, a basic claim compels a subject's assent because it registers his immediate awareness of an object whose *esse* is, for him, *percipi*; and for many recent thinkers, a basic claim compels our assent because it is spontaneously made by a responsible person who has proved himself a reliable observer respecting the kind of thing his claim concerns (it might be a brown pig).

A special feature of the background assumptions presupposed by the acceptance of an observation claim is that they cannot all be directly justified by observation. Since one of the assumptions presupposed by the acceptability of any observation claim is that there is at least one reliable observer (whether he is conceived as man, spirit, or Humean bundle), there is no plausibility to the idea that all of these assumptions are necessary truths. This means that the body of assumptions relative to which a basic claim is accepted as true must be capable of some kind of inductive (or empirical) support. Such support obviously cannot be given by instantial induction, for all forms of instantial induction presuppose such assumptions. Since the certainty of an empirical claim is conditional on the certainty of the assumptions it presupposes, it follows that the acceptability of an observation claim presupposes the acceptability of some nonclassical form of inductive reasoning. This, however, is directly contrary to the foundations picture of empirical knowledge.

In Chapter V it was argued that our basic assumptions concerning observation—let alone such pervasive assumptions as that involving the regularity of nature—gain an indirect support from the success we have in operating with them. There is simply no way, it was argued, to guarantee this success in advance. Not only *may* we encounter difficulties with our basic assumptions, but we have actually done so since the very dawn of human intelligence.* A very important example of the breakdown of certain basic assumptions was developed in detail toward the end of Chapter VII. It was shown just how common-sense assumptions concerning the perception of sensible qualities such as color become subjected to revision as the result of accepting a new theory of matter. This example was developed to emphasize the important truth that when our basic assumptions are revised, the significance of even our observation claims may drastically change: we may end up by reinterpreting our ideas of what we are actually observing. The possibility of this reinterpretation brings out another error of the foundations picture, namely its assumption that the concepts involved in basic claims are logically immune to rational revision.

At the end of Chapter VII it was suggested that changes in certain of our background assumptions may even require a reinterpretation of the concepts used in introspection. This possibility turned out to be unusually enlightening because it put us in a position to appreciate how mental concepts proper could be the partly norma-

---

* For a useful discussion of how our basic assumptions regarding nature have changed from the time of the ancient Greeks (when the world was conceived as a living animal whose behavior is to be explained by final causes) up to the present, see R. G. Collingwood, *The Idea of Nature* (Oxford: Clarendon Press, 1945).

tive, socially inherited products of centuries of cultural development. In regarding these concepts as either innate furniture of the
human mind or as something automatically developed in each man's
solitary consciousness, traditional philosophers were singularly unsuccessful in accounting for their peculiar intentionality or reference, their formal interrelations with other concepts, and their
specific role in guiding behavior. To perceive clearly that the concept of thinking is really as artificial—as man-made, normative, and
subject to change—as the concept of a checkmate, is to take a giant
step toward resolving some of the oldest issues in the philosophy of
mind. In particular, to appreciate the essentially normative rather
than empirical character of mental reference—or of the "intentionality" of belief, purpose, and intention—is to understand a basic
truth hidden to most traditional eyes, namely that so far as the
brute facts of nature are concerned, reality need not be viewed as
divided into two utterly distinct realms of matter and spirit, extension and consciousness, or mechanism and purpose.

Since theoretical science constantly generates new theoretical
principles concerning the nature of matter, brains, and even mind,
it follows that some of the oldest questions of philosophy—relating
to what we actually observe or what we ourselves are really like—
can be successfully answered only by reference to scientific developments, actual and sometimes even potential. For this reason, the
discussion of mind and nature given in Chapter IX went far beyond
the confines of common sense, and introduced ideas that may seem
strange or grotesque to a philosopher who, in accord with the fashion of the day, is largely content to restrict his attention to the
analysis of ordinary discourse. Common-sense concepts and the
logic of ordinary discourse deserve, of course, to be analyzed and
understood. Yet merely to understand ordinary ideas and ordinary
language is to be in a position to make only a very limited contribu-
tion to such age-old and philosophically basic problems as that
concerning the relation between mind and body. This latter problem, like the traditional problem of perception, arises less from a
confusion about ordinary language (as is often alleged) than from
the attempt to understand the puzzling relation between ordinary
and scientific ideas or principles. To resolve this problem one must
accordingly attend to ideas and principles of both sorts, paying
special attention to basic issues regarding theory construction, in-

ductive logic, and scientific methodology generally. To achieve full success in resolving this ancient problem one must in fact attempt to do what traditional philosophers at their best have always done: to work out an imaginative picture of man and nature in which the basic elements of truth in both ordinary and theoretical claims can find their proper place.

notes

Chapter I

1. See G. A. Paul, "Is There a Problem About Sense Data?" *Proc. Arist. Soc.*, Supp. Vol. XV (1936); repr. in A. G. N. Flew, ed., *Logic and Language*, First Series (Oxford: Blackwell, 1951), pp. 101–116. For more general discussion, see Roderick M. Chisholm, "The Theory of Appearing," in M. Black, ed., *Philosophical Analysis* (Ithaca, N.Y.: Cornell University Press, 1950), pp. 97–112.

2. The classic statement of this point of view is found in Gilbert Ryle, *The Concept of Mind* (London: Hutchinson, 1949).

3. G. A. Paul, in Flew, *Logic and Language*, p. 115.

4. See esp. Maurice Mandelbaum, *Philosophy, Science, and Sense Perception* (Baltimore: Johns Hopkins University Press, 1964), and R. Harré, *Matter and Method* (London: Macmillan, 1964).

5. On this see, e.g., J. L. Austin, *Sense and Sensibilia*, G. Warnock, ed. (Oxford: Clarendon Press, 1962), Ch. 3.

6. See e.g., Martin Lean, *Sense Perception and Matter* (London: Routledge & Kegan Paul, 1953), pp. 17ff.

7. See Gilbert Ryle, *Dilemmas* (Cambridge, Eng.: Cambridge University Press, 1954), Ch. 5.

8. This may be called the orthodox view of contemporary methodology. Its classic statement is given in Rudolf Carnap, "Testability and Meaning," *Phil. Sci.*, III (1936), 420–460. Although Carnap did not himself say that the language of observation is the language of everyday life, the examples of observation terms that he cited were ordinary terms such as "red." It has, however, become a commonplace, especially in the work of philosophers in-

fluenced by the later Wittgenstein, that theoretical terms gain meaning only by coordination with the language of everyday life. On this see J. J. C. Smart, "Theory Construction," *Philo. & Pheno. Res.*, XII (1951); repr. in A. G. N. Flew, ed., *Logic and Language*, Second Series (Oxford: Blackwell, 1953), pp. 222–242.

9. On this see Ernest Nagel, *The Structure of Science* (New York: Harcourt, Brace and World, 1961), pp. 120–121, and Arthur Pap, *An Introduction to the Philosophy of Science* (New York: Free Press of Glencoe, 1962), Ch. 3.

10. See Nagel, *The Structure of Science*, pp. 129–140.

11. David Hume, *A Treatise of Human Nature*, L. A. Selby-Bigge, ed. (Oxford: Clarendon Press, 1888), I, iv, 6.

12. See Ludwig Wittgenstein, *Philosophical Investigations*, trans. G. E. M. Anscombe (Oxford: Blackwell, 1953), *passim*, and Norman Malcolm, "Review of Wittgenstein's *Philosophical Investigations*," *Phil. Rev.*, LXIII (1954), 530–559; repr. in Malcolm, *Knowledge and Certainty* (Englewood Cliffs, N.J.: Prentice-Hall, 1963), pp. 96–129.

13. For a nontechnical exposition of Russell's theory of descriptions, see his *Introduction to Mathematical Philosophy* (London: Allen & Unwin, 1919), Ch. 16. The technical development of the theory can be found in A. N. Whitehead and Bertrand Russell, *Principia Mathematica*, 2nd edn., Vol. 1 (Cambridge, Eng.: Cambridge University Press, 1927), *14.

14. The phrase is Nelson Goodman's; see his *Fact, Fiction, and Forecast* (Cambridge, Mass.: Harvard University Press, 1955), p. 37, where references to the relevant literature can be found.

15. See such works as Karl Popper, *The Logic of Scientific Discovery* (New York: Basic Books, 1959) and *Conjectures and Refutations* (New York: Basic Books, 1962); Steven F. Barker, *Induction and Hypothesis* (Ithaca, N.Y.: Cornell University Press, 1957); Grover Maxwell, "The Ontological Status of Theoretical Entities," in H. Feigl and G. Maxwell, eds., *Minnesota Studies in the Philosophy of Science*, Vol. 3 (Minneapolis: University of Minnesota Press, 1962), 3–27; Paul K. Feyerabend, "Explanation, Reduction, and Empiricism," in *Minnesota Studies in the Philosophy of Science*, Vol. 3, 28–97; and Wilfrid Sellars, "The Language of Theories," in H. Feigl and G. Maxwell, eds., *Current Issues in the Philosophy of Science* (New York: Holt, Rinehart & Winston, 1961), pp. 57–77, and in Sellars, *Science, Perception, and Reality* (London: Routledge & Kegan Paul, 1964), pp. 106–126.

16. See Grover Maxwell, "Philosophy and the Causal Theory of Perception," *Graduate Review of Philosophy*, VI (1964), 9–21, and also "Remarks on Perception and Theoretical Entities," in R. Colodney, ed., *Pittsburgh Studies in the Philosophy of Science*, Vol. 4 (Pittsburgh: University of Pittsburgh Press, 1967).

Chapter II

1. See Ludwig Wittgenstein, *Philosophical Investigations*, trans. G. E. M. Anscombe (Oxford: Blackwell, 1953), Pt. I, secs. 243–270, and also Norman

Malcolm, "Review of Wittgenstein's *Philosophical Investigations*," *Phil. Rev.*, LXIII (1954), 530–559; repr. in Malcolm, *Knowledge and Certainty* (Englewood Cliffs, N.J.: Prentice-Hall, 1963), pp. 96–129.

2. A similar experiment is described in Donald O. Hebb, *Organization of Behavior* (New York: John Wiley, 1949), p. 36.

3. His likely behavior is verbal hesitance. See Hebb, *ibid.*

4. Cited in Hebb, *ibid.*, p. 32.

5. E.g., by Norman Malcolm, "Knowledge of Other Minds," *Journ. Phil.*, LV (1958), 977; repr. in *Knowledge and Certainty*, p. 140.

6. See Malcolm, "Review of Wittgenstein," *Phil. Rev.*, p. 532; *Knowledge and Certainty*, p. 99.

7. See Wittgenstein, Pt. I, secs. 256–272, and also Malcolm, "Review of Wittgenstein," *Phil. Rev.*, pp. 532ff; *Knowledge and Certainty*, pp. 98ff.

8. See Wittgenstein, Pt. I, sect. 354.

9. See Rogers Albritton, "On Wittgenstein's Use of the Term 'Criterion'," *Journ. Phil.*, LVI (1959), 845–857.

10. See Wilfrid Sellars, "Some Reflections on Language Games," *Phil. Sci.*, XXI (1954), 204–228; repr. with changes in Sellars, *Science, Perception, and Reality* (London: Routledge & Kegan Paul, 1964), pp. 321–350.

11. See Michael Scriven, "The Logic of Criteria," *Journ. Phil.*, LVI (1959), 857–868.

12. G. E. Moore, "Proof of an External World," *Proc. of British Academy*, XXV (1939); repr. in Moore, *Philosophical Papers* (London: Allen & Unwin, 1959), pp. 127–150.

13. See Milton H. Erickson, "Experimental Demonstrations of the Psychopathology of Everyday Life," in S. S. Tompkins and H. A. Murray, eds., *Contemporary Psychopathology* (Cambridge, Mass.: Harvard University Press, 1944), pp. 524–525.

14. Here I am indebted to Hector-Neri Castañeda, "The Private Language Argument," in C. D. Rollins, ed., *Knowledge and Experience* (Pittsburgh: University of Pittsburgh Press, 1963), pp. 88–105.

15. See Wittgenstein, Pt. I, sect. 654.

16. See Max Black, "Notes on the Meaning of 'Rule'," *Theoria*, XXIV (1958), 107–136; repr. in Black, *Models and Metaphors* (Ithaca, N.Y.: Cornell University Press, 1962), pp. 95–139.

17. A clear discussion of modern theoretical semantics can be found in Richard M. Martin, *Truth and Denotation* (Chicago: University of Chicago Press, 1958).

18. This view seems to be defended by Stuart Hampshire in *Thought and Action* (London: Chatto & Windus, 1959), Ch. 1.

19. See R. G. Collingwood, *The Principles of Art* (Oxford: Clarendon Press, 1938), p. 227.

20. Defenders of Wittgenstein's argument generally admit this point; see Malcolm, "Review of Wittgenstein," *Phil. Rev.*, p. 544; *Knowledge and Certainty*, p. 112.

21. See Willard Van Orman Quine, *Word and Object* (Cambridge, Mass.: John Wiley and M.I.T. Press, 1960), esp. pp. 53, 77.

22. This *mot* occurs somewhere in John Wisdom, *Other Minds* (Oxford: Blackwell, 1952).

Chapter III

1. A clear and brief example of how these two theories were tacitly blended together by traditional empiricists can be found in George Berkeley's discussion of abstract ideas in his *Principles of Human Knowledge*, Introduction, secs. 6–9; in A. C. Fraser, ed., *Berkeley's Complete Works*, Vol. I (Oxford: Clarendon Press, 1801).

2. This view is defended, e.g., by Arthur Pap, *Semantics and Necessary Truth* (New Haven, Conn.: Yale University Press, 1958), p. 239.

3. For a discussion of what is essentially the argument that will follow, see Norman Malcolm, "Review of Wittgenstein's *Philosophical Investigations*," *Phil. Rev.*, LXIII (1954), 538; repr. in Malcolm, *Knowledge and Certainty* (Englewood Cliffs, N.J.: Prentice-Hall, 1963), p. 105f.

4. See Ludwig Wittgenstein, "The Blue Book," in *The Blue and Brown Books* (Oxford: Blackwell, 1958), p. 46.

5. A detailed discussion of the following argument can be found in Bruce Aune, "The Problem of Other Minds," *Phil. Rev.*, LXX (1961), 320–339.

6. See Moritz Schlick, "Form and Content," in *Gesammelte Aufsätze* (Vienna: Gerold, 1938), Ch. 8.

7. See William Kneale, *Probability and Induction* (Oxford: Clarendon Press, 1949), pp. 85–86, for the important objection that while the phenomenalist's screeds would actually have to be infinitely long, no rule for constructing them has ever been provided.

8. On this see H. H. Price, *Hume's Theory of the External World* (Oxford: Clarendon Press, 1940), Ch. 5.

9. This confusion is noted by Wilfrid Sellars in "Phenomenalism," in Sellars, *Science Perception, and Reality* (London: Routledge & Kegan Paul, 1964), pp. 76–84.

10. See also sect. II of Wilfrid Sellars, "The Language of Theories," in H. Feigl and G. Maxwell, eds., *Current Issues in the Philosophy of Science* (New York: Holt, Rinehart & Winston, 1961), pp. 60–68; repr. in *Science, Perception, and Reality*, pp. 109–118.

11. Otto Neurath, "Protokollsätz," *Erkenntnis*, III (1932), 204–214.

Chapter IV

1. See T. E. Hulme, "Bergson's Theory of Art," *Speculations* (New York: Harcourt, Brace, 1924), pp. 141–170.

2. Norman Malcolm, *Dreaming* (London: Routledge & Kegan Paul, 1959), p. 15.

3. See R. G. Collingwood, *The Principles of Art* (Oxford: Clarendon Press, 1937), Ch. VI.

4. Norman Malcolm, "Review of Wittgenstein's *Philosophical Investiga-*

tions," *Phil. Rev.*, LXIII (1954), 542ff; repr. in Malcolm, *Knowledge and Certainty* (Englewood Cliffs, N.J.: Prentice-Hall, 1963), pp. 110ff.

5. *Ibid.*: *Phil. Rev.*, p. 541; *Knowledge and Certainty*, p. 109.

6. *Ibid.*

7. *Ibid.*

8. This point is nicely worked out in Wilfrid Sellars, "Some Reflections on Language Games," *Phil. Sci.*, XXI (1954), 204–228; repr., with changes, in Sellars, *Science, Perception, and Reality* (London: Routledge & Kegan Paul, 1964), pp. 321–350.

9. Malcolm, *Dreaming*, p. 10.

10. To be found in Malcolm, "Knowledge of Other Minds," *Journ. Phil.*, LV (1958), 969–978; repr. in *Knowledge and Certainty*, pp. 130–140.

11. Ludwig Wittgenstein, *Philosophical Investigations*, trans. G. E. M. Anscombe (Oxford: Blackwell, 1953), Pt. I, sect. 246.

12. See J. L. Austin, "Other Minds," *Proc. Arist. Soc.*, Supp. Vol. XX (1946), 168; repr. in G. Warnock and J. O. Urmson, eds., *Philosophical Papers* (Oxford: Clarendon Press, 1961), p. 64.

13. See Bruce Aune, "Knowing and Merely Thinking," *Phil. Stud.*, XII 1961), 53–58.

14. Wittgenstein, *Philosophical Investigations*, Pt. I, sect. 246.

15. In Malcolm, "Knowledge of Other Minds," *Journ. Phil.*, p. 577; *Knowledge and Certainty*, p. 139.

Chapter V

1. An astute critical survey of the literature can be found in Arthur Pap, "Disposition Concepts and Extensional Logic," in H. Feigl, M. Scriven, and G. Maxwell, eds., *Minnesota Studies in the Philosophy of Science*, Vol. 2 (Minneapolis: University of Minnesota Press, 1958), 196–224.

2. The problematic locution "logically adequate basis" is taken from P. F. Strawson; see his *Individuals* (London: Methuen, 1959), p. 106.

3. Michael Scriven, "The Logic of Criteria," *Journ. Phil.*, LVI (1959), 857–868.

4. Norman Malcolm, "Review of Wittgenstein's *Philosophical Investigations*," *Phil. Rev.*, LXIII (1954), 545; repr. in Malcolm, *Knowledge and Certainty* (Englewood Cliffs, N.J.: Prentice-Hall, 1963), p. 113.

5. *Ibid.*

6. *Ibid.*: *Phil. Rev.*, p. 546; *Knowledge and Certainty*, p 115.

7. *Ibid.*: *Phil. Rev.*, p. 547; *Knowledge and Certainty*, p. 116.

8. Scriven, *loc. cit.*

9. Norman Malcolm, *Dreaming* (London: Routledge & Kegan Paul, 1959), p. 61.

10. *Ibid.*, p. 59.

11. On this see R. G. Collingwood, *An Essay on Metaphysics* (Oxford: Clarendon Press, 1940), pp. 285–344, and Wilfrid Sellars, "Fatalism and Determinism," in Keith Lehrer, ed., *Freedom and Determinism* (New York: Random House, 1966), esp. pp. 141–150.

12. See Karl Popper, *The Logic of Scientific Discovery* (New York: Basic Books, 1959), esp. secs. 31, 34, and *Conjectures and Refutations* (New York: Basic Books, 1962), Chs. 10, 11.

13. For a discussion of these borderline cases, where men claim to feel pains that do not hurt, see Kurt Baier, "Pains," *Australasian Journal of Philosophy*, XL (1962), 1–23.

Chapter VI

1. For Sellars' views, see esp. "Empiricism and the Philosophy of Mind," in H. Feigl and M. Scriven, eds., *Minnesota Studies in the Philosophy of Science*, Vol. 1 (Minneapolis: University of Minnesota Press, 1956), 253–329; repr. in Sellars, *Science, Perception, and Reality* (London: Routledge & Kegan Paul, 1964), pp. 127–196; and also "Phenomenalism," in *Science, Perception, and Reality*, pp. 60–105, and "Reply to Aune," in H.-N. Castañeda, ed., *Intentionality, Minds, and Perception* (Detroit: Wayne State University Press, 1966), pp. 286–300. For P. T. Geach's view, see his *Mental Acts* (London: Routledge & Kegan Paul, 1957).

2. See Sellars, "Phenomenalism," p. 93.

3. *Ibid.*

4. Roderick M. Chisholm would, for example, reject both ideas. See his *Perceiving* (Ithaca, N.Y.: Cornell University Press, 1957), Chs. 8, 9.

5. See J. J. C. Smart, "Sensations and Brain Processes," *Phil. Rev.*, LXVIII (1959), 141–156, and *Philosophy and Scientific Realism* (London: Routledge & Kegan Paul, 1963), Ch. 5.

6. See Sellars, "Reply to Aune," pp. 286–300.

7. See Sellars, "Phenomenalism," p. 95.

8. See also Chisholm, *Perceiving*, Ch. 8.

9. See R. G. Collingwood, *An Essay on Metaphysics* (Oxford: Clarendon Press, 1940), Ch. 5.

10. See Sellars, "Phenomenalism," p. 93.

Chapter VII

1. See Wilfrid Sellars, "Empiricism and the Philosophy of Mind," in H. Feigl and M. Scriven, eds., *Minnesota Studies in the Philosophy of Science*, Vol. 1 (Minneapolis: University of Minnesota Press, 1956), 274; repr. in Sellars, *Science, Perception, and Reality* (London: Routledge & Kegan Paul, 1964), p. 146.

2. H. H. Price, *Thinking and Experience* (London: Hutchinson, 1953), p. 40.

3. See note 8 of Ch. I, and also Rudolf Carnap, "The Methodological Character of Theoretical Concepts," in *Minnesota Studies in the Philosophy of Science*, Vol. 1, 38–76.

4. This seems to be what Wilfrid Sellars has in mind in his "The Language of Theories," in H. Feigl and G. Maxwell, eds., *Current Issues in the Philoso-*

phy of Science (New York: Holt, Rinehart & Winston, 1961), pp. 57–77; repr. in *Science, Perception, and Reality*, pp. 106–126.

5. I owe this argument to Wilfrid Sellars; see his "Philosophy and the Scientific Image of Man," in R. Colodney, ed., *Frontiers of Science and Philosophy* (Pittsburgh: University of Pittsburgh Press, 1962), pp. 62–69; repr. in *Science, Perception, and Reality*, pp. 25–31.

6. See Maurice Mandelbaum's discussion of Locke in *Philosophy, Science, and Sense Perception* (Baltimore: Johns Hopkins University Press, 1964), pp. 38ff.

Chapter VIII

1. For a survey of this variety, see Gilbert Ryle, *The Concept of Mind* (London: Hutchinson, 1949), pp. 280ff.

2. Franz Brentano, *Psychologie vom Empirischen Standpunkt* (Hamburg: Meiner, 1955), Vol. I, Bk. 2, Ch. 1. An English translation of this section (by D. B. Terrell) is included in R. M. Chisholm, ed., *Realism and the Background of Phenomenology* (New York: Free Press of Glencoe, 1960), pp. 39–61. For a recent defense of "Brentano's thesis" concerning the mental, see R. M. Chisholm, *Perceiving* (Ithaca, N.Y.: Cornell University Press, 1957), Ch. 11.

3. R. G. Collingwood, *The Principles of Art* (Oxford: Clarendon Press, 1938), p. 157.

4. For a discussion of this point, see Bruce Aune, "Thinking," in P. Edwards, ed., *The Encyclopedia of Philosophy*, Vol. 8 (New York: Crowell-Collier & Macmillan, 1967), 100–104; also see Ch. III of this book.

5. See Wilfrid Sellars, "Empiricism and the Philosophy of Mind," in H. Feigl and M. Scriven, eds., *Minnesota Studies in the Philosophy of Science*, Vol. 1 (Minneapolis: University of Minnesota Press, 1956), 253–329; repr. in Sellars, *Science, Perception, and Reality* (London: Routledge & Kegan Paul, 1964), pp. 127–196; also Sellars and Roderick M. Chisholm, "Chisholm-Sellars Correspondence on Intentionality," in H. Feigl, M. Scriven, and G. Maxwell, eds., *Minnesota Studies in the Philosophy of Science*, Vol. 2 (Minneapolis: University of Minnesota Press, 1958), 521–539. For P. T. Geach's view, see his *Mental Acts* (London: Routledge & Kegan Paul, 1957).

6. On this see H. H. Price, *Thinking and Experience* (London: Hutchinson, 1953), pp. 235ff.

7. This consideration seems to weigh heavily with contemporary psychologists who discuss silent thought. See esp. B. F. Skinner, *Verbal Behavior* (New York: Appleton-Century-Crofts, 1957), pp. 434ff, and John Dollard and Neal E. Miller, *Personality and Psychotherapy* (New York: McGraw-Hill, 1950), pp. 110–115.

8. On this see Wilfrid Sellars' papers, "Abstract Entities," *Rev. Metaph.*, XVI (1963), 627–671, and "Notes on Intentionality," *Journ. Phil.*, LXI (1964), 655–665.

9. See Ludwig Wittgenstein, *Philosophical Investigations*, trans. G. E. M. Anscombe (Oxford: Blackwell, 1953), Pt. I, secs. 256–273; and Norman Malcolm, "Knowledge of Other Minds," *Journ. Phil.*, LV (1958), 976; repr. in

Malcolm, *Knowledge and Certainty* (Englewood Cliffs, N.J.: Prentice-Hall, 1963), p. 139.

10. Cf. Sellars' Jonsean myth in "Empiricism and the Philosophy of Mind," *Science, Perception, and Reality*, p. 178.

11. See Geach, *Mental Acts*, Ch. 17.

12. This is Chisholm's standard objection to linguistic theories of thinking. See *Perceiving*, Ch. 11.

13. I have C. S. Pierce especially in mind here. For a useful discussion of his views, which are often very similar to mine, see W. B. Gallie, *Pierce and Pragmatism* (Harmondsworth: Penguin Books, 1952).

14. Wittgenstein, *Philosophical Investigations*, Pt. I, secs. 19, 23, *et passim*.

15. Chisholm, *Perceiving*, Ch. 11.

16. *Ibid.*, p. 171.

17. *Ibid.*, p. 172.

18. The classic statement of this point of view is found in Ludwig Wittgenstein, *Tractatus-Logico-Philosophicus*, trans. C. K. Ogden (New York: Harcourt, Brace, 1922). In this connection also see Rudolf Carnap, *The Logical Syntax of Language* (New York: Harcourt, Brace, 1937).

19. This is only a very rough statement of the position in point. For a more adequate discussion, see Wilfrid Sellars, "Counterfactuals, Dispositions, and the Causal Modalities," in H. Feigl, M. Scriven, and G. Maxwell, eds., *Minnesota Studies in the Philosophy of Science*, Vol. 2, 225–308. An earlier and less complicated approach along similar lines can be found in Gilbert Ryle, " 'If', 'So', and 'Because'," in M. Black, ed., *Philosophical Analysis* (Ithaca, N.Y.: Cornell University Press, 1950), pp. 323–340.

20. This, in effect, is what Willard Van Orman Quine tries to do in Ch. 2 of his *Word and Object* (Cambridge, Mass.: John Wiley and M.I.T. Press, 1960).

21. Wilfrid Sellars, "Abstract Entities," *passim*.

22. For an explanation of this convention, see Sellars, "Abstract Entities" and "Notes on Intentionality."

23. For a useful discussion of the relation between emotions and their intentional objects, see Irving Thalberg, Jr., "Emotion and Thought," *Amer. Phil. Quart.*, I (1964), 45–55.

24. Ryle, *The Concept of Mind*, pp. 118ff.

25. *Ibid.*, p. 135.

26. The logic of practical reasoning is a very difficult, not well-understood subject. My views on it are suggested in "Intention," in P. Edwards, ed., *The Encyclopedia of Philosophy*, Vol. 4 (New York: Crowell-Collier & Macmillan, 1967), pp. 198–201. The best extended discussions known to me occur in R. G. Collingwood, *The New Leviathan* (Oxford: Clarendon Press, 1942), Chs. XIII–XVII, and in Wilfrid Sellars, "Thought and Action," in Keith Lehrer, ed., *Freedom and Determinism* (New York: Random House, 1966), pp. 105–139. An influential recent discussion, with which I disagree, can be found in G. E. M. Anscombe, *Intention* (Oxford: Blackwell, 1957), pp. 57–88.

27. See Dollard and Miller, *loc. cit.*

28. See Wolfgang Köhler, *The Mentality of Apes*, trans. E. Winter (Harmondsworth: Pelican Books, 1957), p. 238.

29. According to W. Ross Ashby, in *Design for a Brain* (New York: John Wiley, 1960), legitimate scientific "variables" ought to be quantities that can be adequately "represented by a pointer on a dial" (p. 14). He says: ". . . all the quantities used in physics, chemistry, biology, physiology, and *objective psychology* are variables in the defined sense. Thus, the position of a limb can be specified numerically by coordinates of position, and the movement of a limb can move a pointer on a dial" (p. 15; my italics).

30. On the "inner" similarities of men and animals, see Donald O. Hebb, *Organization of Behavior* (New York: John Wiley, 1949), Chs. 7 *et seq.*, and on the formal similarities of men and machines, see Ashby, *Design for a Brain*.

31. See Ashby, *Design for a Brain*, and F. H. George, *Cognition* (London: Methuen, 1962), Ch. 13, for elementary remarks by cyberneticians. Hebb, *Organization of Behavior*, Chs. 6 *et seqq.*, speaks of "concepts," by which he means certain "phase sequences" in cell-assemblies, as representing elements of reality in a nonlinguistic way; he should be consulted for his imaginative ideas on what such concepts are like. The general distinction between linguistic or conceptual reference and nonlinguistic picturing is clearly and instructively worked out by Wilfrid Sellars in his papers, "Being and Being Known" and "Truth and 'Correspondence'," both included in *Science, Perception, and Reality*, pp. 50–59 and 211–223, respectively.

32. See Hebb, *Organization of Behavior*, Ch. 7.

Chapter IX

1. Gilbert Ryle, *The Concept of Mind* (London: Hutchinson, 1949), Ch. 1.

2. Cf. P. F. Strawson, *Individuals* (London: Methuen, 1959), Ch. 3.

3. The epithet is H. Feigl's; see his "Mind-Body, *Not* a Pseudoproblem," in S. Hook, ed., *Dimensions of Mind* (New York: Crowell-Collier & Macmillan, Collier Books, 1961), p. 35.

4. See Strawson, *Individuals*, Ch. 3.

5. See Immanuel Kant, *Critique of Pure Reason*, trans. N. K. Smith (London: Macmillan, 1929), p. 187: "Substance, . . . when the sensible determination of permanence is omitted, would simply mean a something which can be thought only as a subject, never as a predicate of something else" (A147, B187).

6. Fred Hoyle, *The Black Cloud* (New York: New American Library, Signet Books, 1959). What makes Hoyle's Black Cloud believable as a (nonhuman) person is the elaborate steps Hoyle takes to show that in spite of the Cloud's enormous physical difference from a human being, it can nevertheless scan the world, send and receive signals, perform deductions, evaluate its own behavior—and do all of this on its own, without external programming.

7. "Basic particulars" in the traditional, ontological sense, not in the partly epistemic sense of Strawson. I shall comment on particulars in this sense below, but see C. D. Broad on the "nature" of a continuant, in *Examination of*

McTaggart's Philosophy, Vol. 1 (Cambridge, Eng.: Cambridge University Press, 1933), 264–278, and also Bertrand Russell, *Analysis of Matter* (New York: Harcourt, Brace, 1927), Ch. 27.

8. A detailed discussion of this point, built on the important fact that states have the logical status of properties rather than individuals, can be found in Wilfrid Sellars, "The Identity Approach to the Mind-Body Problem," *Rev. Metaph.*, XVIII (1965), 430–451.

9. Wilfrid Sellars, "Phenomenalism," in Sellars, *Science, Perception, and Reality* (London: Routledge & Kegan Paul, 1964), p. 97. See also Sellars, "Philosophy and the Scientific Image of Man," in R. Colodney, ed., *Frontiers of Science and Philosophy* (Pittsburgh: University of Pittsburgh Press, 1962), pp. 35–78; repr. in *Science, Perception, and Reality*, pp. 1–40.

10. See Broad on continuants.

11. See Ch. VIII, pp. 222 f.

12. *Ibid.*, p. 219.

13. See Donald O. Hebb, *Organization of Behavior* (New York: John Wiley, 1949), esp. "Introduction," pp. xi–xix.

14. My views on this issue can be found in my "Abilities, Modalities, and Free Will," *Philo. & Pheno. Res.*, XXIII (1963), 397–413, and "Can," in P. Edwards, ed. *The Encyclopedia of Philosophy*, Vol. 2 (New York: Crowell-Collier & Macmillan, 1967), pp. 18–20. Wilfrid Sellars has recently discussed the issue in a very thoroughgoing way in his "Fatalism and Determinism," in Keith Lehrer, ed., *Freedom and Determinism* (New York: Random House, 1966), pp. 141–174.

15. See note 14 above.

16. Esp. Herbert Feigl, "The 'Mental' and the 'Physical'," in H. Feigl, M. Scriven, and G. Maxwell, eds., *Minnesota Studies in the Philosophy of Science*, Vol. 2 (Minneapolis: University of Minnesota Press, 1958), 370–497, and J. J. C. Smart, *Philosophy and Scientific Realism* (London: Routledge & Kegan Paul, 1963), Ch. 5.

17. Smart, *Philosophy and Scientific Realism*, p. 69.

18. See Feigl on "The 'Mental' and the 'Physical'," where arguments of this general kind are very carefully developed. I myself have toyed with this approach, though dissenting from its physicalist conclusions at the very last minute, in my paper, written in 1961, "Feigl on the Mind-Body Problem," in G. Maxwell and P. K. Feyerabend, eds., *Mind, Matter, and Method* (Minneapolis: University of Minnesota Press, 1966), pp. 17–39.

19. See Ch. VI, pp. 151–152. Phenomenal color possesses a kind of continuity because s-color is related to s-extension as color is related to extension. Thus, every s-region of a visual image, no matter how s-small, has s-color. Although the characterization of s-color is purely formal, the s-continuity of s-color is still a quasi-spatial one because the concept of an s-colored image is *modeled* on a spatial expanse. For further remarks on this point, see Wilfrid Sellars, "Empiricism and the Philosophy of Mind," in H. Feigl and M. Scriven, eds., *Minnesota Studies in the Philosophy of Science*, Vol. 1 (Minneapolis: University of Minnesota Press, 1956), 323–324; repr. in *Science, Perception, and Reality*, pp. 191–192.

20. See William Kneale, *Probability and Induction* (Oxford: Clarendon Press, 1949), pp. 96ff, and Wilfrid Sellars, "The Language of Theories," in H. Feigl and G. Maxwell, eds., *Current Issues in the Philosophy of Science* (New York: Holt, Rinehart & Winston, 1961), 57–77, and in *Science, Perception, and Reality*, pp. 106–126.

21. P. E. Meehl and Wilfrid Sellars, "The Concept of Emergence," in H. Feigl and M. Scriven, eds., *Minnesota Studies in the Philosophy of Science*, Vol. 1, 239–252.

22. This view was defended by Betrand Russell in the middle of his *Analysis of Matter*, p. 286 (fn.), though he rejected it in the last chapter: cf. p. 400.

23. I use the term "emergent" in the sense of C. D. Broad; see his remarks on the "nature" of a continuant. For a recent discussion of emergence, and for arguments demonstrating its logical respectability, see Meehl and Sellars, "The Concept of Emergence."

24. It has been briefly discussed in Sellars, "Phenomenalism," pp. 101–102.

25. In this paragraph and in my discussion of the two approaches to sensa, I am indebted to some unpublished correspondence of Wilfrid Sellars.

26. In Sellars, "Philosophy and the Scientific Image of Man" and "Phenomenalism," to which the following remarks are indebted. Subsequent page references are to *Science, Perception, and Reality*.

27. See Bertrand Russell, *Analysis of Matter;* A. N. Whitehead, *Process and Reality* (New York: Macmillan, 1929), and G. F. Stout, *Mind and Matter* (Cambridge, Eng.: Cambridge University Press, 1931), esp. Ch. 3.

28. See Sellars, "Phenomenalism," pp. 102–105, "Philosophy and the Scientific Image of Man," p. 37; and "Time and the World Order," in H. Feigl and G. Maxwell, eds., *Minnesota Studies in the Philosophy of Science*, Vol. 3 (Minneapolis: University of Minnesota Press, 1962), 593–595.

29. Sellars, "Philosophy and the Scientific Image of Man," p. 37.

30. See Sellars, "Time and the World Order," pp. 593–594, *et passim;* also Strawson, *Individuals,* pp. 46ff.

31. Russell, *Analysis of Matter,* p. 287.

32. See Strawson, *Individuals,* Ch. 1.

33. *Ibid.,* and Stuart Hampshire, *Thought and Action* (London: Chatto & Windus, 1959), Ch. 1.

34. Russell, *Analysis of Matter,* p. 285.

35. This is shown in detail by Sellars in "Time and the World Order," pp. 577–583.

36. Kneale, *Probability and Induction,* p. 94. See also G. F. Stout, *Mind and Matter,* pp. 251ff., and Sellars, "Phenomenalism," pp. 103–105.

37. Kneale, *Probability and Induction,* p. 94.

bibliography

Albritton, Rogers. "On Wittgenstein's Use of the Term 'Criterion'," *Journal of Philosophy*, LVI (1959), 845–857.

Anscombe, G. E. M. *Intention*. Oxford: Blackwell, 1957.

Ashby, W. Ross. *Design for a Brain*. New York: John Wiley, 1960.

Aune, Bruce. "The Problem of Other Minds," *Philosophical Review*, LXX (1961), 320–339.

——. "Knowing and Merely Thinking," *Philosophical Studies*, XII (1961), 53–58.

——. "Abilities, Modalities, and Free Will," *Philosophy and Phenomenological Research*, XXIII (1963), 397–413.

——. "On the Complexity of Avowals," in Max Black, ed., *Philosophy in America*. London: Allen & Unwin, 1966. Pp. 35–57.

——. "Feigl on the Mind-Body Problem," in G. Maxwell and P. K. Feyerabend, eds., *Mind, Matter, and Method*. Minneapolis: University of Minnesota Press, 1966. Pp. 17–39.

——. "Can," in P. Edwards, ed., *The Encyclopedia of Philosophy*, Vol. 2. New York: Crowell-Collier & Macmillan, 1967. Pp. 18–20.

——. "Intention" in P. Edwards, ed., *The Encyclopedia of Philosophy*, Vol. 4. New York: Crowell-Collier & Macmillan, 1967, Pp. 198–201.

——. "Thinking," in P. Edwards, ed., *The Encyclopedia of Philosophy*, Vol. 8. New York: Crowell-Collier & Macmillan, 1967. Pp. 100–104.

Austin, J. L. "Other Minds," *Proceedings of the Aristotelian Society*, Supplementary Volume XX (1946), 148–187. Reprinted in G. Warnock and J. O. Urmson, eds., *Philosophical Papers*. Oxford: Clarendon Press, 1961.

——. *Sense and Sensibilia*, G. Warnock, ed. Oxford: Clarendon Press, 1962.

Ayer, Alfred J. *The Concept of a Person*. London: Macmillan, 1963.

Baier, Kurt. "Pains," *Australasian Journal of Philosophy*, XL (1962), 1–23.

Bailey, Cyril. *The Greek Atomists*. New York: Russell and Russell, 1928.

Barker, Steven F. *Induction and Hypothesis*. Ithaca, N.Y.: Cornell University Press, 1957.

Berkeley, George. *Principles of Human Knowledge*, in A. C. Fraser, ed., *Berkeley's Complete Works*, Vol. I. Oxford: Clarendon Press, 1801.

Black, Max. "Notes on the Meaning of 'Rule'," *Theoria*, XXIV (1958), 107–136, 139–161. Reprinted in Black, *Models and Metaphors*. Ithaca, N.Y.: Cornell University Press, 1962. Pp. 95–139.

Brentano, Franz. *Psychologie vom Empirischen Standpunkt*. Hamburg: Meiner, 1955. Portions translated by D. B. Terrell in R. M. Chisholm, ed., *Realism and the Background of Phenomenology*. New York: Free Press of Glencoe, 1960. Pp. 39–61.

Broad, C. D. *Examination of McTaggart's Philosophy*, Vol. 1. Cambridge, Eng.: Cambridge University Press, 1933.

———. "Testability and Meaning," *Philosophy of Science*, III (1936), 420–460.

Carnap, Rudolf. *The Logical Syntax of Language*. New York: Harcourt, Brace, 1937.

———. "The Methodological Character of Theoretical Concepts," in H. Feigl and M. Scriven, eds., *Minnesota Studies in the Philosophy of Science*, Vol. 1. Minneapolis: University of Minnesota Press, 1956. Pp. 38–76.

———. "On the Use of Hilbert's ϵ-operator in Scientific Theories," in A. Robinson, *Essays on the Foundations of Mathematics*. Jerusalem: Manes Press, 1961. Pp. 156–163.

Castañeda, Hector-Neri. "The Private Language Argument," in C. D. Rollins, ed., *Knowledge and Experience*. Pittsburgh: University of Pittsburgh Press, 1963. Pp. 88–105.

Chisholm, Roderick M. "The Theory of Appearing," in M. Black, ed., *Philosophical Analysis*. Ithaca, N.Y.: Cornell University Press, 1950. Pp. 97–112.

———. *Perceiving*. Ithaca, N.Y.: Cornell University Press, 1957.

———, and Wilfrid Sellars. "Chisholm-Sellars Correspondence on Intentionality," in H. Feigl, M. Scriven, and G. Maxwell, eds., *Minnesota Studies in the Philosophy of Science*, Vol. 2. Minneapolis: University of Minnesota Press, 1958. Pp. 521–539.

Collingwood, R. G. *The Principles of Art*. Oxford: Clarendon Press, 1938.

———. *An Essay on Metaphysics*. Oxford: Clarendon Press, 1940.

———. *The New Leviathan*. Oxford: Clarendon Press, 1942.

———. *The Idea of Nature*. Oxford: Clarendon Press, 1945.

Conant, James B. (ed.). *Harvard Case Histories in Experimental Science*, Vol. 1. Cambridge, Mass.: Harvard University Press, 1957.

Descartes, René. *Philosophical Works of Descartes*, 2 vols., trans. E. S. Haldane and G. T. R. Ross. London: Cambridge University Press, 1934.

Dollard, John, and Neal E. Miller. *Personality and Psychotherapy*. New York: McGraw-Hill, 1950.

Erickson, Milton H. "Experimental Demonstrations of the Psychopathology of Everyday Life," in S. S. Tompkins and H. A. Murray, eds., *Contemporary Psychopathology*. Cambridge, Mass.: Harvard University Press, 1944. Pp. 524–525.

Feigl, Herbert. "The 'Mental' and the 'Physical'," in H. Feigl, M. Scriven, and G. Maxwell, eds., *Minnesota Studies in the Philosophy of Science*, Vol. 2. Minneapolis: University of Minnesota Press, 1958. Pp. 370–497.

———. "Mind-Body, *Not* a Pseudoproblem," in S. Hook, ed., *Dimensions of*

Mind. New York: Crowell-Collier & Macmillan, Collier Books, 1961. Pp. 24-36.

Feyerabend, Paul K. "Explanation, Reduction, and Empiricism," in H. Feigl and G. Maxwell, eds., *Minnesota Studies in the Philosophy of Science,* Vol. 3. Minneapolis: University of Minnesota Press, 1962. Pp. 28-97.

Frege, Gottlob. *Translations from the Philosophical Writings of Gottlob Frege,* Peter Geach and Max Black, eds. Oxford: Blackwell, 1952.

Gallie, W. B. *Pierce and Pragmatism.* Harmondsworth: Penguin Books, 1952.

Geach, P. T. *Mental Acts.* London: Routledge & Kegan Paul, 1957.

George, F. H. *Cognition.* London: Methuen, 1962.

Goodman, Nelson. *Fact, Fiction, and Forecast.* Cambridge, Mass.: Harvard University Press, 1955.

Hampshire, Stuart. *Thought and Action.* London: Chatto & Windus, 1959.

Harré, R. *Matter and Method.* London: Macmillan, 1964.

Hebb, Donald O. *Organization of Behavior.* New York: John Wiley, 1949.

Hulme, T. E. "Bergson's Theory of Art," *Speculations.* New York: Harcourt, Brace, 1924. Pp. 141-170.

Hume, David. *A Treatise of Human Nature,* L. A. Selby-Bigge, ed. Oxford: Clarendon Press, 1888.

Kant, Immanuel. *Critique of Pure Reason,* trans. N. K. Smith. London: Macmillan, 1929.

Kneale, William. *Probability and Induction.* Oxford: Clarendon Press, 1949.

Köhler, Wolfgang. *The Mentality of Apes,* trans. E. Winter. Harmondsworth: Pelican Books, 1957.

Lean, Martin. *Sense Perception and Matter.* London: Routledge & Kegan Paul, 1953.

Leibniz, G. W. F. von. *The Monadology,* trans. G. Montgomery in *The Rationalists.* New York: Doubleday, Dolphin Books, 1960. Pp. 455-471.

Locke, John. *An Essay Concerning Human Understanding,* abr. and ed. by A. S. Pringle-Pattison. Oxford: Clarendon Press, 1924.

Malcolm, Norman. *Dreaming.* London: Routledge & Kegan Paul, 1959.

——. "Review of Wittgenstein's *Philosophical Investigations,*" *Philosophical Review,* LXIII (1954), 530-559. Reprinted in Malcolm, *Knowledge and Certainty.* Englewood Cliffs, N.J.: Prentice-Hall, 1963. Pp. 96-129.

——. "Knowledge of Other Minds," *Journal of Philosophy,* LV (1958), 960-978. Reprinted in Malcolm, *Knowledge and Certainty.* Englewood Cliffs, N. J.: Prentice-Hall, 1963. Pp. 130-140.

Mandelbaum, Maurice. *Philosophy, Science, and Sense Perception.* Baltimore: Johns Hopkins University Press, 1964.

Martin, Richard M. *Truth and Denotation.* Chicago: University of Chicago Press, 1958.

Maxwell, Grover. "The Ontological Status of Theoretical Entities," in H. Feigl and G. Maxwell, eds., *Minnesota Studies in the Philosophy of Science,* Vol. 3. Minneapolis: University of Minnesota Press, 1962. Pp. 3-27.

——. "Philosophy and the Causal Theory of Perception," *The Graduate Review of Philosophy,* VI (1964), 9-21.

——. "Remarks on Perception and Theoretical Entities," in R. Colodney, ed., *University of Pittsburgh Studies in the Philosophy of Science,* Vol. 4. Pittsburgh: University of Pittsburgh Press, in press.

Meehl, P. E., and Wilfrid Sellars. "The Concept of Emergence," in H. Feigl and M. Scriven, eds., *Minnesota Studies in the Philosophy of Science,* Vol. 1. Minneapolis: University of Minnesota Press, 1956. Pp. 239-252.

Melden, I. A. "Action," *Philosophical Review*, LXV (1956), 523–541.
Moore, G. E. "Proof of an External World," *Proceedings of the British Academy*, XXV (1939). Reprinted in Moore, *Philosophical Papers*. London: Allen & Unwin, 1959. Pp. 127–150.
Nagel, Ernest. *The Structure of Science*. New York: Harcourt, Brace and World, 1961.
Neurath, Otto. "Protokollsätz," *Erkenntnis*, III (1932), 204–214.
Pap, Arthur, "Disposition Concepts and Extensional Logic," in H. Feigl, M. Scriven, and G. Maxwell, eds., *Minnesota Studies in the Philosophy of Science*, Vol. 2. Minneapolis: University of Minnesota Press, 1958. Pp. 196–224.
———. *Semantics and Necessary Truth*. New Haven, Conn.: Yale University Press, 1958.
———. *An Introduction to the Philosophy of Science*. New York: Free Press of Glencoe, 1962.
Paul, G. A. "Is There a Problem About Sense Data?" *Proceedings of the Aristotelian Society*, Supplementary Volume XV (1936). Reprinted in A. G. N. Flew, ed., *Logic and Language*, First Series. Oxford: Blackwell, 1951. Pp. 101–116.
Popper, Karl. *The Logic of Scientific Discovery*. New York: Basic Books, 1959. First published as *Logik der Forshung*. Vienna: Springer, 1935.
———. *Conjectures and Refutations*. New York: Basic Books, 1962.
Price, H. H. *Hume's Theory of the External World*. Oxford: Clarendon Press, 1940.
———. *Thinking and Experience*. London: Hutchinson, 1953.
Putnam, Hilary. "Minds and Machines," in S. Hook, ed., *Dimensions of Mind*. New York: Crowell-Collier, 1961. Pp. 148–179.
Quine, Willard Van Orman. *Word and Object*. Cambridge, Mass.: John Wiley and M.I.T. Press, 1960.
Russell, Bertrand. *Introduction to Mathematical Philosophy*. London: Allen & Unwin, 1919.
———. *Analysis of Matter*. New York: Harcourt, Brace, 1927.
———, and A. N. Whitehead. *Principia Mathematica* (2nd edn.), Vol. 1. Cambridge, Eng.: Cambridge University Press, 1927.
Ryle, Gilbert. *The Concept of Mind*. London: Hutchinson, 1949.
———. " 'If', 'So', and 'Because'," in M. Black, ed., *Philosophical Analysis*. Ithaca, N.Y.: Cornell University Press, 1950. Pp. 323–340.
———. *Dilemmas*. Cambridge, Eng.: Cambridge University Press, 1954.
Schlick, Moritz. "Form and Content," in *Gesammelte Aufsätze*. Vienna: Gerold, 1938. Ch. 8.
Scriven, Michael. "The Logic of Criteria," *Journal of Philosophy*, LVI (1959), 857–868.
Sellars, Wilfrid. "A Semantical Solution of the Mind-Body Problem," *Methodos*, V (1953), 45–84.
———. "Some Reflections on Language Games," *Philosophy of Science*, XXI (1954), 204–228. Reprinted with changes in Sellars, *Science, Perception, and Reality*. London: Routledge & Kegan Paul, 1964. Pp. 321–350.
———. "Empiricism and the Philosophy of Mind," in H. Feigl and M. Scriven, eds., *Minnesota Studies in the Philosophy of Science*, Vol. 1. Minneapolis: University of Minnesota Press, 1956. Pp. 253–329. Reprinted in Sellars, *Science, Perception, and Reality*. London: Routledge & Kegan Paul, 1964. Pp. 127–196.

———. "Imperatives, Intentions, and the Logic of 'Ought'," *Methodos*, VIII (1956), 227–268. Reprinted, with additions and corrections, in H.-N. Castañeda and G. Nakhnikian, eds., *Morality and the Language of Conduct*. Detroit: Wayne State University Press, 1963. Pp. 159–218.

———. "Counterfactuals, Dispositions, and the Causal Modalities," in H. Feigl, M. Scriven, and G. Maxwell, eds., *Minnesota Studies in the Philosophy of Science*, Vol. 2. Minneapolis: University of Minnesota Press, 1958. Pp. 225–308.

———. "Phenomenalism," in Sellars, *Science, Perception, and Reality*. London: Routledge & Kegan Paul, 1964. Pp. 60–105. (This essay was written and privately circulated in 1959.)

———. "Being and Being Known," *Proceedings of the American Catholic Philosophical Association*, XXXIV (1960), 28–49. Reprinted in Sellars, *Science, Perception, and Reality*. London: Routledge & Kegan Paul, 1964. Pp. 41–59.

———. "The Language of Theories," in H. Feigl and G. Maxwell, eds., *Current Issues in the Philosophy of Science*. New York: Holt, Rinehart & Winston, 1961. Pp. 57–77. Reprinted in Sellars, *Science, Perception, and Reality*. London: Routledge & Kegan Paul, 1964. Pp. 106–126.

———. "Philosophy and the Scientific Image of Man," in R. Colodney, ed., *Frontiers of Science and Philosophy*. Pittsburgh: University of Pittsburgh Press, 1962. Pp. 35–78. Reprinted in Sellars, *Science, Perception, and Reality*. London: Routledge & Kegan Paul, 1964. Pp. 1–40.

———. "Time and the World Order," in H. Feigl and G. Maxwell, eds., *Minnesota Studies in the Philosophy of Science*, Vol. 3. Minneapolis: University of Minnesota Press, 1962. Pp. 527–618.

———. "Truth and 'Correspondence'," *Journal of Philosophy*, LIX (1962), 29–56. Reprinted in Sellars, *Science, Perception, and Reality*. London: Routledge & Kegan Paul, 1964. Pp. 197–224.

———. "Abstract Entities," *Review of Metaphysics*, XVI (1963), 627–671.

———. "Notes on Intentionality," *Journal of Philosophy*, LXI (1964), 655–665.

———. *Science, Perception, and Reality*. London: Routledge & Kegan Paul, 1964.

———. "The Identity Approach to the Mind-Body Problem," *Review of Metaphysics*, XVIII (1965), 430–451.

———. "Reply to Aune," in H.-N. Castañeda, ed., *Intentionality, Minds, and Perception*. Detroit: Wayne State University Press, 1966.

———. "Fatalism and Determinism," in Keith Lehrer, ed., *Freedom and Determinism*. New York: Random House, 1966. Pp. 141–174.

———. "Thought and Action," in Keith Lehrer, ed., *Freedom and Determinism*. New York: Random House, 1966. Pp. 105–139.

———, and Roderick M. Chisholm, "Chisholm-Sellars Correspondence on Intentionality," in H. Feigl, M. Scriven, and G. Maxwell, eds., *Minnesota Studies in the Philosophy of Science*, Vol. 2. Minneapolis: University of Minnesota Press, 1958. Pp. 521–539.

———, and P. E. Meehl. "The Concept of Emergence," in H. Feigl and M. Scriven, eds., *Minnesota Studies in the Philosophy of Science*, Vol. 1. Minneapolis: University of Minnesota Press, 1956. Pp. 239–252.

Skinner, B. F. *Verbal Behavior*. New York: Appleton-Century-Crofts, 1957.

Smart, J. J. C. "Theory Construction," *Philosophy and Phenomenological Research*, XII (1951). Reprinted in A. G. N. Flew, ed., *Logic and Language*, Second Series. Oxford: Blackwell, 1953. Pp. 222–242.

——. "Sensations and Brain Processes," *Philosophical Review,* LXVIII (1959), 141–156.

——. *Philosophy and Scientific Realism.* London: Routledge & Kegan Paul, 1963.

Stout, G. F. *Mind and Matter.* Cambridge, Eng.: Cambridge University Press, 1931.

Strawson, P. F. *Individuals.* London: Methuen, 1959.

Thalberg, Irving, Jr. "Emotion and Thought," *American Philosophical Quarterly,* I (1964), 45–55.

Thompson, Robert. *The Psychology of Thinking.* Harmondsworth: Pelican Books, 1959.

Urmson, J. O. *Philosophical Analysis.* Oxford: Clarendon Press, 1956.

Whitehead, A. N. *Process and Reality.* New York: Macmillan, 1929.

——, and Bertrand Russell. *Principia Mathematica* (2nd edn.), Vol. 1. Cambridge, Eng.: Cambridge University Press, 1927.

Wisdom, John. *Other Minds.* Oxford: Blackwell, 1952.

Wittgenstein, Ludwig. *Tractatus-Logico-Philosophicus,* trans. C. K. Ogden. New York: Harcourt, Brace, 1922.

——. *Philosophical Investigations,* trans. G. E. M. Anscombe. Oxford: Blackwell, 1953.

——. *The Blue and Brown Books.* Oxford: Blackwell, 1958.

index

A Note on the Type

The text of this book was set on the Linotype in Janson, a recutting made direct from type cast from matrices long thought to have been made by the Dutchman Anton Janson, who was a practicing type founder in Leipzig during the years 1668–87. However, it has been conclusively demonstrated that these types are actually the work of Nicholas Kis (1650–1702), a Hungarian, who most probably learned his trade from the master Dutch type founder Kirk Voskens. The type is an excellent example of the influential and sturdy Dutch types that prevailed in England up to the time William Caslon developed his own incomparable designs from these Dutch faces.